RIOTS & REVOLUTIONS

TRAVELS

OF THE

VERY FIRST

FEMALE

JOURNALIST

TO ....

by

Carol Abaya, M.A.

ACKNOWLEDGEMENTS

Many thanks to:
- Newspaper publisher and editor Virginia Amend who relentlessly went through my manuscript line-by-line -- twice;
- My computer guru Ed Perrella, who with his skills -- and patience -- moved around copy effortlessly;
- My orchid loving friend William Silverman, who took pieces in my mind and developed the eye-catching cover; and
- My now long gone mother Sarah K. Goldstein, who gave me the inner strength to write, edit and re-edit my saga.

Copyright©2017 Carol A.G. Abaya.
All rights reserved. No part of this publication may be reproduced, distributed, or transmitted in any form or by any means, including photocopying, recording, or other electronic or mechanical methods, without the prior written permission of the author.

ISBN: 978-1-62249-396-8

Published by
The Educational Publisher Inc.
Biblio Publishing
BiblioPublishing.com
Columbus, Ohio

TABLE OF CONTENTS

Introduction v

Chapter 1. The Beginning (through graduate school and first trip abroad) Decision to become a journalist. Accurate information needed to make positive political decisions. — 1

Chapter 2. India 1962 -- Prediction of Chinese invasion of India. One-on-one interviews with top leaders: Prime Minister Nehru, M. Desai, Chavan et al — 31

Chapter 3. Indonesia 1963. Malaysia confrontation, Riots and destruction. Anti-Americanism. One-on-one interviews with top leaders: President Sukarno, Subandrio, Aidit et al. Philippines 1963, One-on-one interviews with top leaders: President Macapagal, Marcos, F. Lopez, Manglapus et al — 79

Chapter 4. Investigative newspaper reporter. Covered race riots and Civil Rights Movement. Black Panthers were protectione — 97

Chapter 5. Indonesia Communist coup 1965. (Predicted) Only foreign newspaper reporter there at time of coup. Interviewed all major leaders — 157

Chapter 6. Liberia 1966, Jewel of Africa. One-on-one interviews with all top leaders: President Tubman, Talbot, all key Cabinet Ministers — 187

Chapter 7. Israel 1967. Only foreign journalist traveled into occupied areas and interviewed leaders — 219

Chapter 8. Swing through Far East 1968. First foreign journalist allowed to freely travel in Burma. Borneo, interviewed Last Sultan of Sulu 235

Chapter 9. Philippines 1969 to 1972. Demonstrations, political unrest. One-on-one interviews with top leaders: President Marcos, F. Lopez et al. Husband was a Director on the Presidential Economic Staff. 255

INTRODUCTION

* Molotov cocktails rained down around me as I watched another building burn.
* Police held me for several hours demanding I give them my film after I took pictures of anti-American demonstrators.
* Armed soldiers pointed submachine guns mere inches from me as I tried to get into the Indonesian Defense Ministry.
* "There's been a revolution. Heavily armed soldiers are everywhere. We're trapped," my sister-in-law said. The line went dead!

Over the years I have had some extraordinary experiences -- many with significant political ramifications. I was a lone female in a man's world. THE FIRST and ONLY female newspaper reporter to have covered race riots and the civil rights movement in the United States and to travel extensively meeting and interviewing country presidents, Maharajas and even a Sultan. I found myself in the middle of two revolutions in Asia.

I was there in the midst of these upheavals because I predicted several:
- Chinese invasion of India in 1962,
- the 1965 communist revolution in Indonesia,
- the increased tension and acts of violence in the Middle East, and
- the 1972 coup in the Philippines

Once I made up my mind to write this saga, I realized that more than 50 years of life cannot be boiled down to a few, even a few thousand, words. This book was written in stages.

First, my memories in a stream of consciousness manner. For months beginning in August 2011, I just wrote every day with a red pen on yellow pads.

As I was writing from memory I was also going through many hundreds of clippings of my articles that appeared in newspapers and magazines around the world.

Lastly I went through hundreds of letters to my parents at their home in New Jersey, my father at his business and my sister in NYC. . In my Aug. 13, 1959 letter to my parents from London (my first trip abroad), I wrote "Keep these letters as I'm not keeping a diary."

My "pack rat" mother did! The stamps are all gone -- given by my father to a friend of his who collected foreign stamps. My mother even numbered my letters from India, so it was easy to put my story in historical perspective.

I have actually been in more foreign countries (25) than US states (23) and traveled about 400,000 miles.

The letters clearly show my desire to see all and experience all - from family life to the political and economic situation. They also show that even in the midst of political and economic upheavals that friendship, generosity, hospitality and much love met me at every point in my travels. I was welcomed into the palaces of the very rich and the minute huts of the very poor.

In covering events and my travels as a journalist, I quickly realized that certain people were enablers. These people gave me an edge over other journalists. From the Indian Prime Minister to the Presidents of Indonesia, The Philippines and Liberia to Maharajas and the Sultan of Sulu.

Everyone was interested in learning about me, as a lone female traveler, and life in the United States. The humble

Indian Finance Minister even questioned me about American dating habits.

The incentive to write my story came from two experiences in August 2011, when I was on vacation in the Berkshires, Massachusetts. I watched the revolution unfold in Libya and two female reporters in riot gear dodging bullets. In the afternoon, we saw the play "Red Hot Patriot: The Kick-Ass Wit of Molly Ivins." I personally identified with so much.

While Ivins (according to her biography) was "thinking" about the differences between whites and blacks" and "mulling" over inequities in society, I was dodging Molotov cocktails in Paterson, N.J., during one of the first race riots in the country in the mid-1960s.

My own story holds significant historical perspective. First, I was a lone woman journalist who traveled the world at a time when women went to college for a MRS. degree. My experiences, hopefully, will be insightful and provide food for thought for better political decisions in the future.

My original thought was to show that my political predictions came to be because I connected the political DOTS. For some reason political leaders did not — and still do not — connect the DOTS. DOTS (intelligence/accurate information) are critical and will play an even more important role in maintaining civilization as we knew it before ISIS.

Another important factor then - and now - is that too many American leaders do not even want to understand foreign cultures. .

Nowhere is this more evident than in my visit to Liberia (chapter 6) in 1966. Without exception, from the liberal president to cabinet ministers, businessmen and even Peace Corps volunteers, the word "arrogance," described Americans.

In this arrogance and not connecting the DOTS, in 1980 the US crushed the only real democracy in all of Africa.

We (Americans) think that because we have a great country that everyone should follow our path to freedom. Giving "freedom" to others who have never had freedom has been foolhardy. This is why I have come up with my thesis that political man (especially American) does not know how to correctly connect happenings, those political "DOTS." And non-connection of DOTS has resulted in too many human disasters.

The Tree of My Life has three large trunks.

The largest trunk was from the beginning through 1972. My young years consisted of traveling around the world, covering race riots and revolutions, and interviewing various heads of state, one-on-one.

Originally, I planned to write about all three trunks. But as I finished handwriting (in Feb. 2013) about the 1972 coup in the Philippines, I decided that this book would end with the year 1972.

Perhaps the other two trunks will make another book. Trunk Two would cover 1972 to 1991. Trunk Three would cover 1991 through 2012, which greatly changed my life and career directions. You can learn more about Trunk Three on my web site www.sandwichgeneration.com.

The one person who was my staunchest supporter and encouraged me was my mother. Sarah K. Goldstein, born 1905. She graduated college in 1926. Support was both emotional and financial. Encouragement was for me to take risks, to do new things. She provided financial support to enable me to take those risks.

She was my earliest and continual role model -- believing that a woman could be more than a wife and mother. That a woman can do almost anything she starts out to do.

My mother was a pack rat, and when I was working on The Sandwich Generation(R) nationally syndicated column for Jan. 2012 (part of the third major branch), I pulled out her tiny brown book of sayings and my own special cache of tiny books. Words of wisdom by various people. So, I was struck by the following:

"What is worth doing is worth finishing. If it isn't worth finishing, why begin at all?" by Baltassar Gracian.

A number of other sayings from famous people also pushed me forward in this book endeavor.

"No one knows what it is that he can do until he tries." By Publislius Syrus.

"The only joy in the world is to begin." by Cesare Pavese.

And "Miracles happen to those who believe in them," by Bernard Berenson.

The completion of this book was a "miracle." That it has been published unlimited "miracles."

My dream, my passion has been to help others get factual information about events, to better understand world-wide happenings, and to accept the good -- and bad -- in life.

I do hope you enjoy reading this and learn more about people, politicians, and how some individual decisions changed the world.

x

CHAPTER 1

I was mesmerized as I watched events unfold in Tripoli, Libya, that August day in 2011. I was fascinated by the two female journalists, wearing helmets and protective armor and dodging bullets.

In the afternoon, we went to the Shakespeare Theatre in Lenox, MA, and saw the play "Red Hot Patriot: The Kick-Ass Wit of Molly Ivins." Ivins was a hell-raising journalist, a true Liberal, who was a tireless advocate for social justice.

As a result of the above, I mentally relived the past 50 years of my own life.

I personally identified with so many incidents in the play -- from initially being the only female reporter on a daily newspaper in an inner city to dodging Molotov cocktails thrown from rooftops during the race riots of the 60s to standing in front of an Indonesian soldier who had a sizable automatic weapon pointed at my belly.

The day's experiences (watching Tripoli and seeing the play) prompted me to start to write down some of my own experiences and memories.

Hence I began my story as I sat outside at a resort in Lee, Massachusetts. In so many ways, I *was* a pioneer.

My own background and beginnings are humble, and no one has ever come forth as a mentor to take me to the next level of my professional and thinking abilities. Whatever I have achieved has been on my own.

I come from a middle-class family. As a child I lived in an all-white neighborhood. I don't recall any blacks or Asians in my elementary school. Only contact with blacks (called Negroes in those days) was our day maids or some of my father's customers. The subject of blacks wasn't discussed

My neighborhood was mixed with various religions. The differences became apparent at holiday times. I would peddle my three wheeler down the street to the Ellis family on Rosh Hashanah and Yom Kippur. My friend Sandra was in school. It wasn't her holiday. At Christmas I went across the street to help the Hagens decorate their tree. I got gifts for both Hanukah and Christmas. The other kids were jealous.

My maternal grandfather, Morris Katz, came to the US in the early 1900s. He started peddling fruits and vegetables door-to-door with his horse and wagon, going back and forth several times a week across the Hudson River ferry between New Jersey and New York. He married Rachel Dorf, had four children (only three survived), bought some real estate and in 1923 opened two stores in Tenafly, New Jersey. The family lived above the stores. The barn in the back housed cows and a still during Prohibition. My mother used to tell stories about how she had to stand guard while my great-grandfather, Aaron Morris Dorf, made liquor and to warn him if the sheriff was nearby.

My mother, the eldest, was my role model. I always say, she was a woman before her time. She graduated from Pace College (now University) in 1926 and went to work in a real estate office in Tenafly, NJ, owned by the town mayor. This started a long real estate career. She was one of the very few women real estate brokers (as opposed to just a sales agent) in the 1950s in northern New Jersey. She retired in 1995 at age 89 because she couldn't deal with the MLS computer system. She never could understand the NOW movement -- because she had done it all. Graduated college, had a career, became a wife, mother and again a career professional. And at 90 she tutored disadvantaged second graders in reading at the neighborhood elementary school. No one stopped her from doing what she wanted to.

My paternal grandfather, Hyman Goldstein came to the USA in 1890.

In 1894 my grandmother Sarah Victor arrived. They settled in south Jersey. My grandfather had a sizable chicken farm and specialized in eggs (rather than chickens for food). After WW2 they moved to north Jersey to be near my father, Samuel Victor, and his two sisters, Fannie and Mary.

In 1927, my father and his brother-in-law, Harry Albert, opened a hardware, paint and glass retail store in Englewood, N.J. My father retired in 1969, at age 69. The love of his life was Betty White, for whom he did a considerable amount of mirror work in her Englewood home in the 1950s.

My father was active in the small community and in the fifth car in the official opening ceremonies of the George Washington Bridge in 1931. He 'dined' at the White House several times, having received some award or other. A staunch Republican, he treated everyone, regardless of race, with respect. After he retired in 1969, he did volunteer work every day at the Englewood Medical Center until he was 88.

All of the above helped form me -- in an unconscious way. Both parents were hard working, caring about other people. My father was a man of few words, and my mother often worked late. So conversation at dinner was little. I retreated into books and homework. But things were just whatever.

I can clearly see that my interest in writing -- in putting words down on paper -- began in elementary school.

My mother was a "pack rat." I still have the "newspaper" I was editor of in the 5th grade. In junior high as well as high school I wrote about school events for the local weekly paper, *The Englewood-Press Journal.*

* * * *

One of my passions is dogs. The first thing I wanted to be was a vet. But the thought of blood and guts and my dislike of needles ended that dream.

My next dream was to travel -- to be an airline hostess and travel *free.* At that time, hostesses (only females) had to be at least 5'4" tall and weigh at least 110 lbs. I was only 5'2" (now only 5'1") and never weighed more than 100 lbs. until I was in my 30s. Second dream crushed.

In my sophomore year in Dwight Morrow High School, Englewood, New Jersey, I had a dragon of an English teacher - Anita Dincin. She was a dragon to the boys -- especially a few (who shall remain nameless here even though they are all gone) who thought they were hotshots. I always listened intently.

She gave us an assignment -- write a poem or an essay on brotherhood. I never cared for poetry and wrote the essay. I still remember her handing the essay back to me with a number of red corrections. "Rewrite it and give it back to me," she said (without any explanation).

A couple of months later, I remember my mother getting a telephone call at 10:30 P.M. I had won first prize in a brotherhood essay contest sponsored by B'nai B'rith. Mrs.

Dincin had entered my essay without telling me. The prize was a $25 savings bond, a lot of money in those days.

I am also a pack rat, like my mother. If it weren't for her saving all my school papers and letters during my early travels and my taking them from my parents' basement when my mother passed on April 2, 1997, I would not have found the original essay so easily and the program from the award ceremony of February 17, 1953 and a letter to Mrs. Dincin congratulating both her and myself for the essay and my presentation. Also, the blue first Prize ribbon was found within minutes of my shifting through the many rat pack papers.

So, I will quote from it.

"Brotherhood itself cannot be defined simply. In the dictionary you may find these definitions: a relationship as between brothers, an association of persons joined as brothers, and the condition of being a brother.

"But the kind of brotherhood which is emphasized during Brotherhood Week is not defined in a dictionary. Brotherhood, to most people, is more than just the tolerance of people unlike themselves. Brotherhood is the understanding and accepting, without prejudice, all people, regardless of race, color, creed or religious beliefs.........."

I do want to say that basic brotherhood -- as defined in my essay of almost 60 years ago seems to have been lost by man somewhere along the way.

I found writing the essay had been easy. I thought I'd be an international correspondent so I could fulfill my dream of traveling the world - free.

My interest in writing skyrocketed in my junior year in high school. I took a journalism course given by Sally Winfrey. Miss Winfrey loved dogs as much as I did. But she lived in a multi-story apartment house and worked unusual hours. So, she never had a dog. But we would gather in her kitchen to finish up the school newspaper and after feeding us she would have one of the fellows, John Zeeman, go home and bring over his wired-hair fox terrier.

When I graduated in 1955, the dog of a friend of my father had a litter of pups. I asked Miss Winfrey if she would like a puppy. She was so excited. She spent the summers with her sister in Virginia, and when I brought the puppy -- an ugly little thing -- to her, she had already bought a traveling case, dishes, leash etc. ready for her trip south. She had that dog for 18 years, and whenever she saw my mother she said "That was the best gift anyone ever gave me." I kept in touch with Miss Winfrey until her death in 1977. She followed my travels and work until the end. Her sister sent me a note telling me the sad news and said that the ugly pup had been the joy of Sally's life.

Miss Winfrey's encouragement led to my being selected to participate in a special summer journalism program at Medill School of Journalism, Northwestern University, in 1954, between my junior and senior years in high school. The words in my brotherhood essay were replayed.

At that time in history, blacks, particularly in the south, led separate lives from whites. There were several southerners in the program and two blacks. The white girls had never sat in the same classroom with a black, never eaten at the same table with a black, and had never 'talked' with any black, other than household help. I recall that one of the black boys was from Detroit and that his parents were both professionals, one a doctor and the other a teacher. These southern girls really had an awakening experience.

My upbringing was in an integrated suburban town (Englewood, NJ), and so blacks in the classroom and extracurricular activities were common in junior and high school. But even there, in my elementary school days when the neighborhood school was virtually all white, there was a divide between the races. I can still vividly remember one time as I walked to school our cleaning lady got off the bus. I loved big, fat, cheery Molly. I gave her a big hug before continuing on. But one of the other kids on my block questioned me about why would I hug a black person. I do not remember exactly how I answered the question. I guess to me such a hug was not exceptional, as my paternal grandparents lived in the 'fourth' ward and had many black neighbors. And my father had a hardware store and many of his regular customers were black. I helped my father in the store -- even knew the difference between one penny and five penny nails -- and he always treated the blacks with as much respect as his white customers.

My initial scribbled notes for this saga note the great influence of my history teacher, Irene Eckerson -- Mrs. Eckie, as we all called her. (My mother had Mrs. Eckie the first year she taught in the 1920s. And I reminisced with my 88-year-old cousin, Herman Berkman, up in Massachusetts during that 2011 vacation as he also had Mrs. Eckie.) She gave an unusual course in those days - Far Eastern Studies.

We had an Indian exchange student whom I got to know fairly well. We had many interesting conversations about India's position in world politics. At that time India was "neutral" in world politics and would not support either the USA in its anti-communist campaign or Russia, which led the communist world. The Indian student said, "We have a 3,000+ mile border with Russia. We are a poor country. How can we protect ourselves if Russia invades us?" But the American government -- and press -- treated India as an enemy because of its neutrality. It was at this point I decided that if I could write the truth and real story about such situations that maybe the American people would make better decisions.

That course and my talking with the Indian student were major influences on my road to where I am today -- where I still passionately believe that if people have accurate and well balanced information that life decisions would be better. This is where my passion to search for the truth and write about current events in a balanced manner was ignited.

* * * *

Given my desire to write about world events in a balanced manner, in 1955 I finally chose The University of Wisconsin to pursue my journalism career and had enrolled in the School of Journalism. UW had an excellent journalism program. My cousin, Herman, was working on his Ph.D. in urban renewal. (Years later he retired as Professor Emeritus from New York University, where I did my graduate work.)

After my enrolling, the Freshman Dean came to visit my high school (Dwight Morrow) in Englewood and asked me what I wanted to do. I said, "Be a foreign correspondent." She then recommended that for the first two years I take a special program, Integrated Liberal Studies (ILS), which integrated a wide range of disciplines from sciences, language, literature, history, political science, and economics. The Dean said that having a basic knowledge of various subjects would help me write with a better understanding of what was happening in the world. Then she said I could combine ILS with journalism.

Best advice!! So, I sent a letter to the school saying I wanted to switch my major and take ILS. I received an acknowledgment letter that said "You have been <u>accepted</u> in ILS."

I did not understand what the word "accepted" meant until I went to a Labor Day barbecue with my cousin. His friends asked me what I was going to study. I said I was taking ILS. "Oh, you must be smart," they said. "That is a very hard course." To say the least, I was petrified before I even stepped into my first class. More than 200 started the program, and only 97 of us finished. Instead of continuing in journalism, I majored in International Relations, another very special program that enabled me to take courses in history, economics, political science and journalism. I was able to choose those courses that really interested me. In my junior year I was taking graduate courses in political science and economics. So many of those courses helped me write the kind of political and economics articles I wrote after interviewing top officials around the world.

The first ILS science course combined astronomy, climatology, meteorology, and a little geology. The book itself was mundane, taking each discipline separately and dealing with it. However, the professor's lectures were fascinating. He put all these disciplines together and focused on the rise and fall of the Greek and Roman Empires in relation to climate change. He showed how the change in the rain belt in these two countries (which moved further and further north over time) led to the downfall of these great empires. As the rain belts moved north, drought took over the southern parts, which led to crop failures, hunger, citizen unrest, riots in the streets, and the collapse of the political establishment of that time.

Today, global warming is of great concern. How anyone cannot believe there is global warming is beyond me. Today's scientific technology has clearly shown the changes in the ozone level and the many holes, which expand and contract during different parts of the year. And what about those polar bear and the penguins who now have to search elsewhere for food?

* * * *

Wisconsin had a large number of foreign students, most of whom were graduate students, and a very active International Club. I became active in the International Club. My interest in the international arena increased as I got to know more about the cultures and politics around the world. Many of these students were important in later years in my travels and marriage.

My interest in and understanding of foreign affairs was further heightened . It also increased my desire to dig deep into what was going on in the world and write more balanced articles.

THE FIRST OF MANY EXPERIENCES

Over the years my travels took me to Israel (four times), through Europe, India (a year), Pakistan, Indonesia (three times), Burma, Thailand, Hong Kong, The Philippines (three years), Sabah, Taiwan, Japan, Liberia, and South Africa. I interviewed the top leaders in many of these countries and wrote articles that often were against the American government's position at that time. Today (2011) these strong feelings of truth and accuracy show up in my articles about *The Sandwich Generation* (r) (these words trademarked by me) and about scams that take advantage of vulnerable Americans. **The truth can free people from making bad decisions.**

During my senior year at Wisconsin, in 1959, in order to earn some spending money, I worked for the head of the Hebrew and Semitic Studies Department. Menacham Mansour was one of the few experts in Middle East history who translated the Dead Sea Scrolls, which were discovered in 1947. I helped him write a series of radio broadcasts on the information obtained from his translations. That summer he took a group of Christian clergy on a biblical tour of Israel and asked me if I wanted to go with them. As I only had to pay air fare (we were then guests of the Israeli government), I jumped at the opportunity. The group consisted of 15 clergy (including two wives) from various denominations, myself, and Dr. Mansour. We flew to Rome, spent a day or so there, went down to Pompeii, and then took a ship to Haifa.

In Rome we attended a special audience with Pope John XXII. I had bought several St. Christopher medals and had them blessed by the Pope. My mother kept hers in all her cars until her death in 1997. I still have it -- somewhere.

Naples has had a reputation of housing a lot of poor. In 1959, years after the war ended, bombed out buildings were unrepaired. People lived in hovels and hung their clothes on lines put out along the streets. The children, thin and scantily clothed, played in the streets.

Winding roads along the coast took us to Pompeii. Buried in 49 AD, the city sported cobblestones and thick walls of houses, public baths, basilicas, court yards. Intact houses had original paintings and mosaic walls, ceilings and floors.

Kitchen utensils, women's hair clips, and potbellied stoves were common. An intricate city-wide watering system attested to the sophistication at that time.

* * * *

We then boarded the S.S.T. Herzel, at that time the only real Israeli luxury liner.

This was my first trip abroad and my first of four visits to Israel: 1959, 1967, 1978 and 1984.

We landed in Haifa where white modern buildings covered the mountain from the port to the top. The gold dome of the Bahai Temple and the Dragon Silos towered over all.

Unlike Naples, Haifa had been quickly rebuilt after The War of Liberation. The atmosphere was one of progress and pushing ahead, of building a new life. Everywhere trees and luxuriant vegetation, colorful flowers dotted the landscape. Palm and umbrella trees created an atmosphere of unreality.

Our hotel was at the top of the mountain with a panorama view of the city. The only way to really to get to know a city is to walk. And we walked and walked.

Although a seaport, Haifa at night was quiet. Upon reaching the lower part of the city, we heard Israeli music. We discovered a group of children 13 and 14 years old, singing and dancing in the courtyard of a school. Although it was 11 p.m., there were no adults present.

The spirit of revival was also seen on the slopes rising above the port. Romans and Ottoman Turks had stripped off all vegetation. We noted the reforestation program, rows and rows of new trees, many growing amidst rocks. Jews around

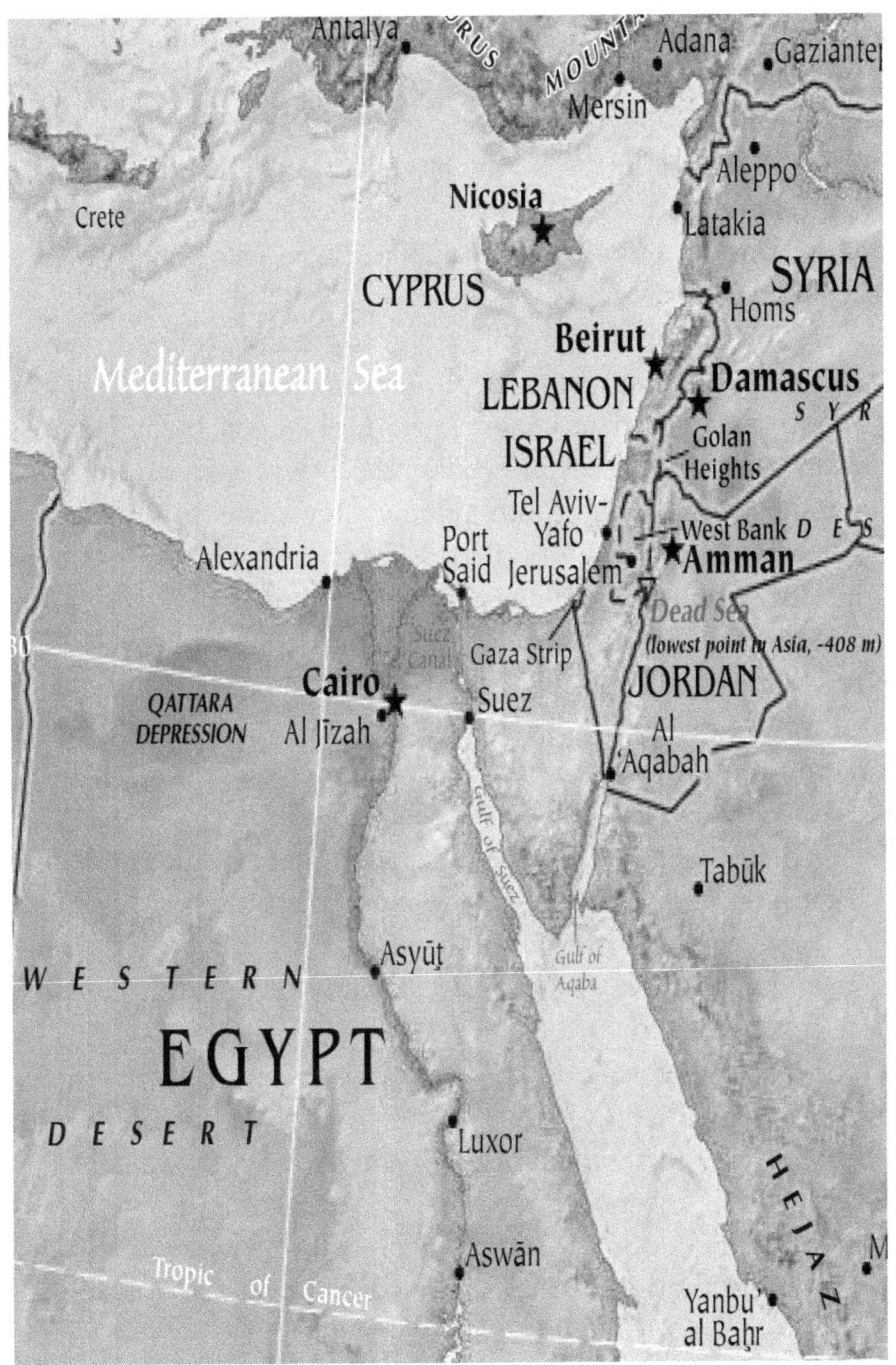

the world donated money to have a tree planted in their family's name.

On July 4, 1959, the US Ambassador had a party. As night fell we stood silently as the Israeli and American national anthems were played. We were in a new state in an old land, looking forward to seeing what had been accomplished in a very short period of time.

The Old Testament was our guide book, and our guide was one of the foremost archeologists in Israel.

We went on to Jerusalem, the Holy City, buried in the mountains and accessible only by steep winding roads. Reforestation was also quite evident. Remnants of the War of Liberation dotted the roadside. Rusty armored trucks and tanks. Deserted Arab villages appeared ghostlike.

The Old City teemed with masses of people and overwhelming noise. Meha Shearim was the center of the very orthodox Jews. They did little or no work, spent the days contemplating the Talmud and lived on charity. My thoughts at that time: they live like parasites on the land.

The City was not a pleasant place. As we walked into the market area, the stench of fish reached our nostrils. Flies and filth covered both foods and humans. Loaves of bread swarmed with flies. The clothes of many of the shop keepers were caked with dirt.

Curious 14-year-old girls surrounded us. Aside from the occasional tourist they had no contact with the outside world. Their few English words were "America is good, isn't it." Verbally our reaction was "Yes, America is good." Our thoughts and our reaction were that we could not comprehend the lives of these Jewish children, curious about us, yet living in filth and poverty.

We continued walking near the barbed wire border between Old and New Jerusalem, keeping our hands down at our sides so the heavily armed border guards would not shoot us. More remnants of deserted buildings from the War of Liberation.

* * * *

Down to Beersheba, the Negev desert which covers 60% of Israel. Desolate, brown and barren. No plants, no human beings. An occasional Bedouin cavalcade with a few camels moved slowly across the eroded soil. One wonders why God called this the land of milk and honey.

One of the outstanding cities we visited was Avdat, located in the center of the desert between Egypt and Jordan. Then deserted Avdat had supported an agricultural and trading population of 10,000. But it wasn't until the mid-1950s that the source of the water for the crops was discovered. A survey by plane showed clearly defined rock walls a short way from the city itself, which stood on a high hill completely surrounded by the desert. The rain water -- only several inches each year -- was collected in these cache basins and used to water the crops.

Israel in 1959 was not well developed. But the Israelis brought together two main elements that helped build the country to what it is today. First, the kibbutz -- THE only true Marxist political community -- where everyone contributed to the whole and everyone was provided with housing, food, clothing, education and medical care. Second, the use of agricultural technology. Israel has little water (as evident in Avdat) and water was -- and still is -- very precious. Amidst the beige sands were green oasis where underground irrigation systems fed the roots of plants, thus bypassing evaporation from the leaves. Thus Israel developed a thriving business of exporting fruits and vegetables to Europe.

My feeling today is that if the Arabs had used such systems that they too could have made their hostile lands fruitful. But sometimes it seems that the Arabs are more interested in political elements rather than providing the basics for their people.

ARTICLES DOCUMENTED THE TRIP

I made arrangements ahead of time to send articles to *The Wisconsin State Journal (WSJ)* -- because the trip was organized through the University of Wisconsin -- and the *Bergen Evening Record*, my hometown paper. My by-lined articles in the *WSJ* read "State Journal Correspondent." In those days there was no Fax, so all articles were airmailed, probably typed on my old Royal portable typewriter, which weighed 25 pounds and which I always carried with me .

My clips tell the story.

Headlines in *The Wisconsin State Journal* were:

<u>Tuesday, July 21, 1959</u> -- Madisonian Reports on Trip to Israel, Progress of Jews

<u>Sunday, July 26, 1959</u> -- Jerusalem Shows Its Age, but Ignores Past as Well

<u>Thursday, August 6, 1959</u> -- In 10 Years, the Negev Struggles From Desert to Vigorous Land

<u>Friday, August 7, 1959</u> -- Equality Stressed in Israel Kibbutz

RIOTS & REVOLUTIONS

These articles focused on what I saw as we traveled from modern city to stark desert and the Dead Sea and Mediterranean. The articles show the vision and hard work of the Jews in rebuilding, in some areas virtually from scratch. Also clearly shown is the drive for the future and enhancing human quality of life. These articles did not deal with politics -- except relating to education and immigration.

My first article in the *Wisconsin State Journal* stated:

"At Haifa, our first glimpse of the Holy Land, the slopes of Mt. Carmel appeared to be dotted with white modern buildings. Soon we could see that buildings covered the mountain. The gold dome of the Bahai Temple and the "Dagon Silos" could be distinguished in the masses of whiteness."

I wrote about the efforts at reforestation and reclamation of the land stripped of forests and vegetation by the Romans and Ottoman Turks.

The first article ends "The general atmosphere is one of progress and pushing ahead, of building a new nation and life."

(Later on in this book I talk about my 1967 trip to Israel and the fact that the Arabs did little, if anything, to reclaim and rebuild the lands they occupied. If Arabs had done 'things' differently, we might not be in the political and highly emotionally charged situation in which we are today.)

My second article to the *WSJ* was from Beersheba and talks about what it was, is and will be. Following is key text.

"Beersheba. The building of a dynamic modern society has gone on at an unbelievable rate.

"With mass immigration, the population has doubled in 10 years. A total of 437 new villages and towns, 578,000 living units, 1,346 new schools, 132 hospitals and clinics, 764 miles of new roads, and 395 miles of railway have been built since 1948......

"The harsh and once unpromising lands of the Negev desert present a typical image of an irrevocable desert. Desolate, barren and brown, eroded by winds and rains, the Negev covers 60% of Israel.

"Before 1949, the Negev was dismissed in a multitude of argumentative documents as impossible for human habitation, destined to remain parched and inaccessible. And when one travels through this area - the bleakest land imaginable - one wonders how it could have been called the Land of Milk and Honey.

"However, scholars knew that once large sections of the Negev had been fertile and productive and had sustained populations ranging from 80,000 to 100,000.

"Today from this area of ungodliness rise the buildings of Beersheba, the vigorous capital of the Negev. ......"

"The clue to the Negev's progress is the bringing of water from the north, where it is plentiful, to the south, which receives only a few inches of rain each year. ...."

In the next article in the *WSJ* as I stood at the barbed wire separating Israel with Egypt, I continued to talk about the spirit of the Jews and the kibbutz -- THE only place in the world where true Marxism existed and was successful. This land-based spirit is also shown in my unique 1967 series in *The Bergen Evening Record* on the "occupied" lands. This spirit continues, even stronger today, as the "enemy" (the Arabs) continues to try to wipe Israel from the world map.

"Life on a kibbutz is looked upon as being the best expression of equality man can find in this word.

"The kibbutz is a communal settlement in which all property is collectively owned, and work is organized on a collective basis. The members give their labor and are supplied with housing, food, clothing, education, and cultural and medical services. ....

"The emergence of Zionism as the concrete expression of an age-old dream to restore Jewish independence in Israel was accompanied by the idea of a return to the soil. ......

"This return to the soil met with overwhelming difficulties. ...."

I talked about the barren land and the tremendous obstacles faced by the settlers, and again the spirit of the people and the country.

The *WSJ* article continues .... "The Israelites are building a country to become a nation among nations. They are building farms and industries from rocks. They are blossoming forth from the desert."

As I stood that day close to the Egyptian border in the Yad Mordechai kibbutz I wrote "Israel is looking to the future, building day by day, yet apprehensive of the still unsettled peace here."

That night, right where we stood that day, Israeli soldiers killed three Egyptians who were trying to cross into Israel to do damage.

* * * *

The first *Bergen Evening Record* article, written from Jerusalem, focused on education and immigration and the problems caused by a multiethnic population. The first paragraph reads: "Educators in Israel today face problems similar to those faced by their American counterparts during the great expansion years following the Civil War and extending to the present day."

That "present day" is still here today with unequal quality of education resulting in a high dropout rate in cities, gang wars, drugs and guns.

My *Record* article headlined "Immigration Causes Problems for Israeli School Systems." And says "As America was an assimilation point for various immigrants and racial groups, so in a smaller sense is Israel just such a melting pot. Since 1948 thousands of immigrants from all parts of the globe have flocked to Israel, bringing with them many diverse languages and customs.

"It is the educators' task to assimilate and raise the living and educational standards of peoples with entirely different cultures and backgrounds. Education is the indispensable instrument for welding together the different elements --the native born and the newcomer -- into a united society.

"Israel's question of cultural atmosphere in the home in correlation to educational levels is not unlike America's education problems born of our influx of immigrants. Both countries endeavor to find the best possible way in which to raise their national standard of living and education, including that of the newcomer, without hindering those who have had a head start by virtue of being native born. ..."

Education is complex. Perhaps the Israelis had been more insightful in philosophy and action than Americans, even in the 21st century. In one of my articles I talked about the aims of the Hebrew University, still the premier educational institution in Israel.

According to my article: "The University has a 3-fold aim: to serve humanity by expanding knowledge, to serve Israel by providing it with professional manpower, by training its future leaders, and by scientifically hastening the process of its development; and to service the Jewish people by helping to redefine Jewish values and to re-create a specifically Hebrew culture."

The article also talked about the technical and trade schools, so "the youths of the nation build themselves into productive citizens and build a greater Israel." Again, Israel was ahead of the USA in establishing educational objectives to meet the needs of both its youth and the nation. We are still grappling with this problem today -- not enough technical expertise to meet the needs of the 21st century.

The next *Record* article focused on Beersheba and the Negev, same as the *Wisconsin State Journal* one. The headline: "Reclamation of Desert Is Important to Israel." The subhead: Portions of Bleak Negev Have Been Restored to Fertility As Nation Marches Ahead. Its beginning tied everything together with "The building of a dynamic society in Israel has gone on at an unbelievable rate."

And the next *Record* article combined a description of the desolate country with the Yad Mordechai kibbutz. The headline: "Rebirth Held Back Without Working Soil." The subhead: "Zionism Accompanied By Return to Agriculture."

My last article for *The Record*, dated Sept. 3, 1959 summarized my impressions and the many challenges facing Israel. So much progress had been made from Independence to that summer of 1959. My 1967 articles further showed the progress, but focused on the political and economic dilemmas resulting from the Six Day War.

The 1959 headline read "Israel Fights to Live, Lacks All Resources."

"Our visit to Israel is over. We leave with a feeling of having seen a modern nation being molded out of wilderness -- a wilderness such as our forefathers never experienced.

"Here the soil is gone from the mountain slopes and water is scarcely found in 60% of the country. Israel has few natural resources, and although a Middle East country lacks precious oil.

"Mass immigration has caused innumerable problems. Problems which must be solved. To remain a free political entity amidst enemies, Israel must build a strong country or perish. Thus, progress comes from necessity."

The article ends: "This land of the Bible, which has lain waste for generations, has, during the last few decades, changed beyond recognition. The barren wilderness has turned into a flowering garden; malaria-infested swamps are now fertile valleys with flourishing settlements; new water resources have been opened up, and the earth yields crops undreamed of a generation ago. Much still remains to be done, but labor, science, and humanitarian work have made common cause and carry on harmoniously towards a common goal."

For the three weeks in Israel, our schedule was hectic. Up at sunrise and after 13 hours either on the unairconditioned bus or sightseeing we'd crash at a hotel. At the same time, I felt as if I had just "tipped the country". So much more! So much dynamism.

TO NEW CULTURES AND FAMILIES

From my experiences in Wisconsin and at New York University, I believe that most peoples were basically the same as far as life values go, regardless of ethnic or country background. I found that even the poor willingly share what little they may have with strangers, especially from another country.

This belief was validated time after time, over the years, as I always tried to get to know average people in every country in which I spent time. I stayed with families wherever possible or visited families of my Wisconsin classmates.

So from Israel, that first trip in 1959, I went to Athens, London, Edinburg and Paris.

In Athens I met the family of one of my Wisconsin classmates, Demetris Spyridakis. His brother, George, managed a small hotel, Hotel Alfa, and I stayed there. I met the whole family, who peppered me with questions about Wisconsin and life in the States.

Needless to say, given my interest in ruins, I found the Acropolis, Delphi and Corinth fascinating. That parts of those cities still stand, after thousands of years, is really amazing -- especially when a building or structure here may only be a couple of hundred years old.

As always the best way to immerse oneself in the atmosphere of a city is to walk the streets. I did this in Israel with the group. And a few of us would do so at night. In Athens, London and Paris I traveled alone. But every day I walked the streets, taking in the past as well as the present. Of course, I was young and had a lot of energy.

The top of the Acropolis, tells the story of the ancients. The Temple of Theseus from 400 BC, the Arch of Hadrian, the Theatre of Dionysos, the Tower of Winds, and so much more. My feet ached, but I continued the next day. An amazing boat trip to Argolis, Corinth, Epodaurus, Mecenas showed the ancient buildings that have stood up over time.

At night, George took me out to dinner. Often to hidden places the average tourist would never find. One dinner with his family. Another night to his cousin's family.

Noted in my diary: HOT!! HOT!! And "the Greek people's warmth was overwhelming."

Given my interest in international affairs, there were many discussions about USA's role in the world. A Foreign Ministry official told me that the US should take more initiative in foreign policy rather than sit back waiting for events to occur.

Aside from my conversations with the Indian exchange student in high school, this was the second time a foreigner criticized American foreign policy and the lack of understanding of the world and other people.

This was re-enforced the next day when I went to the USIS library and spoke with the Director for 1 1/2 hours. The lack of true understanding came out. A larger budget was needed to translate books into the native language. And the availability of cheaper American books would further cement a positive relationship.

LONDON

London is difficult to fully describe because it is so complex. In spite of a lot of rain, I wandered around on foot and found the Indian section, where restaurants offered less expensive lunches and dinners. I loved Indian food even then. I spent many hours in the museums, awed by the masterpieces -- the details and depth perception.

The English had a reputation for being somber and cold. I found them quite friendly. However, I clearly felt the class distinction, an aloofness of lower class from the uppers.

As I'm a people person I sought out people wherever I could. Lunch and then dinner with the family who were cousins of the husband of my cousin. Also I spent a day and evening with one of my Wisconsin classmates, Hasso Rudt Von Collenbeg. We visited the London Tower, the British Museum, and the play "A Raisin in the Sun." If I recall correctly the play premiered in London before coming to NYC. We also went to a concert and ballet. Hasso and I years later planned to get together in Vietnam. Did not happen, as he was killed.

From London I called the parents of one of my Wisconsin classmates, John Crellin, to say "hello" and tell them John was doing fine in the States. His mother said, "Oh, when can you visit us?" On Sunday I took the train to Thorpe Bay. After sightseeing and a long walk on the beach, I had lunch with the family. John's mother looked at the way I ate and said "I wonder if John is going to eat with two hands when he comes home."

From London I took the train to Edinburg to attend the opening ceremonies of the Edinburg Festival. My US travel agent had gotten me a ticket. Cost US$5.

In Edinburg, I visited with still another family of a Wisconsin classmate, Sev Fluss, whose Jewish family invited me to a Friday Sabbath dinner. We talked about the upcoming Festival. They were also going. They wanted to know where I would be sitting so they could find me. I showed them my ticket. "Is this a good seat?" I asked. Everyone looked at each other and said "Yes!" We arranged to meet after the concert.

Before the concert I had dinner at a restaurant on the Village Green, which was crowded with people going to the concert. The maitre'de asked me if I would share my very small table with a female army officer. I agreed and spent an interesting hour learning more about Scotland. The officer had an army car and driver and offered to take me up the steep hill to the castle. Of course, I agreed.

I found my seat. But then I looked around and cringed. I wore a sleeveless denim dress and sandals. I was surrounded by mink, ermine, diamonds and tuxes. Wow! All for $5. Afterwards, I asked Sev's family why they didn't warn me. His mother said, "We were afraid you wouldn't go."

* * * *

The last stop on that first trip abroad was Paris. I spent a lot of time in the Louvre Museum. As in London, the delicacy of the masterpieces fascinated me. At that time, Chagall was little known, but he had one of his first exhibits in a small side gallery of the Louvre. I wasn't impressed by his work then -- and I'm still not. I would buy a loaf of French bread and some cheese and sit on the banks of the Seine watching the boats and ducks.

One night I treated myself to dinner at a fancy French restaurant -- linen table cloths, waiters in tuxes. I had had a little (very little) French in college. When I finished eating, I said to the waiter "Je sui fini ." And motioned that he could take my plate. He asked me what I said, and I repeated it. "Oh, no," he said, "you can't say that." "Why not!" I asked. "I am finished."

"No," he said, "Je sui fini means I am dead." What a booboo!!

I stayed in a small B&B on a side street near the Arch de Triumph. On my last day I met a young Irish couple, who were on their honeymoon. She was a teacher. We spent the day together, and I learned a lot about the poverty in Ireland -- even more than 10 years after the War. Bread and potatoes were the staples. I had about $20 left, and so invited them to dinner -- at a tiny, inexpensive, but very good Italian restaurant I had found. The couple had never seen spaghetti! Once the other diners saw me trying to show them how to use the fork and spoon to twirl the spaghetti, everyone gave advice. We had a jolly time!

AFTER THAT FIRST TRIP

I returned home and after a short stint with one of the encyclopedias I started working for *Time* magazine and went to graduate school at New York University. At *Time,* I was a researcher. At that time, only men were writers, no women writers. I learned a valuable lesson there, which helped me throughout my writing career. I quickly saw that what these men wrote never saw print as they first wrote them. A number of levels of editing changed their carefully crafted words -- and they were making big bucks then. So I asked, "Doesn't it bother you that what you write doesn't get into the magazine?" The unanimous answer was "If you can't accept editing and changes then you should not be in this profession." Another 'best advice.'

The work week was Tuesday through Saturday, because the deadline was 11 p.m. Saturday. The magazine went to press early Sunday morning and was on the streets across the country Monday morning. **Looking back, this** accomplishment was amazing. There were no computers, and every word, in fact every letter, was hand set on large wooden plates that were then put on the printing presses. There was no Federal Express to get the papers quickly to the newsstands.

Another lesson learned was that I am no drinker. One drink was my limit. Reporters have a reputation of being heavy drinkers, and in order to keep the best of the best, *Time* management delivered bottles of Scotch and Rye (favorite drinks of the day) every Friday night to the writers and researchers. On Saturday, gourmet dinners were brought in for everyone. I wonder if this custom is still honored.

Even though we made far less money than the men, researchers welded awesome power. An article could not go to the printer unless I signed off on it. Signing off meant that every word was spelled correctly (no such thing as spell check), each punctuation mark was correct, and the article was totally factually accurate.

I can still remember one story about some agricultural program and policy that was so warped it was factually inaccurate (at least as far as I was concerned). I made the writer change the wording -- otherwise I would not sign off. Reluctantly he did make the change -- probably because we were on deadline and there was no time to debate it.

The only time something inaccurate slipped by me involved the death of some well-known sheik in the Middle East. It was late on a Saturday night -- deadline time -- and I used the information from the *New York Times* obit without checking further.

So, I worked at *Time* during the day and went to New York University graduate school at night -- again majoring in International Relations. My MA degree in Government

/International Relations was January 1963. I commuted from New Jersey every day, often returning home late at night, only to get up very early the next day and repeat the process. My parents paid for my years at Wisconsin, but then I was on my own. I guess when one wants something bad enough one finds a way. Actually *Time* reimbursed my tuition after I completed each course. They wanted their staff members to be as educated as possible.

Several things during those years influenced the rest of my life. First was the ongoing discussions at NYU about world politics and what we would do when we would have the power to make changes. A great lesson learned by listening to others with differing opinions.

Second were connections with colleagues from overseas which made my travels in India and Indonesia extremely fruitful.

CHAPTER 2

NEW ADVENTURES BEGIN

In the 1950s there was great competition between India, supposedly a democratic country, and China a communist country. I became fascinated with the differences in ideology and the fact that both had millions of starving people to feed. Which one could better feed its multitudes? In 1957 a communist administration was voted in in Kerala, a very poor southern Indian state. The communists ruled from April 1957 through July 1959 when they were voted out of office.

The objective of my Master's thesis, titled "Kerala: A Unique Experiment," was to analyze how the communists in Kerala operated. Whether they could work within a larger democratic environment or whether they tried to work within a strict communist structure. My thesis was published in India in 1963. In the Introduction, I said,

"India - land of the elephant and mythical dancing snake - with its teeming population and not enough food, trapped in a crazy-quilt pattern of religious restrictions, poverty and backwardness, is the key to the success or failure of democracy in underdeveloped areas of the world. This key will lock or unlock the way for progress and that vital leap from a pre-industrial society into the atomic era and a democratic government.

"..... two antagonistic philosophies and ways of life -- international communism and democracy -- are competing for the souls and stomachs of the peoples of the world... which country and system can give its people more fastest?"

I had two unique advantages in researching and writing this thesis. First, I had access to all of *Time*'s correspondents' filed information and spent hours in the morgue. Second, our area's Congressman, Frank Osmers, was a friend of my parents. I would find him, the city's police chief and my father playing craps on the living room floor. Osmers enabled me to have unlimited access to State Department files. I spent days culling the reports. Besides getting information on the Kerala situation, I read State Department reports on the activity of the Chinese in Tibet. In the early 1960s, the Chinese Communists were building roads from China itself, through Tibet to the northern most corner of India, the state of Assam. Heavy equipment and tanks were brought in, according to the reports. My conclusion -- the Chinese were going to invade India. Why else would they build roads in this forsaken area? Because India was persona non-grata by the United States, China thought it would have no opposition to the invasion, which would divert Indian resources away from feeding its people and building up the country. *So, by early 1962, I predicted the invasion. But no one - not even Mr. Osmers - would listen to me.*

I decided to go to India to see for myself. Beforehand I got press credentials from *The Press Journal,* a small weekly paper in Englewood, NJ, my home town. Of course my parents knew the publisher. From my clips I see I wrote a number of articles for *The Boston Globe* and also had press credentials from that paper. In India, I wrote articles for the US Information Service. These articles appeared in a number of Indian language papers. When I left India in September 1963

I made arrangements to write articles for the India News & Feature Alliance as well as *The Boston Globe*.

I had spent a tiring summer (1962) working full time at *Time* and writing my thesis -- actually wrote it in six weeks. When I gave it to my advisor, (Thomas Hovet) his comment was "This is too journalistic. It's not scholarly." But he did accept it. So, I was ready for a relaxing month on board a Dutch freighter, going from NYC to Bombay.

* * * *

I left for India on October 15, 1962 on the Dutch freighter, MS Neder Elbe, (nine passengers and a month at sea). I traveled alone -- rare in those days for a female to travel alone, especially to the countries I wanted to visit.

My plans were to stay in India for a year, travel around, and then go on to Indonesia, The Philippines and Japan. Several of my Wisconsin classmates, who had become friends, were from India, and I stayed with their families in different parts of the country. Through an educator at NYU, Vera Michels Dean, I was introduced to the Private Secretary, Vishwanath Y. Tonpe, to the Indian Finance Minister, Morarji Desai. One of my NYU colleagues was from Indonesia, and he wrote to relatives in Indonesia, with whom I stayed for a month. One of my Wisconsin International Club colleagues, Val Alipio, was from The Philippines, and he wrote to his family there. Still another classmate was from Japan (Tomeo Kambayashi, a manager at Nippon Telegraph and Telephone Company), and I kept in touch with him during my stay in India. Beginning in my senior year in high school, I corresponded with a Japanese girl, Masako Nishii, whom I was anxious to finally meet. My contacts were in place. So even though I was traveling in unknown and foreign territory I felt safe.

Except in Indonesia in 1965 when anti-Americanism was at its height, people all over were friendly. So many took me around the various cities, showing me everything from luxurious hotels, casinos, palaces to the poor inner streets. Everyone was protective of me as a single, lone female. Often they put a car and driver at my disposal. My gut instincts helped me meet and spend time with good people and avoid the creeps (like in Thailand in 1968).

* * * *

The beginning of the trip was quiet. But as we neared Spain we saw Russian war ships heading toward the United States and learned they were headed for Cuba to protect Cuba from an invasion by the U.S. Ship to shore communications in those days was dicey and rarely could a full message get through or be heard clearly. We learned little -- except that there might be a confrontation that could end in an atomic war. We also learned that the Chinese had indeed invaded Assam, India's tea province.

Once we were in the Mediterranean, communications were fairly good. So we were able to keep up with what was happening with Cuba and India. All of us were apprehensive as the news from India was not good. The Chinese had penetrated pretty far into India and had captured a regional airport. I had never experienced a war, but planned to continue with the plans to travel around India.

I was correct in my prediction. And I was going to be there.

On the ship my cabin mate was a missionary, Mary Dorsey, who had been in the states for cancer treatment and was returning to India. We became fast friends and remained friends throughout my stay in India and later when I returned home. Our first stop was Tripoli, Libya, -- pre Gaddafi. We were able to get off the ship for a short time. Standing on solid ground for the first time in days really felt good. The second stop was supposed to be Ben Ghazi. But the political situation there was in an uproar. The captain deemed it unsafe for us to go ashore. We rocked away from shore for a day or two and then went on. I can't remember if any goods were unloaded.

The next stop was Alexandria, Egypt. The first day, all of us went on a bus tour of the city. At night I went ashore with the ship's First Mate and saw the night life.

The next day I did not go ashore with the group. Traveling with so many gets cumbersome having to wait for the slower people and missing what I wanted to spend time seeing. The First Mate arranged for me to go into the heart of the city where I looked up TIME's correspondent. Although a Sunday, the local correspondent was in the office trying to make arrangements for a photographer to go to the border of Saudi Arabia to take pictures of the deposed Iman. The month before the old Iman died (I did the story while at TIME) and his son took over. However, a coup ousted the son and he was in Saudi Arabia. The correspondent Abu Said was waiting to make arrangements for a photographer. He put a car and driver, who spoke good English, at my disposal. He took me through the American University of Beirut, and tremendous natural caves that had just been opened to the public. Then Abu and I went to lunch and sat on his terrace which overlooked the Hills of Lebanon as we waited to hear about a photographer.

Abu was an extraordinary person and believed, as I still do, that getting the truth out to the peoples of the world was very important. In fact, as we sat on the terrace I mentioned a TIME correspondent who had been beaten up because he had written an anti-Nasser article that appeared in TIME. Nasser gangs had cut up Abu's feet and backside in revenge. I went back to the ship for a few hours rest, and then returned to Abu's where he was having a birthday party for one of the women at the American Embassy. We then went to a casino.

At the casino I kept looking at a young man by the name of John Smith who worked at Morgan Guarantee Bank in NYC. I asked him if he had visited the NYC TIME offices. He said "no." We started talking. He was from New Jersey. Where? Englewood. His father was John Smith the coach at the high school, and when he was little his family lived next door to mine. We remarked that perhaps as kids we had snowball fights.

As the ship was supposed to leave at 10 p.m., I left shortly after cocktails.

* * * *

The others on the ship had hired a guide to take them into the mountains to old ruins. Even before they left the dock, two guides got into a fight about who would take them. They had returned before I did, but told Mary of cars breaking down, the driver being arrested because there were too many passengers in one car, the car breaking down again and again and the driver being arrested several times for having too many people in the car and not having a license.

We then stopped briefly at Beirut, the financial capital of the Middle East. A beautiful, modern city. It hurts me to see what it has become.

Next stop was Port Said, Egypt, a large important port at the northern end of the Suez Canal.

As Mary and I left the ship a young boy, who was about ten years old, convinced us to hire him as a guide. We saw the city as no other tourist would. We drove through the streets in a horse drawn carriage. Children waved to us. The kid took us to out of the way sights, ones never seen on a formal tour. We walked and walked through clean, garbage free and beggar free streets until we got blisters. Two things still stand out in my mind. First was a Russian Orthodox church, located behind very high walls. The church was laden with 18 carat gold statues and intricate stained glass windows. If a person just walked by, he or she would never know about the beauty inside those walls. Our young guide knew how to get in via a side door. We rested our sore feet, and Mary spent time praying.

Second, were the bakery shops -- full of tantalizing smells and even better tasting pastries. We had the best baklava we had had in a bakery owned by a relative of our guide.

By that time we were weary and as we walked back to the ship I can remember we stopped in the middle of the street relishing the pastries. There was no car traffic and even fewer people walking around. We had the street to ourselves. We looked at each other and said, at the same time, "We should get more and take them back to the ship." But we were tired. "I'll go back and get some for you," our guide said. We gave him some money -- with the thought that we would never again see the boy or the money and certainly not those luscious pastries. But the boy did return with a bag full of baklava.

The mention of baklava reminds me that food on the ship was the highlight of the day. Breakfast at 8:30 a.m., which I never made; tea at 10 a.m., lunch 12.30 p.m., tea at 4 p.m., supper at 6:30 p.m., and tea at 8:30 p.m. Four star chef on board.

The Suez Canal, closed when Israel fought its War for Liberation, had recently re-opened.

I remember walking around and around the deck, as the ship went from one lock to another. On both sides one saw only empty desert, sand and more sand. Once in a while, nomads and several camels could be seen struggling across the sand. A truly hostile land. Mary and I wondered how the nomads made a living and where were their families. The last time Mary had gone to India, her ship went around the tip of Africa and took much longer than our scheduled one month.

* * * *

Our last stop was Aqaba, Jordan, directly across from Eilat, Israel, which I did not visit during any of my four visits there.

On the Jordanian side of the Red Sea one could see sand, and more sand, an army post and some stucco houses and Bedouin huts. Materials for the Jordanian army were unloaded from our ship.

As usual Mary and I avoided the other passengers and went out on our own -- by foot --to get to the town itself. There were no buses in Aqaba. Transportation was by car or on foot. There really wasn't much to see. When we did meet anyone, that person was very friendly. We started talking with a man who was in charge of the road construction, which would connect a new road from Aqaba to Amman (the capital). He invited us for tea. Then a young man who owned the only Casino in town drove up in a big, dated, Buick. He invited us for tea at his casino. We sat in the garden overlooking the bay, drank Arabic coffee and talked. Then he drove us around and stopped at a school. We wanted to see what it was like. Most of the teachers spoke English and were very friendly. They showed us around and we spent some time there. They all had a terrific sense of humor, and Mary and I really had a ball. The thing that impressed us most was that here in the middle of nowhere the Arabs were friendly and eager to share their life with us. We wanted to give some money to the fellow who owned the casino, but he refused. This was very unusual "as most Arabs would just as soon take the shirt off your back."

In my Oct. 27, 1962 letter to my parents I wrote "My impression is what is happening now in India will definitely affect the Cold War. If India is lost, it is the beginning of the end of democracy."

INDIA AT LAST: POOREST OF THE POOR

China's invasion of India in October 1962 was an early prime example of the failure of intelligence. In this case, not picking up and connecting the dots by the Americans and the blinders on the eyes of the Indians. I still find it unbelievable that I, sitting around the other side of the globe, saw what was going on and understood very clearly China's intent.

After a month on board, we finally anchored off shore at Bombay around 1 a.m. Nov. 15th. The shipping agent came aboard around 1:45 a.m. I sat on deck with the First Mate and Chief Engineer watching nothing really happening. I went back to the cabin and around 2:30 a.m. someone knocked on the door. Is Mrs. Dorsey here? John Dorsey walked in. Mary had said that if there was any way John could get on board even before everyone was allowed to get off, that he would.

They hadn't seen each other in more than a year, so I left the cabin.

A launch came around 10 a.m. to take us ashore. I did not expect anyone to meet me, but the port's Chief Inspector came on board and took me quickly through customs. Then as I got on solid land, my friend Sybil Benjamin and her father were there. Sybil, a Jewish Indian, and I became friends in New York, and she had spent time in Englewood with me and my parents. She said she had received a letter from my mother giving my arrival time. A welcome sight!

As I said earlier, my prediction that China would invade India came true while I was on my way there. Chaos reigned in Bombay when I arrived. Indians had been shocked, surprised and were scared. Their army was small and totally unprepared for war. In spite of the fact that the US considered India an enemy because of its neutral political stance, the US sent in troops, weapons and supplies. C-130 transport planes quickly moved in.

Before I left the states, arrangements had been made for me to stay with cousins of one of my Wisconsin classmates, Indravadin Popitlal Shah.

Thus began my travels, in an in-depth way, into another culture.

Staying with families (something I did whenever possible) gave me insight into family life, its dynamics and familial relationships that I would not have gotten if I had stayed in a hotel.

There were a number of cousins living together in Bombay. At first I got confused because they all looked alike. Ramniklal M. and Leela Shah and Krishnagant and Rashmi

RIOTS & REVOLUTIONS

Shah were the primary occupants. Others came and went. We figured out that I.P. and Krishna were third cousins once removed.

The family lived in an apartment over stores in a very busy and crowded part of the city. The apartment consisted of six rooms plus kitchen, bath and toilet. The toilet room was a hole in the floor with two places to put one's feet, like the squat toilets in Israel. No toilet paper. I was glad I had plenty of tissues. There was running water only three hours a day. One hour in the morning and two hours at night. During those times buckets were filled and water was stored and used for bathing and cooking.

I was given the best room in the apartment -- the only one that was air conditioned. I was treated as a special person.

The Shahs were strict vegetarian and ate with their hands, as was the Indian custom. They did not even have a fork or knife as regular tableware. I used a spoon for everything.

The first morning, my host wanted to show me around the neighborhood so I would not get lost. The city teemed with water buffaloes pulling carts, bikes, and pollution spewing trucks and cars. I stood at the curb and looking to my left for traffic. I have told this story many times over the years. I went to step off the curb, and my host grabbed the back of my blouse and pulled me back. A huge water buffalo was bearing down on me. I might have died that first day.

As we walked through the streets I saw a sign that had the schedule of the new Defense Minister Chavan who was going to speak at a rally that night. One of the Shahs and I went. There were probably 5,000 to 10,000 people at the rally. I showed my press card and was taken to the front row. My camera was hard at work taking in the faces of those present.

Like most upper class Indians, a car and driver was a must. Often I had their services. This enabled me to get to appointments and rallies. Public transportation, such as it was, was impossible.

Rashmi and I became close friends, and she often came to my room just to talk. She was intrigued that I set my hair each night with bobby pins. Rashmi, 27, graduated college in psychology and worked for three years before getting married. For the past two years she did nothing in the house -- had plenty of servants-- or even outside the house. Social status forbids a wife to work after marriage. This conversation was repeated many times when I attended I.P. Shah's brother's wedding.

In Bombay I spent a lot of time with Sybil and her large family. On my third day, we went to the Elephanta Caves. The caves were 1,300 years old and held special meaning to the Hindu religion. We took her two nieces and nephew. Although it was hot, Eric, the nephew, insisted on wearing the red shirt I had bought him. We returned to her house, had lunch, rested and then went her sister's for tea. Then we took a train ride to a suburb to another sister's house. We walked along the beach where a war rally was going on. The Jewish community was small, but Sybil took me to Sabbath services. . Her brother in Calcutta took me into the synagogue there, which was locked up most of the time.

A few days later, I visited Sybil's school, and then we went shopping. Later we visited her sister in the hospital who had had a hernia operation.

Every day some event was going on to arouse support for the war effort.

I started going to whatever rally I could. I interviewed the head of the Indian Citizens Defense Committee and had lunch with the American USIS officer and his wife.

The Indians were all emotionally aroused and demanded the resignation of the Defense Minister Krishna Menon. The people demanded strong measures against the Chinese and called for a united India. This was probably the first time the country was united for a specific cause since independence. Banners and posters filled the streets.

The Indians finally realized that it was impossible to negotiate with the Chinese, in spite of a supposed cease fire. The Indians also had trouble with Pakistan, which refused to let Indians cross their territory to get supplies and troops to Assam. Thus everything had to be transported over rugged terrain or flown into the war area.

On Nov. 20, Chavan gave a farewell speech to a group of troops going to war. Never having seen soldiers going to war -- never experiencing war per se, I was choked up. They were so young and inexperienced. Stock and commodity markets fell quickly, and controls were put in place to prevent a crash. The night before at dinner I could feel the tension in the air. Everyone was waiting to see what would happen next.

Through my friend Tonpe, I met a couple of businessmen who gave me an insight into the politics and economics of India. One of the businessmen, Indru Advani, invited me to lunch a couple of times during my stay in Bombay. The lunch consisted of both fish and chicken as well as varied vegetables and rice. "Why both fish and chicken?" I once asked him. "You're staying with vegetarians, and I don't want you to get sick while you are visiting my country." After lunch he would take me sightseeing, often to stores that tourists did not visit. In one store, silks of all kinds adorned the shelves and tables.

RIOTS & REVOLUTIONS

For some reason, he zeroed in on table cloths. He gave me a cock and bull story about needing a wedding gift for the son of friends of his. I say 'cock and bull' story because the day before I left Bombay, he gave me a large Kashmir silk, hand embroidered table cloth that I know cost him the equivalent of US$500.

The second businessman, Harshavadan J. Shah, was a contractor, owner of one of the biggest construction companies in India. Two of his sons were overseas studying -- one in Germany and the other in Connecticut. While I was in India, he visited both of them. He also visited my parents in New Jersey, when he visited his son in Connecticut. He was a vegetarian, and I had warned my parents. So, my mother made many of the traditional Jewish dairy dishes -- blintzes, borsht, potato pancakes.

When he returned to India he told me that was the best meal he had on his whole trip. He especially complained about his stay in Germany as Germans, he said, were not understanding of his dietary needs.

In 1970, Mr. HJ Shah attended an international building conference in Manila. Needless to say, my husband and I treated him to a typical Filipino dinner. During dinner I said I was unable to find good curry spices. He called his wife in Bombay, who put together her special combination of spices and air mailed a packet to me.

As I have said, living with families gave me an understanding of Indian values, which were very similar at that time to the Jewish values I grew up with. Of course there were differences. But in some substantive areas the reasons were for practical and health reasons. For instance, Hindus do not eat beef. Originally not for basic religious reasons, but because there was a time when there was not enough milk for children. To protect cows from being slaughtered and to have enough milk for children, the custom of not eating beef began. Over time not eating beef did become an integral part of the Hindu religion. Originally a similar, yet different, reason Jewish people do not eat pork. If pork is not cooked thoroughly, illness can occur. To avoid illness, Jews began avoiding pork, and this became an integral part of the Jewish religion.

* * * *

From Bombay I went to the northern city of Ahmedabad to attend the wedding of I.P.'s brother, Chandra P., a doctor. I met I.P.'s parents, three brothers and a sister as well as numerous aunts, uncles, cousins, nieces and nephews. I.P.'s brothers spoke English, but his parents did not. Everyone treated me royally, opened their hearts to me, and wanted me to stay longer.

Usually weddings of the upper class lasted several days. But because of the war with China, the ceremonies were only one day -- beginning at dawn and going well into the night. The wedding procession traveled from family member to family member, honoring the elders. Breakfast, lunch and dinner were served to all the wedding guests - dozens of them. I was carried along in the joyous spirit. As the day went on and night approached, the family members assigned to help me drank more and more. For breakfast and lunch, someone always remembered to tell the cooks that I was American and couldn't eat very hot spicy food -- which was the custom as the family originally came from south India. Special portions were set aside for me. But by dark, everyone was so caught up in the celebrations, no one told the cook to leave out the chilies. Now I love Indian food, and if I had to choose one ethnic food I would have to eat for the rest of my life it would be Indian. But the food that night was so hot, I could not bear it. Another brother of my friend and the groom together with a number of cousins, who were intrigued that an American attended the wedding, took me out to a restaurant so I wouldn't be hungry. The cousins kept peppering me with questions about life in America.

The Indian saris (women's dresses) were elaborate and woven with 18 carat gold threads and jewels. The colors were awesome -- deep colors, to pale or pastels. Later in my visit in India, I went south and spent time with I.P.'s parents. Mr. Shah took me to a textile mill, where I bought some silk embroidered with gold (which I had made into dresses for myself and my mother for my sister's wedding), and Indian raw silk that I had made into matching suits for my parents.

Chandra, the groom, was a doctor, and the bride was a college graduate with a law degree. But upper class Indian women did not work, even if they had a college degree. The degree was "added" to the list of accomplishments for the marriage contract. Something similar to our custom in the 1950s that a college degree for a woman was really an MRS. degree. You went to college to catch a husband.

I had several interesting conversations with both young women and even some of the older ones who were college graduates. A college degree equaled more value in the marriage market and had nothing to do with earning a living. Given the immense poverty in India I thought it was a shame that women, who would not contribute to the economy, took up the limited number of seats in colleges that men, who had to work and support families, should have held. When I made this observation, the women just shrugged their shoulders.

They're-enforced what Rashmi had told me that even though she was a college graduate that she could not work now that she was married.

I returned to Bombay after the wedding because on Dec. 2, a new nylon plant was to be dedicated. The plant, Bombay Textiles, was owned by the uncle of one of my Wisconsin classmates, Manhar Bhagat. The Finance Minister, Morarji Desai was to be the guest speaker. Tonpe was also there. He introduced me to Morarji. I took a number of pictures with Desai, the American Consul General, and plant owners. Desai wanted to know why I was taking pictures. So I said if he wanted to know anything about me that he could ask Tonpe. Desai said he never took information second hand, only first hand. I said he could get information from me first hand as I was planning to go to Delhi. He said ok. That broke the ice and Desai and I met on a regular basis for the rest of my stay in India.

Just before I left Bombay, Rashmi and Sudha (the other married woman in the apartment) cornered me and put on a sari. Looked fairly nice -- surprisingly. They made me keep it on until Krishna came home and took a picture. Later as I was packing, Rashmi gave me a sari for myself. Ramniklal's wife gave me a silver filigree dish. In turn I gave Rashmi some perfume and Krishna a Waterman pen and cartridge. I gave Ramniklal a cuff link set.

I.P.'s family treated me like family, and I would have liked to stay longer. I asked my mother to be sure to invite all my Indian friends still in the States for Christmas. For years my parents' house was like Grand Central Station, with foreign students and various high government officials coming to visit and often staying overnight.

Before I left the States, I.P. gave me an order to find him an Indian wife -- a pretty woman, soft-spoken and above all well-educated. He never dated Indian girls in the U.S., but wanted to marry an Indian. At the wedding, I.P.'s cousin had spread the word, and so a number of single young women were glad to talk with me. I did not find anyone I felt would be good for I.P.......

Years later, when my husband and I were living in the Philippines, I.P. returned to India to find a wife. After more than a year of searching, he wrote me that he had given up and was returning to the States. Then he did meet "the" one -- a beautiful, well-spoken and confident woman, with multiple degrees in chemistry.

Staying with families, I quickly learned that basic life values, especially in the upper classes, were similar to ours and based, surprisingly, on The Ten Commandments.

However, the big difference involved who welded the power in the family, business and government. In India, men had *all* the power. In the Indian government, power was concentrated in the hands of a very few. And government officials in the various states, if they worked for the central government, had virtually no power to make individual decisions.

* * * *

After several weeks in Bombay, I went to New Delhi which I used as a base for the rest of my stay. At that time there was only one first class hotel in New Delhi. So many companies owned apartments or houses so their executives would have a safe place to stay when doing business in New

Delhi. Tonpe arranged for me to stay at a house owned by one of the large Bombay companies.

One of the first Americans I met was Edith Marshall, wife of retired Brig. Gen. Theodore Marshall. Ted was a top advisor to the US AID program. They had a sizable house which had a little attached apartment with its own entrance. I stayed there twice when I had to leave my then "permanent" residences. Ted liked to tinker with various projects. Good tools were hard to come by. So my father, who owned a hardware store, sent over a sizable tool kit. As they were connected to the Embassy, we bi-passed customs. Ted was thrilled. Edith said she always knew where to find Ted when she couldn't find him.

When they returned to the States we periodically visited. They bought a house on the water in Maryland. Ted insisted on buying a boat, but had never driven one before. We had to drive for several hours in order to pick up the boat and drive it back to the house. Ted was at the helm, and put a large dent in one side when we stopped for gas. Then the boat got tangled in seaweed. Luckily we finally got to Ted's dock at dusk time. No one on board knew where the lights were. So Edith made Ted take a Coast Guard course before she would get on the boat again. We stayed in touch well into the 1970s.

After a few months in New Delhi the company needed the rooms where I was staying because several of their executives were coming to Delhi. So I had to move. I stayed a few weeks at the Marshall's and then went to South India.

* * * *

Tonpe had many rich friends. Initially one, who owned a car dealership, put a car and driver at my disposal. The driver would come in the morning and stay all day, whether or not I needed him. After a while I felt bad that he had to sit around in the heat. So another of Tonpe's friends, a Member of Parliament, lent me a car, one of the few automatic ones in India at that time. I can't tell you how many times I went to the left side of the car to get in -- without remembering the steering wheel was on the right. He also put a car and driver at my disposal for my 6-week car trip through south India. All these cars and drivers were gratis.

On the weekends, Tonpe and I liked to wander through the very old part of Delhi. The shops were fascinating, and the street vendors' food delicious. Tonpe knew a lot of people and heard from one antique dealer that the Dali Lama had brought in some of this Tibetan temple hangings and needed to sell them to have money to live on. I still have three: one from the 17th century, one from the 18th century and one from the 19th century. I had the hangings dated by an expert at the Museum of Art, but unfortunately never kept the paperwork.

NEW LEADERS

When India had to fight the war against the Chinese, Prime Minister Jawaharhel Nehru (old that he was) knew he needed a strong, fair and honest Secretary of Defense. Nehru appointed the Governor of Gujerat (where Bombay is located), Y. B. Chavan.

I met with Chavan in Bombay a few days after his appointment as Defense Minister. He was surprised by the appointment and told me "I really don't know what to do."

A week or so later, I met him in his new office in Delhi -- a huge room with a long elaborately carved wooden desk at one end. There were five phones on the desk -- all black, the kind reminiscent of the 1920s and 1930s phones in the US. As we talked, a phone rang. He hadn't been there long enough to discern which phone was ringing. He picked up one by one until he found the right one -- the fourth one.

Chavan proved to be a strong leader, mobilized the rag tag Indian army and worked closely with the Americans and British who sent in arms, supplies and army trainers. With the help from the US and UK, the Indian army stopped the Chinese just north of Tezpur, a key city in Assam, which was the gateway to Calcutta.

The Chinese were repelled and retreated a few months after the invasion. Given the American attitude that the Indians were an "enemy," the Chinese had not expected the Americans to react as swiftly and as strongly as we did.

ANOTHER WAR FRONT

On December 29, 1962, Indian and Pakistani officials met face to face for the first time since the War of Independence to discuss Kashmir, a disputed part of India. The meeting was in Rawalpindi, Pakistan, and I was the only female reporter. As was my habit as a reporter, I asked a lot of questions. Next day *The Pakistan Times* ran a front page story about my questioning the officials. .

The headline read: U.S. and NOT THE LADY IMPATIENT.

After a number of questions went unanswered, the article reads "When will the new maps of the borders be released?"

wanted to know the only lady correspondent among the host of foreign correspondents.

The article continues "She was told" In due course, ...

"She persisted. But how soon can you get them printed?

"The External Affairs Secretary, Mr. Dehlavi, said 'you are a woman and I know women are always impatient.' This sent the gathering into peals of laughter." the article said.

"But her reply, the article said, "Oh no. I am not impatient, but the people in the US are."

* * * *

Ali Bhutto, the Pakistani representative and later Prime Minister, was very intelligent and understood the Indian stance. He tried to bridge the gap, unsuccessfully. I was very impressed with him and glad when he was elected Pakistan's Prime Minister. I was devastated when he was killed, supposedly for corruption. While I am sure corruption was indeed rampant, I doubt he was personally involved.

Kashmir is still a bone of contention between India and Pakistan. Even though at that time most Kashmiris were Muslim they told me when I visited that they voted to be a part of India because they feared a strict Muslim state (Pakistan). The Kashmiris felt they would have more freedom as part of India.

I picked up a vicious stomach virus from the food on the train during my return to India. I was able to get penicillin through the doctor at the US Embassy, but spent New Year's Eve in bed vomiting and with diarrhea. What a way to celebrate. I still remember my disappointment at missing a big party. For years afterwards, whenever I was tired and run down, the virus would strike and I had to stay in bed for days.

TOP INTERVIEWS

Back in New Delhi, I met with Finance Minister Morarji Desai a couple of times in his office. But we kept getting interrupted by some secretary or other. So Tonpe and Desai decided it would be better if we met at Desai's house, after supper. He was much more relaxed than he had been in the office. On Jan. 15, 1963 we began regular meetings.

Desai was probably one of the most honest and humblest people in the Central Government. To relax at home during our talks Desai, dressed in the traditional white cotton dhoti, spun cotton thread into material. We would talk as his hands moved back and forth across the loom.

When we first met so briefly in Bombay, Desai said he liked to get information from people first hand. That first more informal meeting was a surprise. By that time he knew that Tonpe and I were "seeing" each other. Desai ended up interviewing me. He wanted to know about the American dating system, the difference between "necking", "petting" etc. As he was a very humble person these questions surprised me. When I left, I couldn't help but laugh. Could anyone imagine the US Secretary of the Treasury asking a journalist such questions? Before I left that night, Desai said that I was different from most Americans he had met. I asked how. He said I was less aggressive and more quiet.

As he was a staunch socialist and I was a staunch capitalist, we had many interesting conversations. Economics was a key topic of discussion, and he clearly recognized the deep divide between the rich and the rest of Indian society. To even the playing field, he felt that no one should be able to inherit riches from a parent, that all those riches should go to the central government. Ford Foundation had given India a $5 million grant (a lot of money in those days) for an agricultural project. Feeding the people was a major problem then - and now.

Our conversation went like this. Me, "I know you think the rich shouldn't be able to pass down their riches to their children. But you just received $5 million from the Ford Foundation. If the Ford family had not been able to keep its wealth and pass it down, you would not have received this money." Silence as he thought about it. "Well," he said "we can agree to disagree about socialism and capitalism and still be friends," And so it was. We would get into tough and sometimes heated discussions, but our mutual respect never diminished.

MEETING NEHRU

I had my first interview with Prime Minister Nehru on January 14, 1963. We spent 30 minutes, one-on-one with no one else in the room. We talked about Kashmir and my impressions of the Indian-Pakistani talks I witnessed in Lahore, Pakistan, in December.

Then I switched to the Chinese invasion. I asked him outright, "Did you have any intelligence that the Chinese were building roads in Tibet to your Assam border and were bringing in tanks?" "No!" "Did you expect China to invade?" "No!" "Were you surprised that America came to help you so quickly?" "Yes."

Nehru's desk was situated in front of a large row of windows, so I couldn't really see his facial expressions because of the shadows. He had a bad cold and apologized. And as we talked, Nehru's head began to nod. And as I sat there during the last few minutes of the interview, I thought to myself, "He's a tired old man."

Over the years I have had trouble understanding how Nehru and the Governor of Assam, an army general, did not see what the Chinese were doing in Tibet and figure out the Chinese were planning to invade.

However, now looking at my clips I see I explained the "why no DOTs connection" in a December 2, 1962 article for *The Boston-Sunday Globe*. Nehru and the Indian people had relied heavily on V.K. Krisna Menon, who assured everyone that India could (quoting Menon) "live in peaceful coexistence with China. We have enough weapons to defend our country." Menon was leftist, if not communist. As a result of the Chinese invasion, Menon was forced to resign his government positions.

In my article, I said "Prime Minister Nehru has been extremely naive in his belief that one could sit over tea (the Indian custom) and solve the problem of the invasion of India.

"Until now he had relied on Menon to act as his mouthpiece. With Menon gone, Nehru is without his mouthpiece as well as without any philosophical basis for dealing with the Chinese. Shrewd as he may be, Nehru does not seem to know how to push the Chinese back. The fall of the vital airstrip at Walong, which is well within India's borders, is indicative of this."

Shortly after the invasion and the fall of the airport in Assam, the Indian government asked for and received military help from the United States. On November 21, 1962, the US Air Force began ferrying Indian troops and supplies to the almost inaccessible regions of India's northern Border. Hercules 130 planes were used and went on daily flights. I wrote about one Air Force Captain who oversaw the operation.

In that December 2 *Globe* article I said, "It seems doubtful that the Chinese expect to invade India on any large scale. All she has is abundant manpower. She cannot keep up a continuous supply line of food, ammunition and fuel over an extended period. China's air force is small; it is doubtful that Russia has given her long range bombers. Her ceasefire proposal is a result of an estimated loss of more than 13,000 men, compared to the 4,000 for the Indians, and an inability to keep men and supplies coming."

* * * *

In late February 1963, I headed to Calcutta. Another one of I.P.'s brothers, Krishnavdan, worked at a jute factory, Birla Jute Company, just north of the city. I stayed there a couple of days and then went to Tezpur, the capital of Assam, the state invaded by the Chinese.

As usual, Tonpe arranged for me to stay in a government guest house and for government officials to take me around. After days of waiting, I finally got permission to go up to the border area. We went up to the area the Chinese invaded. I can remember being surrounded by tea plants -- and not much else. One wondered why the Chinese chose that place to invade. Even though northern Assam was hundreds of miles from Calcutta, the Chinese goal apparently was to get to Calcutta to take control of the largest shipping area in India.

Controlling Calcutta would have given them closer access to Europe and the Middle East.

By the time I arrived in Tezpur the Chinese had stopped fighting about 50 miles north of the city. I was able to get to the towns the Chinese had controlled and which had been reclaimed by the Indians. I had heard about all the chaos during the fighting - from the escape of the Dali Lama and thousands of Tibetan refugees.

On Nov. 20, 1962 an Anglo-Burmese man, Charlie Hall, was the agent for the steamboat company which ran a ferry service across the wide river. He told me his story. In a 48 hour period, Hall helped evacuate 38,000 people from Tezpur. A few days later, 10,000 Tibetans came down from the hills and needed to be evacuated. Hall felt he had to help them, especially the women and children.

I found the area fascinating because besides massive tea farms, the area housed various tribal people, including headhunters. And the jungles were excellent for tiger hunts.

As was my habit when meeting officials connected to the invasion and familiar with the area, I asked if they (1) knew about the road building activities that had gone on for several years, and (2) if they were surprised. "No" and "Yes" were their answers. They praised the Americans and the help given by the US and UK. The invasion actually only lasted a few months and was over before my first interview with Nehru.

The Chinese pulled out of India in late November 1962. But they used the border area and Tibet as a constant threat to India. On February 18, 1967 the Chinese sent three divisions of troops into Tibet and the border area. But they did ot cross the border.

I celebrated my 26th birthday in Tezpur. When the officials heard it was my birthday, they gave me a party and invited a number of government and army officials. I never was a big drinker and got pretty high on the strong beer, native to that area. They all laughed at me.

I returned to K.P.'s home before going to Calcutta itself. The house was basic, with few amenities. Aside from where dishes were washed, there was only a small porcelain sink located in a hallway to wash face and hands. When something broke down, fixes took a long time.

While I was in Tezpur, K.P.'s little daughter dropped a metal pitcher in the sink and broke a large chunk out. In order to get it fixed quickly, KP told the plantation manager that I had dropped something and I was coming back in a few days. In order to save face before an American, the manager quickly replaced the sink.

Beforehand, Tonpe and my American Embassy friends in New Delhi said I could not stay in any hotel in Calcutta because there wasn't one that was clean by our standards. So I stayed with the family of the director of the Ford Foundation. I wanted to see the city -- poverty and all. A driver took me around. I had heard stories about the beggars, but nothing prepared me. I was emotionally devastated. Adults who had had their bones broken as babies were now crippled and could only beg to get food. Women, also crippled, were carrying young, sick babies, begging for the basics. The beggars were organized by mob people and only received a minute portion of the money they collected. This system still exists in Kolkata (formerly Calcutta) today.

On March 23, 1963 I had another meeting with Chavan, the Defense Minister. He knew I had been to Tezpur and wanted to find out my impression. He had been there a few days before we met, and we shared impressions.

STILL NO INTELLIGENCE

After the Chinese invasion, the Governor of Assam, an army general, was moved to a southern state. Hyderabad was the capital and my first stop on my 40 day car trip through south India. As was my custom when interviewing officials, regardless of level, I met with him one-on-one. Gen. S.M. Shrinagesh and I talked about the invasion. Again I asked "Did you expect the Chinese to invade? "Were you surprised." Again, "No" and "Yes."

In the marble rotunda of his palace in Hyderabad, the Governor had a 3-D model of Assam, the Tibetan border, and the advances the Chinese made. I was able to more clearly see exactly how far north I had been able to get.

We talked at length about Chinese political philosophy, which clearly showed me why China invaded. We talked about Mao's books "On Guerilla Warfare" and "On Contradictions," Mao's political philosophy. I suggested the general go to the American consulate and library and read these books. I knew all of the American libraries in India had these books. He did and he did read both books.

After my travels through the south, I took a plane from Madras to Delhi, which had a several hour layover in Hyderabad. I called the governor's private number - just to say hello, and was told by his secretary that the governor was at the airport. So, I tracked him down.

We talked and talked until my flight was called. He begged me to stay over so we could talk more. He said he understand the premises in "Guerilla Warfare" but didn't understand the political concepts (On Contradictions) because they were so far removed from Indian thinking.

I did not stay because I had an important commitment in Delhi .

In spite of Menon's assurances to Nehru, to this day I don't understand the complete lack of intelligence about China's intentions and activities. After all, both the US State Department morgue and *Time* magazine files contained the information which led me -- sitting behind a desk in New York -- to predict the invasion. I did not have to be a rocket scientist to come to the conclusion I did.

AMERICANS HELP TO FEED MILLIONS

While the Indian government supposedly rejected capitalism, American capitalism was evident in a number of agricultural programs.

I mentioned earlier in this story that feeding the masses would determine who (India vs China) would win the game. India was an active player. In 1962 (before the Chinese invasion) the Peace Corps, Kansas State University, the US Agency for International Development, and the Osmania University College of Agriculture collaborated on a chicken raising project. The aim was to provide food, eggs and meaningful employment to rural based Indians.

In my August 9, 1963 article for the *American Reporter*, I described how 19-year-old Albert Snyder from Eldorado, Ohio, developed a chicken raising project. Snyder described the demonstration project as "not only a learning experience, but also an earning experience. Chickens take less space to grow and produce results quicker than various agricultural foods."

THROUGH THE SOUTH

On March 20, 1963 I began a six week (42 days) trip through south India in a jeep with a driver who spoke several Indian dialects. Some days we traveled 10 to 12 hours day.

My travels took me to Hyderabad March 20; Bangalore March 29 to April 3; Mysore April 4 to 6; Cochin April 9 to 12; Trivandrum April 13 to 19; and Madras April 28 to May 2.

Wherever we stopped I visited with political leaders, businessmen, factories, universities, medical facilities, schools and more. Fortunately I did not have to drive. The roads were often packed with cows, sheep, goats, dogs, bikes, rickshaws and people. After each stop I was able to curl up on the back seat and sleep. By the end of this trip, I felt I could not mentally -- or physically --- absorb anything more.

Heat, mosquitos and often dusty roads plagued me. However, the friendliness of all peoples and the generosity were unbelievable. And often with no prior notice people were willing to show me around and share their life with me.

The Member of Parliament who loaned me a car in Delhi, paid the driver, his food, and for gas (then $1.00 a gallon). His family ran a large sugar refinery and I spent the day there before reaching Bangalore. Given all the gratis housing and more, I spent about $150 a month.

My stay in Hyderabad has already been described, as the Governor had been the Governor of Assam during the Chinese invasion.

In Bangalore, I stayed with I.P. Shah's family. They had a large house and several smaller ones on their land. They had two Peace Corps young men living with them. Mr. Shah spoke some English - more than he had at Chandra's wedding. Mrs. Shah understood a little and spoke even less.

This was her first experience with an American female and she was curious as to what I did, especially setting my hair every night. The Peace Corps boys and I had many interesting conversations, as they talked about their experiences.

Mr. Shah was in textiles and took me to several mills. I was surrounded by shelves and shelves of magnificent materials. I bought navy raw silk material enough for two suits for my parents and pure silk with 14 kt gold embroidery for dresses for my mother and myself for my sister's wedding, scheduled for November 1963. I had the suits and dresses tailored when I got back to Delhi. My parents wore their matching suits for years.

* * * *

Mysore was the next stop. I spent over a half an hour with the Maharaja (also Governor) of Mysore. A very bright man, although he had no political power. He lived in a huge marble palace and as I walked through marble halls with 25 foot ceilings, my eyes were all around me.

The Maharaja had his own private game sanctuary, and my treat was riding a huge elephant. I had thought that the ride would be rocky as the elephant was so big. But his gait was very smooth, and I enjoyed spotting other animals as we rode through the area.

Tonpe had also arranged for me to meet the Speaker of the Mysore State Legislature. The Speaker had 12 women legislators to tea with me. They spoke some English and we talked about the role of women in Indian politics. There were many more Indian women in politics than was the case in the United States. It was OK for a married woman with a college degree to be in politics, but not to work for pay.

CAROL ABAYA

* * * *

As I mentioned earlier, power in India was in the hands of a few, and the "top" controlled virtually everything. Even key officials outside of Delhi could not make individual decisions that went against the established process.

When I was in south India, I met many central government officials who worked on state projects. . One official had taken things into his own hands and made a decision -- a very reasonable and thoughtful one -- that brought down the wrath of Delhi. There were two factories under his jurisdiction that made matches. Something very simple. But each box had to have a government stamp/label on it to show that taxes had been paid. One factory received its supply of stamps and the other one did not. The official would have had to close down one factory, thus putting the workers out of work. So the official split the labels packet, giving half to each plant, hoping that the next packet would arrive in time to keep everyone employed. The officials in New Delhi were outraged that he made this unilateral decision. I had to have my friend Tonpe intervene so this official, who really cared about the workers, would not get fired.

We then spent a week in Kerala, the southern state that voted in a communist regime in 1957 and about which was my Master's thesis. A Franciscan brother had written in-depth about the regime, and I used his book (filed in the US State Department morgue) as a frame work for my own discussion and analysis of what happened. I wanted to meet and talk with him, in a way to verify my own work. By asking Kerala state officials, I was able to track him down -- a two-day drive from the capitol of Trivandrum, and into unbelievable wilderness. My tireless driver (who spoke 4 or 5 major Indian dialects) drove me from village to village until we found the monk. I had a copy of my thesis, which I gave him, and later we corresponded. He said he found my analysis not only accurate but intriguing.

While Kerala was a lush state as far as vegetation is concerned, the people were very poor. At the same time, everyone was friendly and helped us whenever they could. We were scheduled to stay at a government guest house in a national reserve park. My driver spoke 4 or 5 major Indian languages, but not Malialam, spoken only in Kerala. He tried to get directions. But the people didn't understand him, and he didn't understand them. At one point, he returned to the car, throwing up his hands, and said "Maimshab, they're hopeless here."

We finally found someone who understood the driver and reached the guest house late in the afternoon. We were fed, and then left alone. The driver slept in the car because he was afraid someone would break into it and steal my things. I shut the wooden shutters to be safe myself. When it was time to go to sleep, I turned off the lights, but left a candle in the bathroom. After a short time, unable to fall asleep, I heard a clatter - inside. I got up, searched the room and the bathroom and saw nothing amiss. I returned to bed. This happened several times. In the morning, when I went into the bathroom I saw a rat scurry out through a hole and bite marks around my cake of soap, which was in a soap dish on the sink. So, my mysterious visitor was a rat.

The Reserve was a jungle, with all kinds of animals. My second ride on a huge elephant. WOW! They sure are big animals. In spite of her size, the elephant loved to be rubbed near her ear and her gait was as smooth as the one in Mysore.. And surprisingly her skin was smooth and soft.

Elephants are known to be both gentle and highly vicious. In 2,000 when I was in South Africa going through a reserve, a large elephant started coming toward the jeep. The driver said "Take your pictures fast! We're out of here! That guy is vicious and can overturn the jeep in a second!"

We stopped in several cities in Kerala, and in Ernakulum (near Trivandrum) there was one of the last Jewish communities in India. Indian Jews were supposed to have been the Seventh Lost Tribe. I spent the Second Seder with the S.S. Koder family, who were of Sephardic background, hence why they were called the Lost Tribe. They had a small synagogue with six Torahs, dating to 1568 A.D. The Seder Service was in Hebrew and followed the order we had at home -- even with matzos.

Madras was my last stop. Madras was one of the cleanest cities at that time. Very wide streets were lined with pink stucco government buildings. By that time I was exhausted from the heat and talking with so many people. But the stay was interesting because while I was there the communist party tried unsuccessfully to again gain control of the Kerala state legislature.

In my May 12, 1963 article in *The Boston Globe* I wrote:

"The Communist slogans are not those expected from an opposition party in a recently invaded country where defense buildup receives top priority. Their economic appeal in the impoverished people of Kerala is strong.

"The poor man," their slogans read, "should not be taxed too much -- withdraw unbearable taxes," "Nationalize unscheduled banks and scrap prohibition because it has proved a fiasco. Don't increase bus fares, and withdraw taxes on kerosene," were the communists' words.

In that *Globe* article I said "Kerala is unique as the state where a communist government was elected only to be violently deposed after 27 months. (April 1957 to July 31, 1959.)"

My article continued: "Today the communal picture is as bad if not worse than it was in 1957. Communal ties are strong and feelings run high. Political parties continue to exploit the differences between the castes.....

"Yet despite these conditions so favorable to the spread of communism, communists in Kerala are in trouble. Identified with the Chinese Communist invaders, the Kerala Communists seek to convince the people the party is working for India's integrity."

Then back to New Delhi, with that stop in Hyderabad and the visit with the Governor.

The heat and humidity was terrible. I had to sit back and think about my trip. What I had learned. What my view of India was and that I had traveled more there than I had ever traveled in my own country.

* * * *

I had to find another permanent place to stay. I couldn't impose on the Marshalls for more than a few weeks. They wouldn't take any money.

Then H.J. Shah, the Bombay contractor, stepped in. The previous year his company had rented an apartment on the top floor of a new building. It was empty as they had never used it. It was in the Lloyds Bank Building and on the main street in the new commercial section of Delhi. Very convenient to get around. I borrowed one of the Marshall's servants to help me clean the apartment, which consisted of a very large living-dining room area, a very large bedroom and full bath, a smaller bedroom and full bath (the only room with a wall air conditioner), a kitchen and servants room.

Mr. Shah had ordered living and dining room furniture and beds. Besides cleaning the apartment I bought dishes, curtains, and other household items. Mr. Shah paid. I finally moved in on May 22, 1963.

I also had to hire staff - who spoke English.

The caste system provided employment for the multitudes. I hired a cook, John, a Christian who also did light housekeeping and grocery shopping. But he would not wash floors or toilets. A second person was hired for those chores. Neither of these two would do laundry. So a laundry man was hired and came in once a week. As I was on the top of the building I had a postage-sized grass patch and flowers. A gardener was needed. So for myself I had four servants. As I never liked housework (and still don't) or cooking, this help was fine with me.

A cook/housekeeper, a servant to do the floors and bathroom, a laundry man, and a gardener. I paid more than the Indian going rate. When my Indian friend Nilima Das, who was still in the states, heard how much I paid the servants, she told my mother that I was wrong to pay so much. My answer to my mother -- which was very rational -- was that Indian families paid servants very little and always had to worry that the servants would steal. So Indian women walked around with a large ring of keys as everything was locked up. My housekeeper, who spoke good English, had good references, and so I did not lock up anything except my passport and financial records. Whenever the sweeper or washer man was there John and his son kept a close eye on them.

For the first time I was able to reciprocate entertaining friends who had been so generous to me. And it really was the first time, Tonpe and I had some private time together.

I told John, the cook, that Tonpe did not eat beef. Besides chicken and fish, I asked John what else could be gotten at the market. "Veal," he said. "Are you sure that is ok?" I asked. "Yes." A month or so later, Edith asked me what I was feeding Tonpe. "Chicken, fish and veal," I said. Edith gasped. "Don't you know that veal is young calf?" I didn't. Neither of us ever told Tonpe that I had given him beef.

I've always loved dogs, Remember in the beginning of this story I said the first thing I wanted to be was a vet. One of the American families was going to the States for a lengthy vacation. So I took care of their dog, a feisty but lovable Lhasa Apso. Most animals can sense whether a person is "good" or sense if the person is afraid. Each animal reacts differently.

Except for John, the main servant, the others were all afraid of the dog -- tiny that it was. Whenever possible the dog would attack the servants' feet. I had to close him in my bedroom when the others were around.

I had the dog a couple of months and noticed he was infested with blood sucking ticks. I took him to a vet, who shaved off all the dog's hair and coated him with pink medicine. A pink, bowlegged dog, who also wobbled, emerged. As I walked into the building to the elevator, everyone who was in the lobby laughed, pointed and laughed some more. We finally discovered that the ticks were coming into my bedroom from cracks in the concrete walls. I had to hire an exterminator.

* * * *

A couple of weeks later, Tonpe took a vacation for the first time in the 17 years he had worked for Desai. We went to Kashmir where friends of his (an Indian man and Swedish wife) had a house boat. Kashmir was probably the most beautiful part of India. The area is riddled with lakes, so we had a number of boat rides.

According to my letters home, I seem to have periodically gone on a buying spree in India. Kashmir was a highlight. I bought a 30 inch carved walnut coffee table with four little tables and two etched brass table lamps (which I still have in my living room) and a brass floor lamp (which I have in my office.)

To mar the vacation, a continuing presence was the Indian army, a quarter of which was in Kashmir because of the dispute with Pakistan. Armed soldiers were everywhere. In spite of the talks in December 1962, which I had attended, nothing had been resolved.

* * * *

During the whole time I was in India and afterwards for many years, Mary (my cabin mate on the way to India) and John Dorsey were close friends. Their Christian mission took them into some of the poorest areas on Delhi. I walked with Mary through narrow smelly streets, hospitals for the very sick and poor, and schools. They both spoke some Hindi, so were able to really get to know the Indians and their life and thinking.

We had long talks about what was going on -- as a result of the Chinese invasion as well as the Hindu mentality.

RIOTS & REVOLUTIONS

Getting back to my thesis on Kerala and whether or not democracy or communism would prevail, we realized that India was at a critical time in its history.

We agreed that the subtle politics of Russia and China completely snowed Indian leaders. Leaders walked around with blinders on their eyes and mind and so reality passed them by. Some of the happenings were so appalling that Americans could not understand events. As a result many of my articles did not see print because editors did not believe what I wrote.

In discussing Hindu mentality, we were all discouraged. John felt it was sometimes hopeless to try to help the Indians because John said they were a lazy, self-centered, and a selfish lot. They had been in India for 12 years trying to instill Christian ideals of honesty, morality, etc.

John always told the story of a trip he had going north of Delhi. He had to take several trains and had been warned that he should not fall asleep because whatever he had would be stolen. He was very tired and after putting his trunk under the seat fell asleep. When he woke up, needless to say, the trunk -- filled with Bibles -- was gone.

THE END BROUGHT TROUBLE

In August 1963, as I walked into the Parliament's press section, I was accosted by the Finance Minister's press secretary. "Did you write it?" he asked. "Did you write it'" he asked agitated. "What are you talking about?" I asked. "That article...." he stammered, "that article that is to be in *Playboy* magazine." I hadn't written anything that would have created this reaction. Puzzled, I asked "Why are you asking me?"

The press secretary said that the Indian Embassy in Washington was told that there would be an article in *Playboy* that was written by a Western journalist, who claimed to have interviewed Nehru. Nehru's date book was checked, and I was *the only* foreign correspondent to privately meet with and interview Nehru -- on two occasions.

I told the press secretary that I had not written anything for Playboy. The Indian government was really worried as there was talk of wild parties in Nehru's compound -- by his son and daughter. (I never paid much attention to these stories.) So when the October issue with Nehru's article came out -- with no named writer -- there was a box that said the Indian government denied that any interview by a Western reporter had occurred. Needless to say, I read the article very carefully. Everything in it came from Nehru's public speeches, articles in Indian papers, or his political writings -- with which I was thoroughly familiar. There was no hint of any sexual misconduct in the story.

Even before my travels south, the political scenario heated up after a new budget was introduced which doubled the money for the army and increased taxes for everyone. The country was in an uproar. In March, Parliament convened and many Members of Parliament heckled the speakers. I found this disconcerting as Desai was one of the speakers. Even though he was heckled his quiet sense of humor and retorts came through. But he and Nehru were blamed for the invasion.

Unhappiness increased dramatically. In July the smear campaign against Desai, Tonpe and myself began in earnest. I never thought I'd be a pawn in communist politics.

The communists, headed by Menon, had tried unsuccessfully to discredit Desai for years because Desai was very anti-communist. Mid-July, using the communist press, *Blitz* newspaper, a vicious and filthy campaign began. Initially it was just against Desai. Because this was unsuccessful, the communists started targeting people around him -- including Tonpe and myself, by name. At one point, Desai told Tonpe that we were "being watched." Once I had my own apartment, Tonpe would come to dinner several times a week, either with other friends or alone.

After the first several articles, Nehru himself intervened and told the editors to stop writing trash about Desai, Tonpe and myself. These articles stopped. However, the fact that I was mentioned at all ended my hopes of getting a job with the US Embassy and USIA.

After a break, Parliament reconvened August 13 and a No Confidence Motion against Nehru was introduced. Nehru and Desai bore the brunt of the attacks. I spent hours each day sitting in the press section. Parliament was in chaos and I described that it was like a three ring Circus. While many expected the Motion to pass, many were surprised that it did not. Very few voted for it.

However, the communists continued their attacks against Desai. And on August 24, 1963 Nehru, in order to appease and quiet them, ousted six top Cabinet Ministers, including Desai. S.K. Patil, Food Minister and pro-American, told me that Nehru "was a fellow traveler if not a communist." I never felt that Nehru was a communist. A socialist, yes. However, in some ways he was very far removed from the average Indian.

On September 1, the day before I left, I met for the last time with Desai. He seemed to have taken Nehru's decision fairly well. He talked about the changes that were going to happen in his life. He realized he had life easy as Finance Minister. He had to move to a small house, in which he did not have room for Tonpe. So Tonpe moved into my apartment.

I had made many friends during my stay in India. They were all as sad as I was to see me leave. Edith and Ted Marshall, Mary and John Dorsey, Neena Mehra, Bali and others came to the airport and stood near the runway. As I got on the plane I had trouble not breaking down. Tonpe stood here until the plane took off, looking very sad indeed.

* * * *

Those last few days, I was busy packing up to leave for Indonesia and making arrangement for shipping some of the things I bought. My thoughts were as follows: I cannot leave India without talking about the abject poverty throughout the country. The Indians basically were -- and are -- a people who liked cleanliness -- even though they did not think about the quality of water they used to wash their clothes or even self. Their mud or straw huts were always clean inside. Outside garbage was in the streets, which were also littered with animal droppings -- cows, pigs and chickens -- which were often recycled as fuel. Flies and rats were commonplace.

I saw all this, and just took it as "this is the way it is." However, when I visited Calcutta and saw the poverty and the dozens of beggars, I was emotionally upset. Begging was big business. The "controller" recruited young girls to beg, carrying babies (many times not even theirs), whose limbs were deliberately broken. These babies then grew up to be severely handicapped and misshaped adults whose only source of income -- and food -- was from begging.

I left India with mixed feelings. An easy life style, given the household help I was able to easily afford. But overpowering all the wealth I saw was the poverty and the hopelessness felt by the lower castes. There was a growing middle class, and, as everywhere else, education was the key. But then again, education, in many ways, did not provide gainful employment that could help the country develop so everyone could have a better life.

CHAPTER 3

ON AND ONWARD

I flew to Singapore September 2, 1963, but missed my flight to Djakarta, Indonesia. As there were only two flights a week, I was stuck in Singapore for two days. We were put up in the Raffles Hotel, first class luxury at the airlines expense. $15 a day, which was a lot in those days. The city was cleaner than Indian cities. The poor were better dressed and stores had many luxury items (TVs, refrigerators, etc.).

My interest in Singapore at that time was that Malaysia and Indonesia were fighting over this city state, both claiming ownership. So I took advantage of the unexpected time there. I went to the US Consul and met with the Political Officer who knew people in New Jersey. He said there were 700 Jews there and two synagogues. In fact, the first Chief Minister of Singapore was Jewish. I met with him the next day. Then I was able to fly to Djakarta.

Because my New York University classmate, Han Ong, had connections at the Indonesia Consulate in New York City, I was able to get a student visa. Neither my classmate nor I mentioned the fact that I was working for *TIME*. I would not have gotten a visa if the Indonesian government knew I was working in the media. Han Ong also made arrangements for me to stay with the sister of a friend of his in Djakarta -- the Nurs. Mohamed Nur el Ibrahimy was a retired professor and had four children, two sons and two daughters --daughters

Hanim (20) and Susanna, and two sons Nyazi (22) and Ramzi (16).

Mr. Nur had been a popular political science professor and a senator. But in 1961, Sukarno dissolved the party and forced Mr. Nur out of his professor job. He was never able to get work again.

Wherever I've traveled people have been extremely generous in sharing their homes, food and selves. The Nurs gave me a large room, lit by a single small light bulb hanging from the middle of the room's celling. The only toilet was on the other side of the house. Even then there was a nightly "pit" stop. I used my flashlight (never traveled without one) to walk as quietly as possible. But as soon as I opened the door of my room, the sounds of huge cockroaches scurrying away filled the air. And the rats... Running water was a problem throughout the city. And the Nurs' home was no different. Buckets were kept under open faucets to gather the few drops. I became very adept at bathing and washing my hair with one bucket of water.

The family played a key role in my long-term future, as it was through the elder son, Nyazi, that I met my husband, Angel, and moved to the Philippines.

Djakarta was more primitive than modern, except for small areas around the palace and the British Embassy. Transportation was a big problem. Taxis were only available at a hotel, and there were only a few of these. The Nurs did not have a car, and two seated bicycle rickshaws were the main means of transportation.

The Nurs would not take any money from me for the room or food. So when I learned that Mrs. Nur loved ice cream -- served at the Hotel Indonesia -- I would hire several rickshaws after dinner and take the whole family to the hotel.

RIOTS & REVOLUTIONS

* * * *

At that time, Indonesia was also on America's "enemy" list because President Sukarno was neutral politically and stayed out of -- or at least tried to -- the Cold War. Sukarno and his key advisers were anti-America and the number of foreign correspondents was limited. In 1963 I was THE only American newspaper reporter in Indonesia and went in on a student visa.

The US called Sukarno a 'bad' dictator. I'd say Sukarno was a strong leader, but not necessarily a bad dictator. I look at a dictator as a leader who prohibits all freedom of speech other than his own party's political activities. At that time, there were three allowed political parties/groups: National Party, Christian Party, and the Communists. The military played a key role in keeping Sukarno in power. Because the communists were allowed to play a role in the government, Sukarno was often called a communist. He was far from being a communist and did not endorse either Marx's or Lenin's political philosophy.

Sukarno did rule with a firm hand. The three political groups balanced the political scene, and Sukarno would allow one to become more dominant -- and then (like Nehru did in India) the rug was pulled out from under that party. So while the parties were able to recruit and speak publicly, they were careful not to anger Sukarno. It was an interesting juggling scenario.

Corruption in Indonesia was rife, and Sukarno had millions stashed in Swiss banks. But there were many stories about how he funded various projects from his supposed own personal funds because he didn't trust other government officials to properly manage the project. Sukarno's successor, Soeharto, was not only a mean, hardnosed dictator, but also more greedy.

Before the Sept. 16, 1963 anti-Malaysian demonstrations and storming of the British Embassy, the country seemed fairly stable -- except for the skyrocketing prices of food. Sukarno seemed to have everything under control. However, there were some Americans who said that he "creates" a crisis every 2 1/2 weeks to keep the people's minds off the skyrocketing cost of living. Teachers' salaries were 2,000 rupiahs a month. But an egg cost 20 R; meat 500 R. a kilo; 1 chicken 50 R, and a shirt 6,000 R.

My Indian friend, Tonpe, had contacted the Indian Embassy in Djakarta. However, several employees were involved in illegal activities and the government shut down their car operation. Finally after a number of days, an official there introduced me to Kumar, who had his own car and had driven for Indian officials and foreigners. I hired him for the duration of my stay. I used the rickshaws at night because Kumar had a family and did not want to work after dark because of safety problems.

As in India I wanted to meet top officials. One often gets a sense of where a country is and where it is going by meeting one-on-one with the power brokers. So, I wanted to meet President Sukarno. The security at the Palace was multilayered, and I could not get in to speak with anyone who would help me. Because of his connections, Kumar knew where most of the top Indonesian officials lived -- including the head of Sukarno's security corps, Brig. Gen. Sabur, Commander of Army Strategic Reserve. One night, after dinner, as dusk fell, Kumar took me to Sabur's home. I knocked on the door and asked to speak to Gen. Sabur. A servant invited me in. Over the traditional tea, I explained to Sabur that I was a student who studied international relations at NYU and was spending a month in Indonesia. I said I would like to meet Sukarno. Within a few days, I had an appointment -- one-on-one with Sukarno.

In the early 1960s Indonesia and Malaysia were fighting (arguing) about Singapore. Both wanted to rule/own it. The British supported Malaysia. The day before my Sept. 17 appointment with Sukarno, Indonesian students broke through the gates of the British Embassy and burned cars in the compound. The students, who had been bussed into the city by Sukarno, also broke windows and started some fires. I was having coffee at the Hotel Indonesia, just across from the Embassy, and was able to get upstairs into a room overlooking the supposed 'spontaneous' demonstration. I still have my pictures, both still and movies.

When I met with Sukarno the next day, he was glowing about the "spontaneous" demonstration (his words) by the students. He asked me -- believing I was a student myself -- what I thought. My answer "It seems a shame that students during their school vacation went about destroying things, when they could have been doing good deeds and projects." Sukarno was taken aback -- for a few seconds.

Then he started talking about how well the economy was. Again, I reacted, "Well, I have been here 10 days and the price of rice has tripled. How can you say the economy is so good?" He leapt out of his chair, went into another room and came back waving a report from his Economics Minister. He opened the report and showed it to me: "Prices are remaining stable." Again I told him about the price of rice increasing so much in a short period of time. Like too many leaders,

Sukarno relied on information supplied by people who wanted to protect their jobs and did not tell the truth.

We spent 40 minutes one-on-one and discussed a variety of topics. Then Sukarno's secretary came in to remind him he had a Cabinet meeting to attend. I guess few had ever "discussed" reality with Sukarno. At any rate, he took me into the meeting and introduced me to all the members. This opened the door for me to be able to meet other key officials and the heads of all the political groups.

There is the old saying "It's not what you know; but who you know that counts." This certainly was as true in Indonesia as it had been in India through the help of Tonpe, the Indian Finance Minister's Private Secretary.

Having been acknowledged by Sukarno in a positive way, I was able to meet with Subandrio who had been the Indonesian representative to the UN and was disliked by the US because he was supposed to be a communist. Subandrio was a staunch socialist, but not a communist. I didn't have a formal appointment, but my driver took me to Subandrio's house, on a weekend. I was invited in, served tea, and we spent time discussing various subjects. Subandrio was concerned about the growing influence of the communist party.

I also met the head of the Christian party - at his home - and the head of the communist party before I started a 12 day car trip traveling around Java and over to Bali. Traveling by car gives an insight into the country as a whole, its people and culture one would not get on a train or in a plane.

* * * *

RIOTS & REVOLUTIONS

Actually the day after my meeting with Sukarno, I was in Bandung, the second largest city on Java. A group of students were demonstrating in the village green, waving banners and chanting anti-British and anti-American slogans.

Kumar parked a block or so away. I grabbed my cameras and ran to the square. I spotted a two-story building -- the only one in the area -- and ran inside. There were people in uniforms milling around, and I asked if I could go in. Heads nodded "yes," On the second floor, I was able to get good pictures of the demonstrating students.

After a while, to my dismay, I learned that the building was the police headquarters. The police were not happy that I took pictures and started questioning me and demanded identification. I was allowed to go to the car and quickly pinned my press card into my bra. Then I showed my passport and student visa.

The police still weren't satisfied and wouldn't let me go. They wanted the film from my cameras. I refused! I said I was a "friend" of Sukarno. They didn't believe me. I gave them Gen. Sabur's telephone number and said "Call him. He is head of Sukarno's security guard. He will tell you I'm o.k." They took Sabur's name and telephone number, went to another room and huddled in conversation. I don't think they called Djakarta, and I was only released after two or three hours. I had instructed Kumar to call Sabur if I wasn't released.

The rest of the trip through Java was smooth. Poverty was everywhere, but not as intense as India. Java's vegetation was lush and wild food was available.

We arrived on Bali at dusk, and the car had a flat tire. Kumar was very uneasy -- an Indian driver and American tourist in a strange area. Villagers from two nearby villages came out when they heard a 'white' woman was there. In one village, a wedding party was going on. I was invited to attend and treated as a special guest, had a front row seat, and was served tea, fruit and other wedding food. The wedding was Hindu, as most of the people on Bali were Hindu. The same colorful saris, music and dance movements that I saw at the wedding I had attended in India.

Except for a few green fringe areas and a couple of oasis, Bali was a wasteland, covered with ash from a volcanic eruption a few years before.

I stayed in a small guest house on the beach. There were a couple of resort communities, not much else. Sukarno had a palace on Bali that was built on a hill. At the bottom of the hill were ancient ruins and a pool. I've always been fascinated by ruins -- ancient civilizations and life. I was wandering around when two uniformed guards approached and asked who I was and what I was doing. I said I was a student of international relations and visiting. One of the guards had been to the States and spoke some English. We spoke about my experiences thus far in Indonesia, and he recalled some of his experiences when he visited the US.

The guard told me about the many attempts on Sukarno's life, and the political undercurrents in Indonesia. There was a pause in our conversation. I still remember it so clearly! Then the guard said, "It could never happen in America!" "What?" I asked. "No one would try to kill your President."

Fast forward! On November 22,1963 , I was returning to New Jersey after a visit to the Indonesian Consulate in NYC. As I stepped up into the bus, the driver, who recognized me (my great uncle owned the bus company), said "Did you hear? Did you hear?" "What?" I asked. "Kennedy has been shot, killed."

Fast backward to my conversation with the guard at Sukarno's Bali palace. It had happened here!

Back in Djakarta, I met again with Subandrio, the head of the Christian Party, and some of the top leaders in the communist party. I was probably THE only foreign correspondent who met and talked at length with the communist leader, Aidit. Subandrio and I met several times, and he invited me to a communist youth rally. There were some 10,000 students. Needless to say I was the only white person in the place. Anti-American sentiments were expressed, and I felt a little uneasy because everyone seemed to be staring at me.

IMPRESSIONS SENT TO INDIA

Communications in the early 1960s were primitive compared to today. In India my articles were snail mailed to American papers via the American Embassy diplomatic mail system. In Indonesia, I used the Indian Embassy diplomatic mail system.

Because of my long-held passion to pass on accurate information about happenings wherever I was, in Indonesia I wrote about the mood and political reality in Indonesia for several Indian papers. In my articles in Oct. 1963 in *The Eastern Times* and the *Nagpur Times* I made some insightful observations.

In *The Eastern Times* Oct. 13, 1963 article, headed "Indonesia Troubled," after a month's stay there, I wrote

"I left with the feeling that things were going to get worse before they get better.... I traveled by car through the rich, luxuriously vegetated islands of Java and Bali, witnessed the

September 16 stoning of the British embassy and the burning of the ambassador's car, spoke privately with President Sukarno for 40 minutes (on September 17) and was afforded the warmest hospitality and cooperation by the military as well as the average 'joe.'

"Politically a veneer of calmness covers much embarrassment by government officials and dismay by some citizens about the sacking and burning of the British Embassy and Commissary, the Cricket Club, more than 30 cars and the contents of 50 British homes. Under the surface the stream of political forces -- the military vs the communist party -- is torrential.

"Economically the people live day by day watching the price of rice skyrocket and the value of the rupiah shrink.

"On September 17 Sukarno (however erroneously) compared the damage done the day before with that in the Alabama racial demonstrations, the Boston Tea Party and the two World Wars.

"Glass and cars can be replaced. The principle" Sukarno told me, "was more important than a few broken windows."

* * * *

While the Embassy compound was damaged on Sept. 16, on the 18th (the day after my meeting with Sukarno), students rampaged through the streets hitting British homes and other buildings. Sukarno apparently had not foreseen the widespread damage by these gangs. According to my article Sukarno tried to stop the rampage, but was unable to.

"The most plausible explanation seems to be that Sukarno wanted an angry mass demonstration to protest the setting up of Malaysia and the burning of the Garuda Bird and also to divert the people's attention from the rising price of rice to an external threat."

Further on in the article I described the economy. "The economy of Indonesia is chaotic; the cost of living index has risen from 100 to 2,000. The price of rice in September doubled. A 'beetcha' driver (Peddler of 3-wheeled bikes) earns more than a university professor or civil servant."

"Professors earn $5 a month, civil servants $4. Cabinet Ministers $5.50. They all must have several jobs in order to eat and have to sell personal belongings and household effects or engage in black-market deals. Village pawn shops are crowded as villagers bring in some meager possession in order to eat that day."

"Prices of vegetables usually shipped to Singapore have plummeted. The Bali tourist trade has already felt the pinch as vacationers avoid troubled countries."

In spite of the political chaos when I left Indonesia, I ended this article with: "Indonesia is one of the richest countries in the world, abounding in national resources yet to be exploited. Most of the people, resigned to their fate, are surprisingly cheerful in their belief of a better future."

In the *Nagpur Times* article my approach was entirely different, giving an historical perspective of Indonesia at that time. Much of what I said in this article can be transferred to the African countries that gained independence from the colonial powers and as a result are still having stability problems today.

The headline read "Sukarno's Efforts through Military Development."

"Indonesia, a tropical archipelago of lush vegetation and wondrous natural resources, was quite unprepared for independence after World War II. Unlike the British in India or America in the Philippines, the Dutch did not even try to prepare the Indonesians for self-rule by giving them educational opportunities or by developing a native civil service.

"Dutch colonial policies deeply affected the way of life and thinking of the Indonesians. Few were able to obtain a higher education. The Dutch, however, did allow them to become doctors. Today MDs are in many key government positions. They were the only educated group at the time of independence. The civil service was practically exclusively Dutch. So the country had no native government infrastructure.

"Because (1) of the absence of civil service administrative personnel; (2) of deficit financing, (3) 80% of the budget goes to the military and (4) of the lack of investment capital, Indonesia's transportation and communications systems as well as irrigation and flood control have continued to deteriorate. Unlike many new countries which have set up ambitious development plans, Indonesia does things step by step. She has no overall analysis of the size of her problems, what resources are available and what is needed and feasible.

"In January 1963, President Sukarno laid down the jobs of civic mission as engineering, rehabilitation and major projects such as road, bridges, village reconstruction. Civic mission plans to go to the people in the interior will thus build roads and bridges and dams with relatively little red tape and with the active cooperation of the leaders from President Sukarno down.

"Having attained some political stability last year, Dr. Sukarno felt it better to use the military forces and organization for development rather than to demobilize. As Dr. Sukarno feels it necessary to extend his influence and gain the solid support of the people in the interior, the program was undoubtedly given impetus for political rather than economic reasons. President Sukarno has no head for economics and his advisers paint a rosy picture as the price of rice spirals."

The rest of the *Nagpur Times* article deals with how Sukarno used the military to complete public works projects.

Meeting all those leaders in 1963 -- with the implicit approval of Sukarno at that Cabinet meeting -- helped me immensely in 1965 when the communists staged a coup that quickly failed. I had predicted an "explosion" in Indonesia and was there when it happened. And all these contacts kept me up on what was happening. It truly was "It's Who You Know."

THE PHILIPPINES: VERY PRO-AMERICAN

After a month in Indonesia, I went to the Philippines for a two-week stay there. The Philippines in 1963 was a strange mixture of armed goons on the streets, tinned roofed shacks, beggars, and modern luxury houses and compounds surrounded by ten-foot high cinder block and concrete walls, empty streets in the newer sections because of the goons, and crowded, smelly streets in the old section of Manila.

Unlike India and Indonesia, where the governments were not too happy with the US, the Philippines government and people in general were pro-US because of the Clark Air Force Base, which provided hundreds of jobs for Filipinos. Also, the US ruled the Philippines for 50 years, having taken over from the Spanish in 1898. A democratic Filipino government was formed July 4, 1946. The US Constitution formed the basis of the Philippines Constitution.

I stayed in a small hotel a block away from the American Embassy and about six blocks from the Hilton Hotel, the only major hotel in the city at that time. My first stop whenever I travel and plan to spend time in a foreign country is the US embassy. One, to make contacts and get information about the latest news and happenings. Two, to get referrals to enable me to interview top leaders. And three, to let US officials know that I, an American journalist, was in the country -- just in case of a natural or political disaster.

As I recall, I was able to get an appointment -- one-on-one -- with President Diosodado Macapagal. I found him to be a sincere person and he really wanted to do good for his country. However, while he had support from the army, he was not a strong leader who could manipulate the democratic system. He was strongly pro-American.

I quickly learned that a Senator Raul Manglapus was pro-American and had attended Georgetown University in the US. I was quickly able to get an appointment with him.

Manglapus and I hit it off immediately, and he had a great time telling me about his American experiences. Toward the end of the meeting, he asked me if he could help me with anything. I said, "Yes. I want to meet (then Senate President and later President) Ferdinand Marcos." Manglapus picked up the phone and called Marcos directly. "Hey, Ferdie," he said, "I have an American reporter who wants to meet you." Immediately a one-on-one meeting was set up.

At my first meeting with Marcos (Oct. 1963), I was impressed by his political philosophy (based on American values), his sincere interest in working for the people, and his understanding of how to make the democracy work. The meeting was in his home office late in the afternoon, and he then invited me to have supper with the family. This was my first meeting Imelda -- who was very gracious about having a stranger suddenly appear at the dinner table. The children were there and very young at the time. The boy asked me a lot of questions about America.

In 1965, Marcos was elected President and inaugurated Dec. 30. I wrote him and congratulated him. Somewhere I still have his answering letter.

I can't remember if it was Marcos or Manglapus who introduced me to Fernando Lopez, head of a prominent business and political family, and vice-president at that time. Later, he was also vice-president with Marcos. I met Lopez on a Sunday morning and ended up having brunch with his extended family. Everyone was gracious about having a stranger in their midst.

Like Marcos, Lopez was very astute, understood the country's problems, and how democracy could work in a positive way.

I only stayed in the Philippines for two weeks and did not meet Marcos or Lopez again. I did meet Manglapus several times as he put a car and driver at my disposal. He didn't even like me walking the short distance to the Hilton because of the armed goons on the street corners. But I got to know some of the goons who always waved and became protective of me if a "bad" goon approached me.

I spent two days in Bagio, a northern mountain resort town. Beautiful! I stayed with the family of one of my Wisconsin classmates, Val Alipio. Val was still in the states. As a special treat, I was taken (we walked) up a very narrow, winding dirt road that was on the very edge of the mountain. Barely wide enough to allow someone to pass and go down.

Dogs, chickens and pigs abounded. Word has always been that dogs were just as much a part of the food chain as chickens and pigs.

Returning to Manila, I stopped by the Palace to say goodbye to the President's Private Secretary -- with whom I later kept in touch and who was so very helpful when my husband and I returned to the Philippines in August 1969.

* * * *

My last two weeks were spent in Japan. Another Wisconsin classmate, Tomeo Kambayashi, was a top manager in Nippon Telegraph and Telephone Company. Few Japanese spoke English in those days, and it was impossible to travel without a translator. (At least in India, train agents spoke enough English to let me know when the train would stop where I was getting off.) Tomeo arranged for one of the secretaries, who spoke a little English, to take her vacation when I was there. With a friend of hers (who spoke no English), we traveled to Kyoto, a resort town, and to Nagaoka, where I spent the weekend with the secretary's family.

At the Palace in Kyoto, we walked around beautiful gardens with sculptured trees. Next door were tennis courts, each court filled. "Oh," I said, "You have adopted another American sport." (Japanese have always loved baseball.) "Yes," the secretary said, "But you have adopted one of our favorite sports." She said the word a number of times, but I could not understand. Finally I said, "Write it!" Scrounging for a piece of paper, she wrote WRESTLING. There was no way she could pronounce the consonant combinations. We had a good laugh.

The weekend proved interesting. Of course, the first thing you do when you enter a Japanese home is to take off your shoes. Second, they end their meals with a bowl of plain white rice. I really got teased when I added soy sauce to my rice. And then they tried to get me drunk on sake (traditional rice wine). I was never a drinker and have since learned that I am allergic to wheat (base of liquor). So on sake, I never get a reaction. More laughs over my soy soaked rice and sake.

In my last year in high school I started corresponding with a Japanese girl, Masako Nishii. We traded information about our lives and dreams. Japan, at that point, was still reeling from WWII and there were strict import restrictions. High import taxes were placed on most everything. Books and used clothes were exempt.

Masako loved to read, so I was able to send her books. She loved picture books. I also bought new clothes for her, especially warm for winter as there was no central heating. In order to avoid taxes, I bought new clothes, removed the sales tags, and washed them before I sent them.

We corresponded while I was in college and in India. We were looking forward to finally meet when I planned to go to Japan after India. Just as I was leaving India I got word that she had passed away. Over the years she had been hospitalized for TB and later major depression. My friend Tomeo took me to meet her family, who really wanted to meet me. None of them spoke or understood English. Tomeo translated. We were all in a very solemn mood. It was an uncomfortable visit. Tomeo and I only stayed a short time.

I never was a city person and so really didn't like Tokyo. Too crowded. People pushing and rushing to get wherever. Worse than NYC. In other countries, the people were friendly, helpful to strangers and spoke at least a little English. Few Japanese spoke any English.

In October 2012 Hurricane Sandy desiccated New Jersey, New York, and Connecticut. THE worst storm ever in the mid-Atlantic region. The Japanese Ambassador at the NYC Consulate visited our area to share our pain. After the press conference, I told him the above stories - about my soy sauce and sake experiences in Japan in 1963. He laughed. All the county's officials could not understand why the Ambassador was laughing, and I did not enlighten them.

CHAPTER 4

CHALLENGES, RIOTS, AND FUN

The next phase of my life -- five years on a daily newspaper -- is probably the most fun, exciting, learning and doing part of my life. My deep seated need to tell people the truth about events was evident then and still prevails.

November 1963: After returning from Asia, I went to an employment agency in NYC to get a job. I got one immediately with an encyclopedia -- as a production assistant. I really wanted to write, but I figured I needed to get my foot in the door. I wasn't very good as I did not realize the importance of tracking the different elements in the process. It was only years later, when I became editor of a real estate investment magazine, that I had to track all those little what I thought nonsense things. (In 1974 I quickly learned the importance of those little details when I worked on three different issues of a magazine at the same time.) So I did not last long at the encyclopedia. Back to the same employment agency.

In April 1964, I can still remember sitting with my rep as he went through his jobs list. In the adjacent room I heard another rep talking on the phone to his client. "*The Record* is looking for a reporter. Call Carl Jellinghaus for an appointment."

My ears picked up, and I asked my rep about the reporter job. "They want someone with reporting experience," he said,

"You don't have any!" And he refused to recommend me for the job.

By that time (1964) five years had passed from the time I had traveled in Israel and wrote several stories for *The Record*. Screw that employment agency guy, I thought.

The next day, I drove to *The Record* in Hackensack, NJ, just a few miles from home. I asked to see Carl Jellinghaus about the reporter job. I was able to see CJ then and there. He took one look at my resume -- actually just my name -- and said "Didn't you write for us before?" "Yes," I said, "when I was in Israel." Imagine that. After five years he remembered my name in a positive way!

I was hired on the spot (April 1964) -- and didn't have to pay the employment agency fee (equal to one week's salary.)

While CJ hired me immediately, he wanted to be sure I -- and my mother -- did not have trouble with the hours -- 3 p.m. to 11 p.m., Sunday through Thursday. He told me he had hired another young woman, whose mother wasn't happy with the hours and called to say her daughter would not return to work.

For me the hours worked fine. When I was home during the day, both my parents were at work. So I had the house (small as it was) to myself. When my parents were home at night, I was at work. We all had our privacy and quiet. When, a couple of years later, I was switched to day hours, being home with my parents was terrible. I ended up at my cousin's house, three houses from my parents, at night. So I got my own apartment -- just across from my mother's real estate office and two blocks from my parents' house. I often came home to find my mother had stocked my refrigerator with things she liked (like yogurt) but which I never ate. But it was

RIOTS & REVOLUTIONS

MY space and I treasured it until I married in July 1969 and moved to the Philippines.

In early 1964 *The Record* bought a Paterson paper, *The Paterson Morning Call*. So the job was working for *The Call*. *The Record*'s masthead declared that the paper was "Independent, Liberal and Progressive." So *The Call* also was a liberal, crusading paper. Nothing or no one was sacred (even during one of the country's first child abuse murder trials).

I was *the first* Call girl, and except for one female hard news reporter on *The Record*, was **the only female to cover hard news.** The society editors were female. Several female beat reporters were hired a year later.

I started at $90 a week. In the next two months, I got three raises. When I got married, I was making a considerable amount more than my father, who owned his own business -- a hardware store. I was making all of $150 a week - a good amount in those days.

The Record news room, which then also became *The Call* newsroom, was rather small, with rows and rows of desks right next to each other. Because our work shifts were different (*The Call* was a morning paper, and *The Record* an afternoon one) reporters from both papers had to share the desks. I was one of the first new *Call* reporters hired and lucked out. I found the only empty desk and confiscated it for myself. So as all the activity swirled around me, I did not have to worry about being displaced by *Record* people or having to displace another reporter when I came into the office.

However, I wasn't so 'lucky' when it came to my writing skills. After a few weeks trial period writing obits, I was given other assignments before being sent out into the wilds of Passaic County.

I can still remember one night. I proudly (yes, a great word) handed my typed (and crossed out -- no computers in those days) story to the new city editor, Mark Stuart, a little guy with a booming voice. As I got back to my desk, Mark was standing by his, waving that piece of paper and yelling "Goldstein, this stinks! Rewrite it!" It took me six months before I was able to write a really sharp, crisp news story.

You have to remember that by that time I had finished college and graduate school, and had my thesis published, traveled around the world, and interviewed various heads of state. I thought I was a good writer!

At that time, in 1964, *The Record* was building a new printing plant on the banks of the Hackensack River. (Paper was shipped in by boat). Top line German presses were installed. The new news room was humongous, and the reporters' desks were smack in the middle. We all finally had our own desks. *The Call* reporters were clustered together, and *The Record* reporters were in another area. A new photo lab also was built. Don Borg, owner and publisher, insisted on the best -- including one of the first FAX machines. There was only one major problem with those machines. Special paper had to be used, which was highly flammable. I remember standing by the machine waiting for a late breaking story and pictures of a huge fire/explosion to come through. I started to pull the paper out and flames shot up. We quickly learned not to touch the paper while information was still being sent.

An exciting five years, filled with turbulent times and my 'beating' the competition over and over again. Just great for my ego!

My first assigned beat was West Paterson, Totowa and Little Falls. I had heard of Totowa because I attended an overnight camp there when I was 10 or 11. I learned quickly that the towns formed a ring to the west of Paterson, the county's largest city and one of the country's first industrial cities.

These towns were typical American middle class, with a few upper/larger houses, but no mini - or mega-mansions like those that are built today.

There was a SAT test essay (2011) that asked whether a person can get further from listening or talking. I am a listener -- always have been. And people told me (and still do) things they would never tell others -- much less a reporter. They talked because I asked a few key questions -- and listened.

I never was afraid to ask questions of those who were involved in whatever was going on.

A December 11, 1965 *Call* editorial was headed "The Duty To Ask." It was lengthy, but basically dealt with a complaint from the West Paterson superintendent of schools. The editorial read "According to a report (to the board of education) Mr. R... said Miss Goldstein has bypassed the superintendent to talk to principals, has questioned a school clerk on a matter of tenure, has asked a teacher for an opinion concerning the Education Association. In each instance, Mr. R... persists in stating Miss Goldstein committed these acts illegally. He winds up in a grandiloquent flourish with the charge that Miss Goldstein disregards what he calls the ethics of authoritative relations, whatever that is."

The editorial continues "The word illegal is Mr. R... and Mr. R.. alone. Since when is it illegal for a teacher to be questioned about a teachers' organization? Under what statue is it illegal for a reporter to ask questions of a school principal? (The school principal was also township mayor). Why should legitimate inquiries concerning the educational establishment be filtered through the office of just one man?......

"No segment of public life should be free from scrutiny....the bedrock of our right to know what is being taught our children would be undermined...." There is more, but you get the idea.

My job was to cover everything that happened in those three towns -- police, town council, board of education, planning board, zoning board, community organizations and more. I made the rounds, introducing myself to everyone and started each work day visiting the police departments. The police record book was a public document and open to whoever wanted to see it. And the police were always accessible to talk with. Today you don't even see a human being when you walk into the local police department, have no access to police officials without an appointment, and certainly no access to the police record book. Reporters have to depend on a friendly policeman leaking information or wait for an official statement. Of course, today police are swamped by reporters, while in the past there were only a few of us looking for information.

To recap everything in those five years is impossible. Three papers covered those towns; *The Call*, a morning paper, and *The Paterson Evening News* and *The Passaic Herald News*, both evening papers. I was the only hard news female reporter. There was a lot of competition among the three of us. I could not even count the number of times I beat the competition with stories they did not have that day. I'll talk about each town separately for historic purposes.

* * * *

RIOTS & REVOLUTIONS

I just talked about my asking questions. Always asked questions - and got answers. I seem to have saved clips only from controversial or unusual happenings and about interesting people in the three towns. Even in those days there seemed to be a lot of international exchanges and of course my education centered on international affairs.

The first article I saved, dated April 20, 1964, deals with birth control and the Planned Parenthood organization in Paterson. The Paterson organization was established in 1938, and probably was the first in the country. At that time, 1964, birth control -- even mention of it -- was a no-no. Any government employee or social worker or welfare official who mentioned birth control to a client could - and often was - fired. Roe vs Wade changed our society and gave women rights they never legally had before. I remember stories of so-called midwives who used wire hangers to abort a fetus. I still cringe today (2017) of talk of overthrowing Roe vs Wade.

West Paterson was originally a farming community - dairy, fruit, and vegetables. And the hills of Garret Mountain (originally named the First Watchung Mt.) contained 450 acres that were visited in the 1950s and 1960s by 1.5 million people a year. A mecca for pleasure seekers.

Today few people remember the important historical roles the borough played in American history. In an extensive article dated June 5, 1965 I noted that one company, General Precision "manufactured many of the vital steering control instruments found in Mariner IV, the spaceship now on its way to Mars..."

West Paterson was also the site of a number of movies filmed in the "colorful mountains. One movie, The Great Train Robbery, a western produced by E.S. Porter, greatly changed the motion picture industry." Filmed in 1903 -- although only 12 minutes -- this was the beginning of 'live' action films.

Three things stand out in my mind from those first years: the Mafia (Joseph Muccio) trying to buy me off so I wouldn't write anything negative or emotional; the drowning of a young black boy who was a gifted artist; and the approval of some 1,000 apartments on the side of Garrett Mountain and residents picketing against construction of so many apartments.

The May 1964 headline read "Schoolboy Artist Drowns in Pond. Lad's Rescue Attempt Fails."

The young artist -- John Oliver, 16, was to have received an award from the Optimist Club of Paterson for his art work. His picture is in my article. He was at the lake with friends. He was an athlete, but slipped off a ledge into deep water and got severe cramps. The other boys did not know how to swim. This was before cell phones, but someone managed to call police. I was at the police station when the call came in and followed police and EMS to the scene. I remember standing at the lake's edge as the lifeless body was raised with grappling hooks and brought to shore. I stood close by and was extremely upset. The two friends were in shock. Because I was there I was able to write a vivid story, got quotes from the two friends and even spoke with the principal of the boy's school.

The other reporters took the bare-bone information from the police report and got hell from their editors because they missed such a good human interest story.

FIRST GOLD STAR FOR CAROL

For some reason this incident sticks with me, as I know I thought then "What a waste of the life of someone so young and so gifted." (Sort of like the waste of lives of Americans -- especially the very young -- in Iraq and Afghanistan.)

This story marked the start of the competition between *The Call* and *The Herald News* and *The Paterson Evening News*, morning vs evening. The date of the news impacted advertising. Advertisers wanted to be "first."

Besides covering the hard news, I always seemed to hear about interesting people with unique hobbies or charitable works. So each week I would write one or two little feature stories with a picture of the person about whom I was writing. Again, the other reporters got nasty letters from their editors. "Where were you? She's only a female." **More gold stars**! I know the other two reporters were chewed out, because *The Herald News* reporter, Paul Alberta, was nice to me and answered my many questions so I could better put daily events into overall perspective.

In the beginning I started a series of articles on various township officials - Know Your ___, a profile of what they were doing for the community. My clips show stories on West Paterson's mayor and school principal Alfred H. Bauman; Totowa's mayor Samuel Cherba; Little Falls mayor T.W. Edward Bowdler; West Paterson's police chief Alfred O Jackson; Little Falls police chief John Berghorn; and Totowa police chief James C. Pellington.

I mention this because it helped me get to know key news source officials in a positive way. These articles were non-confrontational, and when controversy did happen these officials readily talked with me. This was important in my being accepted as a reputable reporter.

Opposition to apartments in W. Paterson started in 1962 (before my time) when residents in a referendum overwhelmingly defeated the original plan for a high rise project.

When the apartment idea resurfaced in 1965, garden apartments were suggested. Organized opposition began in May 1965 and was headed by a member of the Planning Board, Leo Stuppiello.

This same builder wanted to build 1,000 apartments in West Paterson on the slopes of Garrett Mountain and had filed the papers for planning board approval. Because of its size, the project also had to be approved by the Town Council. The town was small, and residents were up in arms, presented signed petitions, and protested at the meetings.

The protesters readily spoke to me -- the other reporters cared little -- and before one meeting, I innocently asked "Are you going to picket?" "Great idea," they answered. So I had a photographer there taking pictures of the protesters with anti-apartment placards.

My article had a picture, and the story read "Cheering, clapping, stomping and booing characterized last night's Planning Board meeting as an overflow crowd voiced outrage and objections to a proposed ordinance which would allow garden apartments in the borough. An ambulance stood by outside as tempers rose inside."

Another coup for Carol! And **more gold stars**! I continued covering every meeting and protest, which got the Mafia upset. The protesters would not talk with the other reporters.

My clips tell the story.

RIOTS & REVOLUTIONS

May 14, 1965 -- West Paterson in Uproar Over Apartment Plans. 800 apartments were to be built in a high priced (then $40,000) residential area and in an area zoned for 1/4 acre.

May 17, 1965 -- "Residents Plan Protest of Apartment Proposal"

June 16, 1965 -- Anti-apartment Drive Organized

June 22, 1965 -- Garden Apartments Opposed

June 24, 1965 -- Women March for Hours

June 29, 1965 -- Group Organizes to Bar Apartments

July 22, 1965 -- Council to Allow First Apartments. Attorney was told to draw up new ordinance

July 23, 1965 -- Council Assailed on Bias

July 28, 1965 -- Taxpayers Protest Planned

Aug. 5, 1965 -- Taxpayers Threaten Injunction. Apartment Plan Rapped.

August 10, 1965 -- Apartments Hearing Scheduled Monday

August 12, 1965 -- Proposed Project Facilities Held Swamped

August 17, 1965 -- 400 Roar Protests to Apartment Bill

August 24, 1965 -- W. Paterson Plan Board Passes Garden Apartments

August 25, 1965 -- Apartment Foes to Fight

August 30, 1965 -- Plan Board Favors Apartments

Nov. 4, 1965 -- Headline "Apartment War Aided Democrats." Ed Gallo lost his bid for a 4th term on the Council by 1,000 votes.

Dec. 2, 1965 -- 892 Apartments Planned

The Planning board finally got site plans for approval.

I had heard that Joseph Muccio, head of the local mafia, and three of the Councilmen were getting paid off by the developer. The amount in my mind today is $75,000 each. I knew who, but didn't have concrete proof. The three were voted out of office at the next election -- but not before the project was approved. One of the councilmen, Ed Gallo, after the election said to me "I really care about the community. Why?" My answer, "Come on, Ed, don't be naive."

I also knew that the other reporters were paid off each month in cash! An extra $25 a month in cash helped one of the reporters who had a young baby. But I couldn't say anything.

All during the approval and protest process I wrote stories, playing up the protesters -- but always including quotes from town officials. **I always strove to write balanced stories, so readers would have complete and accurate information. This philosophy is a keynote in my mind even today.**

Muccio, the head of the area Mafia, did not like my approach and called me a rabble rouser. Muccio tried to buy me off, first with an unspecified amount of money and then a weekend on his fancy boat at one of the north Jersey lakes. I put off meeting with him after the first offer.

But I really wanted to nail him. I discussed the situation with my editor, Joe McGovern, who decided it would not be safe for me to try to get proof. In those days, a reporter could not even hint about payoffs. Nor would a paper even write about an investigation. Proof was in the form of an indictment before anything was written. Later I'll tell the story of how I had to 'sit' on a mortgage fraud story for six months before a local judge and VA representative were indicted. Different today, when many officials have had their reputations needlessly trashed and their lives turned upside down because of over aggressive reporters. There are still a few of us 'old' *Call* reporters around and we always lament the fact that the media today creates news -- often biased -- and doesn't just report what happens. In talking with another long time reporter about this incident, the reporter said "It was lucky you did not go on that boat. You might have ended up at the bottom of the lake." I had never thought about that at that time. Wow!!

It was only several years later that Muccio stopped trying to bribe me. He made a comment to our court reporter, Evelyn Leopold, who told him, "Oh, Carol doesn't have to work. She only does this because she likes it." Last words from Muccio -- even though I did have to work to pay my own bills. Once I finished college I was on my own.

My naming Muccio as one of the heads of the mafia in the area was really public knowledge. On June 26, 1966 a *Call* headline (by lined article by me) read "Mafia" Sign Picketed, and the article referred to Muccio. Also the signs read (during a dispute for a town charter change) "Vote Yes. Save Your Home, and Get Rid of the Mafia."

* * * *

Little Falls was a quiet middle and upper middle class community where little really happened that produced front page copy. Newsworthy police activity was almost nonexistent. Many residents were professionals who worked in New York City. Little Falls was a major train stop on the commuter line. The town had typical green lawns and white picket fences.

But again I beat the other reporters out on many human interest stories that appeared on the front page of our Local section. Not all meetings of town boards were open to the public in those days. There were closed meetings, called Work Sessions. This changed years later with the Sunshine Law, which mandated that all meetings (except those related to personnel matters) be open to the public.

Little Falls, like West Paterson, had one public meeting a month and all other meetings of the Town Council (W. Paterson) or Committee (Little Falls) were behind closed doors. The Little Falls Mayor Edward Bowdler and I developed a respectful relationship, and for some reason he did not like the other two reporters or newspapers. I would talk with him before the closed meetings to find out what would be discussed. If newsworthy, I would talk with him after the meeting -- even after our official news deadline of 11 p.m.

As I've mentioned earlier, people always talked to me. Everyone thought I was just a female trying to be a good reporter. No one knew I had a Master's degree, had traveled around the world, and interviewed top leaders. I wasn't flashy!

So at least one person on each key board would talk with me either before or after a meeting. As our 11 p.m. deadline became closer I was often on the phone with the mayor, the president of the board of education or the chairman of the planning board. In those days we used the word "Reliable sources said last night...." A rumor circulated that I listened at key holes. Of course, I really was sitting in Hackensack. I used to laugh at this! This procedure went on for the 2 years I covered these three towns.

I had two "deals" working. First, to find out what happened at the meeting. Second, to have the *Suburban News* editor hold space on the front page of the Suburban section of the paper for my story. This way we had the story in the morning paper, and the afternoon papers had nothing.

* * * *

The second thing that stands out was the time high school students in Little Falls picketed the Township Committee meeting to discuss a proposed reduction in the Recreation Program because of budget problems. The Rec Center was the only place teens could safely publicly hang out.

I had talked with both the students and their parents and wrote about the planned protest. I then arranged to have a photographer at the scene to take pictures of the kids with their placards. One time some of the students got into a shuffle with the police and I was there with a photographer. The shuffle was not pre-planned. Because I was at the scene interviewing the students I was accused of instigating the students.

The Aug. 26, 1964 headline read "Enlist Parents Help in Getting Place to Go. Teenagers Circulate Petition."

Sept. 9, 1964 Headline was "Reporter Accused of Inciting Pickets"

The teens had tried the governmental and board of education routes seeking redress of their concerns. But then - as today - too many officials did not listen to the kids and seemed to lack respect for the kids' concerns, needs and wants.

* * * *

In 1964 **Totowa** was the third town on my "beat." Also a quiet suburban town with little dramatic going on. More blue collar than Little Falls, but a mixture. Nothing really stands out in my mind, except the mayor, Sam Cherba, a short, chubby man with an upbeat personality.

According to my clips, the only controversial happening there involved the building of Route 80 - a new major east west highway that begins at the George Washington Bridge. Certain exit ramps, according to the town, would create a hazardous condition for the trucks in that area. The fight went on for several years and halted construction of the highway which now goes from the George Washington Bridge (which connects New York City and New Jersey) across the country to California. Something like the original Route 66 in the early 1900s.

Totowa stories were mostly about people and everyday - yet special -- events.

In the late 1970s, when I was vice-chairman of the Marlboro Zoning Board of Adjustment, I was at a League of Municipalities conference in Atlantic City. I spotted Cherba way down the boardwalk and ran to catch up with him. After a few "hellos" and catching up with intervening years, Cherba said "You know, no one has ever covered my town the way you did!" For him to say that at least ten years after the fact, boosted my ego as a journalist! I never cared whether or not I was "liked" (which the male reporters wanted). I always cared whether or not I was respected as a journalist.

Actually I covered every major happening in those three towns by myself and rarely missed anything important. When I took my yearly vacations and traveled abroad, three reporters were assigned to do what I did!

RIOTS & REVOLUTIONS

RIOTS BECAME THE NORM

As I was covering the suburbs in 1964 and 1965, I wasn't involved in covering the explosive racial situation in Paterson and the beginning of the civil rights movement. For historical perspective, I will note that riots erupted in Jersey City, New Jersey, on Aug. 4, 1964, in Paterson August 11 to 13, 1964 and in Trenton, New Jersey's capitol, August 12.

The Paterson riots started when teens in the Fourth Ward pelted bottles and rocks at police cars. The police moved in quickly in a heavy handed manner.

Newspaper headlines tell the story. I am including them here because unrest in the Fourth Ward simmered for several years and periodically violence broke out. Besides covering civil rights and racial happenings from 1966 to 1969, the ramifications on education were important to me. The riots moved from the Fourth Ward to the downtown, a block from City Hall, and near our office. Many businesses went out of business, and many blacks and whites were afraid to walk the streets, even in the daytime.

Headlines summarized events and the mood.

<u>August 12, 1964</u> -- "Paterson Bans Rallies in Wake of New Clashes. Firebombs and Rocks Tossed."

<u>August 13 , 1964</u> -- "New Rioting Batters Paterson. Molotov Cocktails, Gunfire Mark Outbreak"

<u>August 17, 1964</u> -- "Riot-ending Pact Seen a Pattern for Other Cities."

* * * *

Paterson was a typical American melting pot. Upper, middle and lower socioeconomic classes of whites, mixed classes of blacks and lower class Latinos. Italians, Jews and Gypsies rounded out the population. While 50% of the population was minorities, there were no blacks or hispanics in any important elected or appointed position.

The blacks were petrified of the Latinos who wielded sharp knives and knew how to use them. There were some guns and drugs, but nothing like the ferociousness of today. Weapons of choice were Molotov cocktails, stones, bricks and fists.

In the 1960s Paterson was one of the country's most densely populated cities (#4). One out of every eight was on welfare. There were 25 public schools and 13 parochial schools, yet the level of education was low. The school dropout rate was high. Also, Paterson was one of the most corrupt cities in New Jersey.

In 1964, the marches in the south triggered emotions in Paterson. Paterson had riots that went on for days -- from August 11 to the 13th. The riots started when a group of teens in the Fourth Ward started pelting police cars with bottles and rocks. Why they pelted the police was never determined.

Unrest and more riots in 1966 and 1968, when I was covering Paterson.

In December 1965, two months after returning from the Indonesia coup (more about this later), I was reassigned to Paterson -- to cover the Passaic County courthouse, where Joe Muccio (Mafia from West Paterson) continued trying to bribe me.

I worked days, 10 a.m. to 6 p.m. out of the Paterson office, an old grungy building, a block from City Hall, the County Court House, and the police department. Paterson was a crime ridden, corrupt city, with rough police officers, many of whom were very racist. Rough as they were, they were always polite and respectful to me. They would always apologize if they cursed in front of me. Once when I got on an elevator, police officers got red in the face given their language. My old "friend" Joe Muccio, head of the mafia, was an investigator, and I would often see him at the court house.

I did not wax philosophical about the racial split, about the marches in the South, the race riots themselves in Paterson and Newark. I don't think any of us did. **We all had a passion to report what was happening, as it happened. We did not espouse a particular view** -- except that by our Constitution and the 23rd Amendment everyone is equal and deserved to be heard. So, we interviewed and quoted leaders from all walks of life and colors. None of us bought into the then black philosophy that the whites created all the societal problems and therefore should solve these problems.

I was the only female reporter covering and walking the streets of Paterson's Fourth Ward. Most of the black and some of the hispanic leaders knew me and would talk freely with me. The Black Panthers -- the only group that said blacks need to solve their own problems -- were my "protectione." If I was hassled, I would say, "Go talk with Curtis (Primus)." They did, and then were very helpful.

Looking back we reporters all agreed that these events changed the dynamics of our entire society. Segregation wasn't as obvious in the north as it was in the south. Buses, schools, restaurants were integrated. However, whites would not go into certain black or Latino areas.

These years went by very fast and much is now blurred in my own mind. But there are a few events that stand out. The four I will write about here from memory are:
- summer 1968 riots when I was dodging those lethal Molotov cocktails;

- a conversation with a black minister when I told him that the blacks' problems were created by the blacks and not the whites;
- the takeover of the Paterson Eastside High School auditorium in 1968 by black students for inequities in the school's classes and programming;
- and my threatening to quit in 1968 if my stories were edited at all by the new southern racist city editor DeWitt Scott.

I also started covering the Civil Rights Movement. I quickly developed a positive rapport with the black leaders because I listened respectfully and my articles were balanced and factually accurate -- without any "white" bias. Early articles showed that Paterson police were racist and often over reacted to happenings involving black leaders.

My first experience with black injustice and police over reacting was covering the trial of the head of the Paterson C.O.R.E., Edward R. Carter. There was conflicting testimony in December 1965, and I won't go into that here. But comments by the Passaic County District Court judge Theodore Rosenberg show the system's bias. Rosenberg upheld a disorderly persons conviction of Carter and said on Dec. 22, "Carter was on his way to work and should have continued. The only inference I can draw from Carter's injection into the matter is that the two individuals were Negroes." Carter had claimed that five white policemen were beating two Negroes. Afterwards, Carter said, "Whether one receives justice in Passaic County depends on the color of one's skin."

Perhaps -- maybe more definitively -- this bias continues today with the stop and frisk policies especially in large cities. Also, in many cases in the 1960s as well as today, people are arrested and not told why until much later when they are physically in jail.

In researching this period, to broaden my own notes, I came across a 1973 US Supreme court decision that mandates police tell a person why he has been arrested.

<u>Feb. 18, 1966</u> -- "Judge Disputes Arrest Procedure. Says Police Need Not Advise of Lawyer." The article reads "District Court Judge Theodore Rosenberg declared yesterday that police officers do not have to advise anyone under arrest he is entitled to call an attorney."

The Miranda Rights bill was established by the Supreme Court on June 13, 1966.

* * * *

In addition to ongoing, often emotionally-charged activities by Negroes (the word used at that time), the Ku Klux Klan was unusually active in New Jersey. I covered some of the courthouse happenings, as noted in my article Jan. 5, 1966, "Grand Jury Will Renew Klan Diet Probes Today."

Call reporter Murray Zuckoff had infiltrated the Klan and wrote extensively about their activities in both Passaic County and nationally. Because he had to testify about their activities, he could not write articles about this trial.

According to one article the Klan had distributed 20,000 leaflets "asking white Gentiles to join the Klan." An anti-negro backlash had resulted from the marches down south and the clashes in key blue collar areas of the country, such as New Jersey.

* * * *

Unrest ensued. The headline, July 8, was "Cops Quell Brawl" and the headline on the continued story page was "4th Ward Rock-Hurling Broken Up By 100 police." Several events seemed to merge into the riot.

The extensive and detailed article which included my by-line read "More than 100 helmeted police, many armed with riot guns, last night quelled a rock and bottle throwing spree by a handful of Negroes in the Fourth Ward.

"Before their arrival, however, windows in Levine's Pharmacy were smashed by bottles. ....

"The spree started more than an hour after Edward Carter, chairman of the Passaic County Congress of Racial Equality (C.O.R.E.) made a fiery street-corner speech at the same intersection calling for Black Power and urging Negroes to march to City Hall today to register to vote. ..."

Carter was quoted extensively as reporter Murray Zuckoff, who was on the scene, always took copious notes. Because this incident portrayed racial frustrations and attempts by well-educated Negroes (correct word used then) to get Negroes into a pro-active mode, Carter's quotes have (to me at least) great historical value.

"Before the near riot broke out, Carter called for solidarity against the white power structure here and for the organization of political strength by Negroes in the Fourth Ward, on every block.

"Without any sound equipment, the militant outspoken CORE leader stood on two garbage cans bridged by a heavy wooden board and shouted, above the din of traffic and the firecrackers exploding under a reporter's feet, they should elect Negro representatives who would not be Uncle Tom's. ....

"Change must come this year," Carter shouted to the cluster of people forming a semi-circle around him and about 50 people standing along the tenement buildings on Carroll and Governor Streets. "The house nigger is gone. We must change our leadership. We want to make our own decisions. Even if we make the wrong decision, we want the democratic right to do so.

"Chants of 'Say It right, brother,' 'That's it, that's it', 'Tell it like it is' punctuated his 25 minute speech.

"There must be changes in this country," Carter continued. "We don't need lawyers and doctors running for office. We need some gritty Negroes. We need those who have been beaten over the head by the police. We need someone to say no more slums, no more poverty, no more cheating, and no more taking our women. No more.' ....

According to the article, besides seeking changes in the political power structure, Carter wanted a change in the attitudes of Negroes. This was significant.

"Stop frequenting the corner bar and bring the pay check home so bills can be paid. Stop sending your women to meet the bill collectors at the door. Our women must be respected. We must respect the fruit trees,' he told the cheering Negroes.

"Carter also warned that white owned stores cheating Negro customers would be boycotted." He named some specifically.

"He also rapped the press for what he called prejudicial reporting.

"Remember 1964? The press said it was a riot. It was a social disorder, not a riot. No one was killed. Go back to the 1930s and study how the Italians and Irish made their mark in the community.

"Carter ended his speech with a sing song repetition of the words Black Power, while the audience repeated the phrase each time. The crowd continued to repeat the words even after Carter left. Black Power. Black Power, they chanted and clapped hands.

GOVERNMENT CORRUPTION WAS RIFE.

In January 1966, a trial involving charges of bribes and corruption in Clifton, N.J., went on for months. A Clifton man was found guilty of false testimony in a 1964 grand jury investigation. The case was complicated because of hearsay evidence and sometimes miscommunication between the defendant and some of his friends. The case involved whether or not an owner of an auto business was told he had to bribe someone to get variances and site approval.

My clips tell the story.

<u>Jan. 19, 1966</u> -- "Randazzo Is Convicted by Jury"
<u>March 28, 1966</u> -- "Clifton Perjury Term Appealed"

* * * *

In 1966, besides the riots, Paterson was ahead of the times when it had one of the country's first murder trials for child abuse/death. Because it was a first in Passaic County, I arranged for a photographer to meet me at the Court House, hoping he would be able to get a picture of the accused. We lucked out! During a recess, the man sat on a bench outside the courtroom with his head down in his hands. The photographer got some quick pictures as I held the elevator door open so he could quickly escape. The man's attorney came screaming at me, threatening dire consequences if we printed any pictures. He yelled "I am a friend of Don Borg!" Borg was the owner and publisher of *The Call* and *The Record*. The picture ran front page! I had heard the story of Borg's instructions to reporters and photographers when someone said "I am a friend of Don Borg. You'd better not print that. Or you'd better include me in that picture." Borg's instructions, tell that person "Borg doesn't have any friends!" We always laughed about this, as Borg was one of the finest newspaper moguls around.

The charge: second degree murder. A 21-year-old man was accused of beating to death his 2-year-old stepson. The trial went on for days, and I sat at the edge of the audience bench, - horrified that someone could beat and kill a small child.

The headlines show the 2-week trial's progression, and my articles included the man's confession. He said he slapped the child, pushed him, hit him with a belt and kicked him because the child was slow moving, wouldn't eat and wet his pants. The event happened April 9, 1964. The defending lawyer was Ervan Kushner who later married my husband and me in 1969.

March 15, 1966 -- "First Juror Picked for Murder Trial"
March 17, 1966 -- "Twelve Chosen for Death Jury"
March 18, 1966 -- "Two Say Child's Body Bruised" Article graphically described the injuries to the child.
March 22, 1966 -- "Trial to Hear Statement"
March 23, 1966 -- Worker Admits Beating Stepson." Son died April 9, 1964.
It was at this point that I ordered a photographer, as described above.
March 24, 1966 -- Mother Says She Struck Child

March 25, 1966 -- "Espinosa Jury Returns"
The day before the jury had been unable to reach a verdict.
March 28, 1966 -- "Espinosa Is Guilty"
April 1, 1966 -- "Child Cruelty Admitted. Mrs. Espinosa Also To Be Sentenced."

Following this child abuse case was traumatic for me. But the authorities hoped it would be a wakeup call and maybe stop some of the violence against children. Unfortunately child abuse is even worse today.

* * * *

In further reviewing my clips in 2013 I see my interest in education began even earlier than my stint in Paterson. I did an extensive article "School After School" for *The Call* weekend magazine. The article describes a joint effort between Paterson K district and Paterson State College, located in Wayne. Because the after school centers only had a few students at that time, critics said the poverty cycle would not be broken.

ON TOP OF HAPPENINGS

We had a police radio in the Paterson office, so we always knew when something big (or little) was happening. Sirens blared and a riot alert announcement sounded that hot Sunday early evening June 30, 1968. Trouble in the Fourth Ward!

I was in the Paterson office with a brand new young reporter. As I was the "senior" reporter I told him to stay in the office, while I ventured to the Fourth Ward. I had to park blocks away because the police had closed off streets. I walked to the very active scene as darkness fell. At a key intersection, Molotov cocktails and bricks rained onto the streets. The mayor, Lawrence F. (Pat) Kramer, and the police and fire chiefs stood in the middle of the intersection sporting white construction helmets. When Kramer spotted me he wanted to give me a white helmet so I wouldn't get hurt. I refused to wear one. "Are you crazy?" I asked. "You're prime targets. With my dark hair, they will never see me." They acknowledged my point, but kept on their helmets!

I spotted several black leaders and went over to speak to them. By 10 p.m. -- close to our story deadline -- I had to get back to the office to write my story. Kramer had a couple of police walk me back to my car so I would be safe. So my story covered the event itself, the whys, description, and quotes from the mayor, black leaders and bystanders, who were more than willing to talk with me.

Another coup for me! First, no other newspaper reporter was at the scene, so my competition did not have a 'colorful' story. Only what they got from the police report. Second, I had pulled rank because up to that time *The Call* editors tried to keep me out of explosive zones. I had such fun! And of course, the next day I did follow-up interviews and stories. More exclusives! People always were willing to talk to me! And trusted me! I still marvel at the ease people talked to me! Makes me feel good!

August 1, 1968 -- "Grand Jury Visits Scene of Disorders". This relates to the July 3 police raid in the 4th ward. Witnesses testified that police had thrown tear gas bombs into the headquarters of the Southern Christian Leadership Conference offices and also smashed windows.

RACIAL DISCUSSIONS

I can't remember the exact date of my lengthy conversation with a key black minister. I do remember meeting him in a tacky neighborhood coffee shop in the 4th ward. Worn flooring, cracked plastic seat cushions, and chipped formica table tops -- but clean. I was the only white person there! Yet I didn't feel uncomfortable.

We talked about events in the south and the role of Jews leading marches. We talked about the holocaust, and he compared the treatment of the blacks in America to the treatment of Jews in Germany.

Then he started the James Baldwin white guilt philosophy -- which I didn't buy. The black philosophy at that time was that the whites had to solve all the blacks' problems and give the blacks everything -- especially that we whites had to develop black pride by what was taught in the public schools. I had great problems with this stance.

Going back and forth with some questions and historical facts, the conversation (my words to him) went something like this:

Me: "While the slave traders were white, the African tribal chiefs 'sold' their own people for guns and baubles. So white people cannot take all the blame. Your leaders turned against your people." He acknowledged I was correct.

Me: "I am Jewish and proud of this. I 'got' Jewish pride from my family and synagogue -- not from the public schools or universities. I went to Sunday school and Hebrew school. We always celebrated the major holidays at home and the lessor ones in Sunday School. That's where I got my pride from."

I continued "You are a minister. What have you done to help your people become prideful of who they are? What have you, as a minister, done to help families better understand the American Society?"

He said he hadn't thought of things this way and acknowledged he was derelict in what he should have done. He also acknowledged that the Black Panthers (who rode into town on motorcycles from Chicago) was the only black group that said blacks had to solve their problems and not expect whites to do everything. Unfortunately the Panthers across the country got into drugs and trouble. However, in a sense they were the forerunners of the Guardian Angels in big cities who are active today in protecting the average people in the street.

* * * *

In 1968 and 1969, racial tensions skyrocketed. Martin Luther King, Jr. was killed April 4. Robert Kennedy was killed June 6, and President Lyndon Johnson signed the Civil Rights Act of 1968 on April 11 (The Fair Housing Act). In Paterson, tensions skyrocketed with the June 30, 1968 disturbance.

A group of black high school students took over the Eastside High auditorium and boycotted classes. They invited Mayor Pat Kramer to meet with them at the school to discuss their concerns. They wanted Kramer at the school so everyone could ask him questions and express their concerns. Kramer refused to go to the school. I spent hours in the balcony of the auditorium listening and observing. The students were well behaved and did not destroy or break anything in the school.

The kids wanted the mayor to see that they were good kids, interested in education and wanted to be able to take advantage of the American dream. Kramer continued to refuse to go to the school. Kramer felt if he went to the school that he would be showing weakness... that the blacks would think he would give in to demands and manipulate him. He invited the kids to send a delegation to City Hall, so he, not the kids, could control.

I was the only reporter inside the school and the only one everyone -- students, school officials and the mayor talked with. The students asked me to intervene. I tried hard to convince Kramer to go to the school, but he still refused. The kids only gave in after a number of days, and after I suggested they could gain more by going to see the mayor.

Kramer, unlike his predecessor Frank Graves, set himself apart from the minority groups. Graves moved around the community and was at ease with all peoples. Kramer was not. This aloofness was Kramer's downfall in the 1990s when he ran for the NJ State Senate.

The situation in Paterson schools is told in the movie "Lean on Me."

* * * *

During those troubled times, we got a new news editor, DeWitt Scott, at *The Call* -- born in the south and racist. One night during the high school sit-in and boycott he edited my story so it seemed as if the kids were really bad troublemakers. And he wrote a very inflammatory headline. I got frantic calls at home from black leaders and the mayor asking why the headline. I was furious when I saw the headline and read the story which was under my by-line. I told Scotty that if he ever touched my stories again, I would quit and he would have to deal with the blacks. He never again touched my stories. I resigned in June 1969 when I became engaged and shortly afterwards moved to the Philippines.

* * * *

Paterson's mayor Pat Kramer and I became friends. He always tried to get me to move to Paterson from Englewood. "It's safe" he told me. *The Call* office in Paterson was on a side street which had no parking. Parking was in the back of the building, and the lot was so small we all left the keys in our car so people wouldn't have to leave the office to keep juggling cars. One night at 11 p.m. I went out and my car was gone -- stolen. Fortunately one of the other reporters was still there and took me home.

First thing the next morning I called Kramer. "Pat," I said "You're always telling me how safe Paterson is and I should move here. Well, last night my car was stolen from our lot!" Silence on the other end of the phone. "You're kidding me," he said. "No," I said. "I wouldn't kid about something like this." He reported it to the police. I reported it to the police. I called several of the black leaders I knew. Word was out on the street that Carol's car had been stolen. Thirty-six hours later my car was found on a street in the 4th Ward. Damage was minimal, being a bent wheel spoke. My black friends and the Paterson police worked fast!

FLOATING ASSIGNMENTS

In 1966 and 1967, besides covering Paterson, I "floated" in other towns. I can remember going into the Hackensack office one Sunday and was told a chemical plant in Hawthorne had exploded on Friday and was still smoldering. I had never before been in Hawthorne. I had to park blocks away because 'sightseers' wanted a glimpse of a disaster. I can remember walking toward the smoking site and hearing an older couple walking away from the building. The woman said to the man, "I'm disappointed. I expected to see more." For some reason - as evidenced today on TV -- people loved to hear about other people's miseries and tragedies. George Rosner, the father of a friend of a friend, died in that explosion. Several days passed before firemen could walk inside the building. They found Rosner dead, sitting in his chair which had been slammed against the wall.

This story and follow-up ones were traumatic for me.

The caption on one of our pictures read "Tons and tons." "Rescuers pick through tons of debris searching for 7 bodies still missing!"

Another picture shows the stream of cars which jammed Hawthorne's streets. Cars came from all over New Jersey, New York, and even Connecticut.

My article headed "Scene Attracts Onlookers" recaps what I remember.

"Why did they come?"

"We just took a ride,'" one man said. 'We came to see what was going on.'

"One woman, who walked 12 blocks to the scene, told a police officer, 'I'm disappointed. It's not much."

Playing a prominent role in locating 3 of 4 bodies recovered, was a German shepherd, whose owner came from Manhattan. Headlines and pictures "German Shepherd Assists Hawthorne Blast Workers."

Looking now at my articles I can remember that I stood close by when they brought out Rosner's body. I was shell shocked when I got his name from police. I knew him.

The company, Morningstar-Paisley division of International Latex Corp and the town immediately started an investigation. Headline "Hawthorne Opens Blast Probe."

According to my Monday, February 20 1967 article several men were still missing. And according to the article

"A 3-man rescue team and Passaic County coroner, John Kotran, picked their way through glass and falling walls in order to free Rosner.

"Kotran, still trembling from the experience, said Rosner was seated in his chair with a pencil in his hand. "There was a piece of paper on his desk. I had to pry the pencil from his hand."

MORE FLOATING ASSIGNMENTS.

In the 1960s housing developments ate up farm land in western Bergen County, NJ. Post World War II housing boom. A little man, maybe 5'4", owned a petting zoo in Fair Lawn which attracted people from all over the tri-state area. He had elephants, lions, tigers, monkeys and many other animals -- some retired from Ringling Bros. Circus. As houses surrounded the zoo, residents started complaining about the noise and the traffic. The owner Robert Dietch had to find another home for the animals.

So I went out to do a story.

Bob had a pet tiger that he walked in the river on the property and took into house, where the Tiger rested on the couch near the TV. He also had a pet cheetah and other petable animals. After getting the basic information, I had a photographer meet me at the zoo. I had my young niece Ruth (then 16 months old) with me. So my original story had a picture of Ruth petting the cheetah that towered over her. Telephone callers were outraged that I put Ruth at risk.

The Sunday before the article ran on Monday, November 28, 1966, was dark and rainy. I called Bob to double-check some facts. He told me he had a disaster on his hands and that all of his animals were unconscious -- from tainted meat. I sent a photographer.

My story, then headlined "Animals Eat Drugged Meat. Beasts Sleep On and On," hit the wire services at 1 am Tuesday. Included in the semiconscious animals was Bob's $20,000 pet tiger Sabu -- mentioned above -- and a 450 pound lion Elvis (retired from the circus).

As soon as the wires ran the story, Bob started getting calls from zoo directors all over the country, giving advice as to what to do to bring the animals back to full consciousness. Area nurses volunteered to get liquids into the animals.

I can still remember calling Bob at 10 a.m. on Tuesday to see how the animals were doing. He barked "You don't know what you started." He told me of all the telephone calls. Then he yelled "NBC is sending a crew out at 2 p.m. Be here!"

Technology in those days was much different from today. NBC had sent a crew of four men: cameraman, lighting man, tape recorder and reporter. (Today one or two people can handle everything.) First they had Bob lift up one of the barred "rooms" so close-up pictures of the baby tigers could be taken.

My November 30, 1966 article's headline was "Drug-Drowsy Big Cats Slowly Coming to Life." The article read

"Sabu, the swimming tiger, walked and played yesterday for the first time in nearly 3 days after eating drugged meat.

"Several of the other eight tigers and lions, in a semi-comatose state since Sunday's meal began coming out of their drugged lethargy.

"Late yesterday afternoon Robert Dietch.... half lifted his 350 pound pet tiger from his cage.

"With television lights flooding the barn and cameras whirring, Sabu wobbled, then sank onto a pillow. At Dietch's prodding, the tiger began to wake up and wrestled for a short time with his owner. After he tried unsuccessfully to climb on a nearby cot, Sabu was put back into his cage.

"Among the first to recover was Tasha, a tame lion cub. Tasha played for a while outside his cage, but his wobbly legs still showed the effects of the drugs. Elvis, a 450 pound lion, woke up, yawned, blinked his eyes and went right back to sleep. ..."

Sabu, the pet tiger, was in a separate cage in the middle of the barn floor. Waving his hands and jumping up and down, Bob told the NBC crew, "Set up everything in the barn door way. Then I'll take this tiger out." The men blanched. "Who will help you?" they asked. "No one. I'll do it myself."

Inside the barn door was a small office and outside the office was that cot. I stood inside the office, at the door and watched. When Sabu spotted the cot and moved toward the NBC men, the men were really scared. One, I think, did have an "accident." I stood there chuckling as I knew Sabu was tame.

The next day, the State announced it would investigate: "State Probes Tiger Sleep."

"State officials investigating the apparent loophole in regulations, which allows animals headed for the meat market to be killed with drugs. ...."

"The animals were drugged with sodium pentobarbital, which had been used to kill a horse with a broken leg. The horse was fed to the animals when Dietch's regular meat supplier ran short."

I remember I tried to track his new location, but never was able to tie it down.

ANOTHER 'FLOATING ASSIGNMENT'

My ability to cover anything at the drop of a hat and to get people to talk with me was evidenced on Sunday, September 4, 1966 when two gunmen killed a police officer and held a new bride hostage in a motel in Fort Lee, NJ.

Working Sundays, when staff was light, the editors had me covering unusual situations. As a female I was sent out even if the event was dangerous. I remember getting a call from the paper early Sunday morning, as Englewood (where I lived) is next to Fort Lee. I remember trying to find the motel, missing it and having to cross the George Washington Bridge and circle back across it to reach the motel.

Headline on September 5, 1966 article reads "Bridegroom Nabs Man as Fort Lee Cop Is Slain. Police Capture Second in Holdup."

Because the incident was so unusual in that quiet area, the articles I wrote were very detailed.

"An enraged bridegroom of a few hours pistol whipped and disarmed one of two gunmen, now being held on murder charges, within minutes after a young patrolman was shot to death at the Riviera Motor Hotel on Route 4 early yesterday morning.

"Patrolman William Birch, 25, the father of three small daughters, was gunned down by two men, who, police said, had just held up the Hotel. ....

"(James) Belton and (Ulysses) Neil, armed with what was reported to be .38 and .22 caliber pistols, and brass knuckles, entered the hotel office at 12:25 am. ....

"The gunmen ordered (hotel manager Joseph) Vaspol to leave with them. Patrolman Birch arrived as they were leaving and was immediately fatally shot. ...

"Belton ran out the front door just as Mr. and Mrs. Thomas Thompson, who were still in their wedding clothes, drove up. Belton jumped in their car, pointed his gun at Thompson and ordered him to start driving, according to reports.

"Thompson, a recently discharged Air Force official, refused to drive. Belton then jumped out of the car, dragging the 22 year old bride, Sheila, with him, his gun aimed at her head. The angry groom, grabbed a gun from the glove compartment, got out and walked around the car, and hit Belton on the head from behind. After hitting Belton several times with his gun, Thompson reportedly punched Belton, disarmed him and held him for police. ....."

A scary "things don't change" incident. The police officer, William Birch, was gunned down by a man who was a parolee from a Texas jail where he had been serving a 99-year sentence for killing a dentist and was able to get guns. Availability of criminals to get guns and kill has not changed -- and in fact has gotten worse.

Birch left a wife and three very young daughters, ages 3 1/2, 2 1/2 and 15 months.

The next day, I visited the bride's parents, who relived their nightmare.

Headline reads "Bride Rescuer A Quiet Man." According to his father-in-law, "He's a quiet, studious young man and not inclined to violence. ...

"...said he and his wife had come home from their daughter's wedding reception shortly before his son-in-law called them.......... The article then recapped details of the event and reaction from Thompson's family.

The headline on the September 6 front page article was in bright red letters "Ft. Lee Killing Suspect Shot Dentist in Texas."

In writing this story I had even talked with Huntsville, TX, prison officials and recapped the suspect's 1955 murder. Details here are immaterial. Another example of my never ending propensity to continue to ask many questions.

* * * *

Something started during those five years that is with me today and which shaped the last ten years of my life in this new millennium.

As a "beat" reporter - someone who wrote about everything that went on in a town -- I became interested in education -- the system, but not to teach. When I started covering racial issues, I saw that education was the key to changing society. In the summer of 1967 I convinced the editors to let me do a roundup of short stories about the education in each town we covered and what new programs were being introduced for the new school year. This roundup proved so successful that the next year, Don Borg, the paper's owner, used these school stories as a vehicle to get advertising. So in 1968 the very first in the country Back to School special supplement was introduced, written and coordinated by me. Local reporters supplied me with the basic information.

A NEW BEAT

In 1966, a new young reporter was assigned to cover Wayne, N.J. He was a good looking gung-ho new reporter. His goal was to get as much news out of the town as possible. But the mayor, Edward Sisco, did not like *The Call* and called press conferences for 9 a.m., knowing that the afternoon papers could carry the story that day and *The Call* would have to run it the next day. For some reason -- I think to attract more advertisers -- the date of the story was important, and there was keen competition between *The Call* and the afternoon papers.

This reporter made friends easily, and *The Call* ran stories that the other papers did not have. By April, he had antagonized Sisco to the point that Sisco would not talk to him. So, I was assigned to Wayne, to smooth Sisco's feathers and get stories on a timely basis. I covered the town until Sisco got really mad at me, and then the young reporter went back.

At that time Wayne was fairly rural, only about 50% of the land was developed.

I can remember from memory two times Sisco really got mad at me.

In August 1966 Sisco reintroduced a Master Zoning Plan previously vetoed by the former administration.

The proposed changes were in the Old Wayne Area along the always flooding Pompton River. Today flooding still occurs on a regular basis because (1) the US Corps of Engineers plan to straighten the river and decrease the flood area was never implemented and (2) hundreds of new homes were allowed to be built in the zone.

A public hearing was scheduled, but Sisco refused to release the proposed new map and the changes. Of course, that was illegal. But Sisco didn't care that residents would be unprepared to ask questions or protest. He had to control!

As was usual with my reporting techniques and ability to get people to talk with me, one of the men on the Planning Board felt the residents had a right to see the map before the hearing and was willing to give me a copy. Even though Sisco had sworn them all to secrecy. We ran the story and map on a Monday -- a day or two before the hearing. Sisco was furious that *The Call* had the story, while the other papers did not and that someone gave me the information. Sisco called every town employee and official demanding that they tell him if they leaked the information. Everyone denied they gave me the information. And, of course, I would not tell my source. More coups as I was able to cover the night hearing and also get quotes ahead of time from residents who opposed the changes.

On August 25, 1966 the plan was put before the Planning Board and the map was not disclosed to the public ahead of time (except for my article).

Planning Board member John Phelan was the one who gave me the map, which the paper ran before the meeting.

At this meeting Phelan asked that the plan be studied further (in my article August 26.) "Old Wayne Rush Charged."

In the rush to get the changes approved (Monday, August 29) Sisco put "the screws" on Planning Board members. "Planners Back Rezoning" even though the Corps plan had not been considered.

The Plan had to be approved by the Council and a fight ensued there. "Jasinski Wants Answers."

My article read "How can we in good conscience vote on the matter when so many questions remain unanswered," Walter Jasinski asked. "Jasinski also referred to the Corps Plan, which was still unofficial. .....

The whole situation was further complicated by the fact that ownership of a large portion of the Old Wayne Area was unknown. My articles traced the problem.

In the September 28, 1966 story the headline read "Old Wayne Land Ownership Tangled Up. Records Show Many Different Claims."

I worked on this story for weeks, tracing deeds block by block and talking with various US federal agencies. I do not remember the outcome.

* * * *

The next Sisco-Goldstein incident was in 1966 when I was doing a roundup story -- what Sisco had achieved that year.

At that meeting Sisco told me that one company would be removing and moving graves in order to build a large extension to the plant. Needless to say, my ears picked up and my pen was ready to write. "Oh" I said, "where?" Sisco was an information control freak. "You'll hear when I am ready to tell you," he said. I knew darn well that he'd tell the other papers before me.

So, after I finished the interview, I went to the township clerk, who did not like Sisco and did like me. (I can't remember her name, but I think her first name was Dorothy). She scoured the township map and located the old cemetery, which dated back to 1883. I took down all the information. The clerk told me that the health officer would have to be involved. So, I went to see the health officer, Oscar Aquino. "I understand you are going to move those old graves on ___ property," I said. "When?" "How did you know?" he asked. "I just came from the mayor's office," I said. (Not mentioning of course my stop in the clerk's office.) Aquino then gave me all the information I needed to write the first story. By the time I got back to my office, the plant in question was closed, so I couldn't talk with the owner. I was able to send a photographer out, who got a marvelous picture of two young boys jumping over the tombstones. Front page! The July 13, 1966 headline read "Wayne May Move Dead to Aid Industry."

First thing the next morning I called the plant owner who gave me more information. Another story! Another coup! When I first called and identified myself, he said, "Oh, I thought I recognized those tombstones on your front page. They're on my property."

He then gave me the details of the project.

In my initial article I did not name the company that wanted to build because I did not want the other papers to be able to do a story. In my follow-up story I did name the company and quoted the President.

Sisco was furious that *The Call* had the basic story before the other reporters and that I wrote a follow-up that the other papers also did not have. Sisco stopped talking to me. The young reporter went back to cover Wayne. I went back to Paterson.

But moving the bodies/graves wasn't easy. By September, the company, Passaic Rubber Company of Clifton, was so frustrated that it filed a law suit (September 26) to have the cemetery declared a nuisance. The cemetery sat in the middle of a tax-exempt six acre site. The cemetery was abandoned in the late 1800s. No one claimed ownership.

I've said earlier that people away seemed willing to talk to me -- still do -- and so I was alerted to the law suit even though the court was in another county.

MORE ABOUT SOCIETAL CHANGES.

I have always felt that the 1960s was a key pivotal time in our history. Reviewing my articles from that time re-enforces this belief. However, at the time we really didn't understand the broad national significance. We just went day by day doing our job. But even then, I somehow understood the racial upheavals. I guess from my experience in 1954 at Northwestern University and the Medill School of Journalism summer program. I've talked about that previously.

The 1960s was also the beginning of the women's movement and the cry for equalization in traditional male jobs, particularly police officers.

In July 1966, white elitist Wayne, NJ, appointed the first woman as a regular police officer. Males protested the appointment and having to train with a woman. A tricky (my words) lawyer representing the police officers found a loophole in Wayne's police ordinance.

The headline on my July 20, 1966 article is "Sugar-Spice Cops Aren't So Legal".

According to the town ordinance police officers are referred to as "he" with no mention of "she." Perhaps the generic reference of the day and perhaps an oversight. But the clincher was that police officers had to be 5'7" tall and weigh at least 150 lbs. In this case, the woman, Mrs. Gloria Hinderlong, was 5'4" and 120 lbs. .

At that time, state law also talked about "he" and never used "she." So the fight for women's equal rights was on. According to my August 4th article, the Council authorized the town attorney to draw up a new ordinance that would cover women. Part of the "fight" was Hinderlong's initial balking at having to go through police training and being trained in judo and other bodily techniques with the men.

Today, the "he/she" wording is usually used or there might be specific reference to the fact that after an initial he/she wording that the word 'he' would encompass both sexes.

REPORTERS STYLE HAS CHANGED DRAMATICALLY

Intrusive reporters were not so intrusive in those days. And when the core group of us *Call* reporters got together in the late 1990s and early 2000s, we always lamented that the media today is so intrusive and lacks respect for people.

This remembrance brought back another event in Wayne -- the first Wayne young man to be killed in Vietnam. My editor wanted a picture. I was supposed to knock on the front door of this family and ask for a picture. Well, aggressive as I was, this did not sit well with me. I went to one of the neighbor's house, identified myself, and asked if either the husband or wife were friends with their neighbor. I explained what I needed. The wife was a friend and went next door to see if she could get a picture. She came back and said the family wanted to meet and talk with me. Over a drink, the mother pulled out an album, pictures of her son's life and recalled all his achievements in school. I got the picture and a firsthand description of the young man. Still another coup.

* * * *

According to my clips, when I first started covering Wayne in 1966 there was a fight to prevent a heliport from being built in a residential area. The land's owner Milton Neil refused to stop work even though residents and town officials objected.

The headlines on my articles tell the story:

April 22, 1966 -- Wayne Heliport Work Goes On Despite Complaints.

April 25, 1966 -- Heliport Opposition Readied. Wayne to Seek Injunction.

April 27, 1966 -- Ordinance Would Restrict Heliport

May 3, 1966 -- Keagen Will Offer Heliport-Data Bill

May 4, 1966 -- Laguna Lake Heliport To Be Fought at Trenton by Wayne Residents

May 21, 1966 -- Sisco Vetoes Law Restricting Wayne Heliports

June 1, 1966 -- Neil Boosts His Wayne Heliport. New Form of Taxicab

MANY BAD THINGS REMAIN CONSTANT

The 1960s were troubled times in the American society. One would think supposedly intelligent man would learn from such events and make changes so history does not repeat itself. For some unfathomable reason, man does not seem to learn. This "non-learning" is not limited to domestic situations. But as I tell of my travels in later pages, the same kinds of problems remain today (now 2017). I have noted throughout the next pages my own opinion of such problems -- ones that were evident in the 1960s when I was a young woman and still exist today, when I am 80.

My articles particularly in 1967, 1968 and 1969, clearly show certain constant societal elements, and I've noted which elements remain problems/concerns today. Thus my deeper interest in education was born.

My clips and the headlines clearly show several things:
- events as they happened
- educational happenings involving the minorities
- the overall mood of the city
- the deficiencies of the 1960s society as a whole

Jan. 30, 1967 -- NJ Lowest in Nation
Survey Flunks teachers
NJ last in elementary certification and 48th in relation to high school
Mar. 28, 1967 -- Male Teacher Turnover High - 13%
Mar. 27, 1967 -- Catholic Schools Told To Do More for Nonwhite Children - from a keynote speech at the National Catholic Education Association Convention.
April 6, 1967 -- Assaults on Teachers in Paterson Among Highest in State (3rd highest)

May 3, 1967 -- Series on sex education and status of schools in Passaic County

May 11, 1967 -- Priest Denounces Dogmatic Sex Moralizing -- priest's statement was a result of my series

May 9, 1967 -- Swindlers Cheat Income Tax Too?
A real estate scam and tax fraud that involved a real estate broker, lawyer, FHA, and a bank
I had to "sit" for 6 months on this story until an indictment came down

May 1967 -- a series of articles on the beginning of more state involvement and control of education standards.
SITUATION CONTINUES TODAY

May 1967 – a series of articles on the high cost of college education and how it affects families
SITUATION CONTINUES TODAY

June 1967 -- Students Shortchanged
beginning of the discussion of inequities in education and the fact that kids in urban areas are getting "stop gap education"
SITUATION SAME TODAY

June 15, 1967 -- Education Laws Shake Curricula
-1st law mandating education for handicapped
-- home schooling and tutoring also mandated

One wonders why age-old solvable problems still exist

June 14, 1967 -- A series on Unmarried and Pregnant Teens

-- parental neglect and indifference are to blame for school girl pregnancies in low-income families
SITUATION UNCHANGED

-- the articles also pointed out that low income mothers keep babies resulting in more financial pressures on government resources. Middle and upper income teens tended to put up babies for adoption
June 21, 1967 -- Nursing Shortage
-- article quoted 20 to 30% fewer RNs than needed
SITUATION UNCHANGED

July 7, 1967 -- Drug Abuse Is Decried
-- drug abuse is symptomatic of character disorders and adolescent rebellion
SITUATION UNCHANGED

Aug. 17, 1967 -- Labor Demands Outsteps Skilled Supply
SITUATION UNCHANGED especially given increase in technology

Nov. 6, 1967 -- 10% Would Fail Police Mental Test
SITUATION UNCHANGED -- over reacting, beatings and shooting by police clearly indicate the need for more testing as well as training.

Nov. 13, 1967 -- Should Johnny Go To College? The Pressure Tank series.
SITUATION SAME TODAY

College looked upon as THE panacea and specialized education/training is neglected. Today many unions fight for status quo and do not retrain members to meet/deal with reality today. (A Jan 2013 reports shows that 48% of college graduates are over qualified for the job they have.)

<u>Nov. 18, 1967</u> -- Behind The Headlines: The Teachers Who Failed

<u>Dec. 7, 1967</u> -- Pay, Working Squabbles May Wipe Out State College Staffs

* * * *

Headlines from the beginning of 1968 show an increased dissatisfaction with the status quo and frustration about not seeing progress in key societal problems. Problems in the Paterson educational system skyrocketed with demonstrations and strikes.

Emotions from various elements (blacks, whites, hispanic) simmered in the middle of 1968 and then boiled over in the fall. The adult leaders were unable to get any help from the mayor's office, the county, the state, or the Board of Education.

Many words -- just a lot of talk -- flowed, still without any action, and a stalemate prevailed with the Board of Education, whose members had been appointed by the previous mayor.

The inequities in urban education were further widened by a 1973 Supreme Court decision that urban children do not have a Constitutional guarantee to equal education. This problem, especially in large cities, remains -- leaving minorities frustrated, uneducated and into gang wars and drugs.

<u>Jan. 23, 1968</u> -- Picket Line Protests Youth Corps Cutback

Feb. 24, 1968 -- Shoppers Balk at High Prices - Fruits, Vegetables Off List

Feb. 24, 1968 -- Draft Deferments To Be Scarce in Jersey (Vietnam War)

Feb. 24, 1968 -- Draft to Pinch Research

Feb. 29, 1968 -- New Leader of School Board in Paterson Outlines Plans

  --Marion Raushenbach took over. A non-confrontational kind of person, she became bewildered by all the protests and demands from the blacks.

  -- she said at that time that the key to quality education is people, the teachers, the administration, the professionals and the parents and their attitude

  --SITUATION SAME TODAY

Mar. 5, 1968 -- New Policy Aids Deprived Teens

Mar. 14, 1968 -- Youngsters Plug In To Reading

Tape recording to help kids -- one of first uses of technology to help children learn

Mar. 20, 1968 -- Paterson State Students Oppose Marine Recruiters

* * * *

Mar. 28, 1968 -- Mortgage Jury to Hear Final Testimony Today

Mar 21, 1968 -- Animal Welfare Group Hits Proposed New Rule That would allow pounds to give animals to research labs

April 11, 1968 -- Ban On Teacher Strikes Lifted

April 16, 1968 -- Civil Service Balks at Paying Shelter Workers

--was fight to get workers more money at children's shelter -- homeless and abused children

* * * *

April 20, 1968 -- Six Plead Innocent in FHA Case
--N. Haledon judge Vincent Pernetti indicted April 9, after 11 months investigation
--this is story I had to sit on for 11 months before being able to write about it.
--DIFFERENT today at the media jumps on any hint of investigation or wrong doing.

Nov. 23, 1968 -- Real Estate Couple Pleads Guilty in Fraud
Indicted April 1968 FHA fraud
--Haledon Judge Pernetti
-- Mr. & Mrs. Fred Murray of Paramus began
fraud scheme in 1965 that involved 60 properties. Investigation started in 1967

* * * *

April 30, 1968 -- Kramer To Make School 6 Safe
- charges then that girls and teachers were molested
--SAFETY SITUATION TODAY prominent - but now with guns

May 1968 -- there was a sit-in at Paterson City Hall for 4 days and Kramer refused to talk to the leaders.
May 1, 1968 -- Paterson State Teachers Oppose Merit-Raise System
SITUATION TODAY and discussion continues

May 4, 1968 -- 3,000 Students March Monday for State Aid

NOTE: I mentioned earlier about the Sunday riot during which I dodged Molotov cocktails and bricks. Dates here are important.

June 30, 1968 -- After the Puerto Rican parade, several fire hydrants were opened. A man was arrested and beaten. This started three days of rioting.
July 3, 1968 -- Paterson police swept through the Fourth Ward, smashed windows and attacked people on the street.
Sept 23, 1968 -- Spanish Center in The Middle of Poverty Fight
Sept. 25, 1968-- Shouts of Protest End Center Hearing
Dec. 6, 1968 -- Schools Call Off Hot Lunch Plan
Dec. 7, 1968 -- School Boycott Threatened
Dec. 10, 1968 -- School Lunches Promised for Next September

Beginning in May 1968, there were increased demands that Dr. Michael Gioia, superintendent of Paterson schools, quit or be fired. There were increased problems from the influx of disadvantaged kids coupled with old-time administrators and teachers unable to understand and meet new needs. Also there was not enough money to bring in professionals who could handle the problems.

By the fall of 1968, lack of quality education for the minorities became the focus of the primary minority organization, Federation of Neighborhood Council. The Hispanic community had also organized a center, with some government funding.

At the Sept. 5, 1968 Board of Education meeting the Task Force (the trustee body of the Federation) demanded that superintendent Michael Gioia be fired. When the Board refused, the Task Force called for a school boycott. While nothing was done, by Dec. 7, 1968, the Task Force pushed harder for a boycott.

Major problems at Paterson's Eastside High School came to the fore in 1968 and continued through the 1970s. In 1982 the situation was so bad that a black principal -- Joe Clark -- was brought in to fix things. Movie "Lean on Me" tells Clark's story.

Jan. 1969 - Board hired law enforcement agents to provide security at Eastside High School.

SITUATION SAME TODAY IN CITIES - even more pronounced re guns and drugs

Jan. 6, 1969 - An Educator Decides Not to Retreat
A series on Dr. Michael Gioia, superintendent
Jan 7, 1969 - What's Needed: Teachers and Cash
In the fall 1968 Gioia took a leave of absence for health reasons and returned after 3 1/2 months. My series noted his new energy and philosophy and actions.

Gioia stressed that better trained teachers and more money were critical.

"Teachers must be trained to deal with the emotional problems of the inner city child and the sociological impact of the rapidly changing urban scene."

Jan 11, 1969 - 4th Graders in Ghetto, Suburb Look at Each Other's Worlds
Jan 25, 1969 - Eastside Teachers to Study Tensions
A number of high school students were beaten on the way home from school.

-- unrest and trouble in school halls
-- problem of timid teachers who could not deal with unruly kids.
SITUATION SAME TODAY

* * * *

In Feb. the black students boycotted the Eastside High cafeteria complaining that the food was "white" oriented. In the beginning of March, there were after school sit-ins and more appeals to the Board of Education for changes. At one point the school was closed.

<u>Mar. 4, 1969</u> -- Eastside Reopens, Demands Unanswered
-- Mayor Kramer refused to meet with dissident black students. charged the Black Student Organization (BSO) was illegal re geared only to blacks.
-- another sit-in on Friday

<u>Mar. 6, 1969</u> -- Black Students Plan Action at Eastside
-- Kramer still refused to meet the dissident black students
-- students continued to boycott cafeteria food
-- Kramer continued to call BSO illegal

<u>Mar 7, 1969</u> -- Kramer, Students Try to Cool It
-- Kramer did meet white student leaders, but not blacks
-- still refused to meet black students
--- continued to say BSO was illegal
-- discussed 'process' to hear complaints and did not discuss specific black demands.
-- Eastside's Black Students Demands
-- ten demands presented to the Board of Education

<u>Mar.11, 1969</u> -- Student Unrest Boils in Two Schools: Police Lead 250 from Eastside High
-- 4 hour sit-in in cafe - took 100 cops to lead kids out
-- superintendent Gioia to meet with students

-- Board of Education more sympathetic to student demands than was mayor

<u>Mar. 12, 1969</u> -- 60 Arrested at Eastside

--all day sit in

-- 3rd sit-in in 10 days

-- 500 blacks sat in auditorium all day

- on other days students left at end of school day. This day the students remained in the school and police had to carry each one out

-- couple police injured

**---- I snuck into the school and sat in the balcony observing. Students basically were well behaved and not destructive. This was the story headline that *The Call* racist city editor changed and made it seem as if the kids were hoods. And this is the story about which I told the editor I would quit if he touched any more of my stories.

<u>Mar. 12, 1969</u> -- How Board Reacted to Student Demands

-- Black Student Organization made 11 demands which included flying black flag next to US one in hallway, various building problems, maintenance problems and curriculum changes. Also wanted black assistant principal

-- addressed most demands in a positive way, but students still not happy.

<u>Mar. 13, 1969</u> -- Sit-Ins Ask Full Pardon

-- BSO demanded amnesty for kids arrested

--talks continued with Board of Education

-- mayor not involved at all except to claim outsiders were involved and told police to use force if necessary

-- white students demonstrated and "accused school administration of not listening"

<u>Mar. 21, 1969</u> -- Eastside Row Boils Down to a Flag

-- Board and mayor said NO to African-American flag being placed next to US flag

<u>Mar. 21, 1969</u> -- State School Commissioner George Sokalski called black demands "nothing constructive"

-- Kramer finally gets involved and called for various changes

-- various changes that students had made requests for months before and Board did not even reply

-- the blacks were completely frustrated and further demonstrated and complained that no one listened to the blacks.

<u>April 8, 1969</u> -- Eastside to Have Guards

-- in response to complaints, city police in the schools were removed.

-- the school hired security guards. The hiring of city police in March triggered latest demonstrations.

In the next few months, up until the time I resigned in mid-June, education troubles escalated in several venues. Also, more inner city problems came to the fore, and some of these problems still exist today.

* * * *

Again, the headlines on my stories tell the story.

<u>April 11, 1969</u> -- Nixon Move Affects Area Job Corps, Head Start

-- At that time there was the problem of insufficient job training for drop out students and minorities.

-- Even today, many people are repeating the same complaint and are going a step further by saying that there are not enough skilled workers for manufacturing plants and that on-the-job training is too expensive for individual companies. In several situations there have been joint technical school-company programs which reduce the cost for both students and companies.

April 29, 1969 -- Sociologist Is Critical of NJ Drug Education
--PROBLEM CONTINUES

May 1, 1969 -- Drugs Held Balm For Social Pain
--PROBLEM CONTINUES TODAY

May 6, 1969 -- Paterson Teachers Spurn Offer
May 7, 1969 -- Black Sit-In Hits College in Wayne
-- blacks called for Open Admissions and student controlled black studies program
May 10, 1969 -- PSC and Rebels to Air Conflict
-- no decisions on demands after two meetings
-- black students left in the middle of the meeting because they did not get the answers they wanted.
May 15, 1969 -- SDS, Panthers Slate Paterson State Teach-In
May 18, 1969 -- Much Wordage, Little Communication at Paterson State College
June 9, 1969 -- How Passaic Country Cares for "Bad" Kids
-- a Carol special and follow-up of a 1968 Carol investigation
June 17, 1969 -- Paterson Teachers Strike
-- teachers were court ordered to return to work and did not. I was on the phone daily with PEA leaders and wrote stories.
-- At some time right after the strike, there was a court hearing, which I covered. At that time I was handed a Jane

Doe subpoena and ordered to testify because I had been writing daily stories. I refused at first, saying I would have to consult the paper's attorney. I did have to testify, but could contribute nothing that was detrimental to the teachers.

<u>June 18, 1969</u> -- Paterson Schools Stay Shut
--Kramer always took a hard line when it came to disputes -- it was his way or no way and said negotiations were off until the teachers returned to work
-- fight was about salaries

<u>June 19, 1969</u> -- Doors Open, Teachers Still Balk

NOTE: My clips end here as that is around the time I resigned, got married and moved to the Philippines

Originally my Life story was to take the reader to the present. But as I wrote and finished *The Call* story, my foreign travels in the 1960s, and my married life in The Philippines, I decided to end this book in 1972. In that year the second trunk of my Life tree matured.

However there still is more about those early years at *The Call* newspaper to be told here.

WE WERE A FAMILY

Up to now I've been focusing on myself and my interaction between the people in the towns I covered. There was another very important, very dynamic element during those 5 years on *The Call*. These dynamics continue between those of us who were still around in 2011. We were a close knit group.

RIOTS & REVOLUTIONS

* * * *

The first couple of years when I was covering Totowa, W. Paterson and Little Falls, I worked out of the Hackensack office. This meant that I had to travel back to the office at night to write my stories. We worked 3 p.m. (or earlier when things were really happening) until 11 p.m. By then we were all exhausted, but charged up. A core group of us headed across the street to a local bar. The waitress, Stella, always had a fresh pot of coffee ready. We rarely had a drink -- in spite of the myth that all reporters were heavy drinkers. We snacked -- and talked and unwound. Then the owner of the bar built a diner on property adjacent to *The Record* office in Hackensack. Our new landing place -- with Stella a star player. We all kept in touch with Stella until her death in the early 2000s. She always attended our yearly reunions.

As most of us worked Sunday through Thursday, we'd "celebrate" Thursday night by going into NYC to a bar under the 3rd Ave L subway. The bar was frequented by reporters from the *Journal-American* and *NY Post* (both long gone). We'd feel we really were professionals! After that we'd often head to our favorite coffee house in The Village.

Come summer, a large group of us (two or three car caravan) would head up to Bear Mountain, just across the NJ-NY border. We'd spend the day soaking in nature, visiting the zoo, picnicking. Come dusk we'd caravan into NYC, to China Town for dinner. The same restaurant off Mott St., the same waiter. It seems we were constant in our loyalty to "servers." In fact when I took my husband to the restaurant in 1971, the same waiter was there. And he actually remembered our large boisterous group!

Then to the coffee house on Bleeker Street. Several of us would end up at my parent's house around 5 a.m. I'd make breakfast, and at 7 a.m. Judy Megaro and Joe DeFillipis (both gone) would go to mass. I'd go to sleep. Judy would come back for a few hours of sleep. My mother would wake us at noon and feed us. We always were ready to eat! Then Judy and I were off to work at 3 p.m. Often my mother would join us when we got home at 5 a.m. She loved the dynamics of young people. (At 90, she tutored disadvantaged second graders in reading.)

* * * *

In the mid-1990s, Judy Megaro bought a house on Long Beach Island, NJ. Every Columbus Day weekend, we'd have a Call reunion, staying over, catching up on the past year's happenings, walking the beach, and having the cocktail hour on the sand. More food! Judy footed the bill for everyone -- hotels and food. For a number of years, 20 to 25 of us gathered together. Then as several died or could not travel, the numbers fell to 10 to 12 in the last few years. The reunions ended in 2008 when Judy passed on.

CHAPTER 5

FOREIGN SEAS AHOY

There is still another major element to my story. Although my "beat" was Passaic County, NJ, I kept up with foreign affairs, particularly in India and Indonesia, which I had visited in 1962-1963, and wrote articles about current events in a number of countries.

During those five years at *The Call*, each year I would vacation in a different country and spend at least a month there. Then I'd write about my adventures.

1965 Indonesia and the communist coup
1966 Liberia
1967 Israel and all the occupied lands
1968 a swing through Asia

In order to take these trips, I'd borrow money from the local bank, Citizens National Bank. My parents knew the President, Jesse Turner. Then I'd pay it back over the year. My mother taught me early on that as a woman I should have my own credit history. While my income sucks today, my credit rating at last checking was 850.

After my 1965 trip to Indonesia, which experienced a communist coup while I was there, each year Turner asked where I was going - and how much money did I want. He wanted to know where I was going because trouble seemed to follow me.

* * * *

In 1964, I met an Israeli journalist who was covering South America for one of the major news services. His main objective was to find Nazi concentration camp officials who had fled to South America. Then he helped the Israeli government bring these officials to trial in Israel.

He was fascinated by the fact that I had a 1959 picture of my father with Fidel Castro. My father visited Cuba every year from the cruise ship on which he traveled. Shortly after the picture was taken, Castro closed Cuba to outsiders.

This is one of the early examples of US intelligence failing to connect those political DOTs. We put Castro in power ousting Batista. According to this Israeli journalist, Castro was involved (with news pictures to prove this) in EVERY anti-government demonstration in South America in the early 1950's. He was known to have very leftist beliefs. Why would the US think Castro would be better than Batista???

My June 5, 1964 article in *The Call* had a headline "How To Subvert A Continent" and contained information from this Israeli journalist who detailed Castro's communist activities throughout South America.

I described the "fight for man" in South America as a "battle for the soul of man. One of the most unstable regions in the world today is South America. Economically backward, politically explosive....

"With a feudal society in-between the old and new, it is fertile for Communists. And the Communists are sowing seeds.

"Castro spends an estimated $1 million a day in Latin America to subvert and infiltrate, to promote terror and discontent, to distribute arms and propaganda. With Cuba's economy chaotic -- industrial and agricultural production are down, prices are up and the people are hungry. There is the nagging question "Where does Castro get the money and supplies to support his Latin American campaigns?"

"Late reports from Cuba indicate that Russian bloc and Chinese influence are quite noticeable. In addition to the millions of dollars Russia gives Cuba every year, it sends grains, arms, tanks, and planes. There are still some 300 rockets on 30 bases in Cuba.....

"Technically called technicians, 22,000 Russian soldiers are still in 1964 Cuba in military uniforms. There are about 5,000 Chinese businessmen, technicians and group instructors, 1,000 Czechs, and 500 Polish industrial advisors."

My article describes in detail Castro's activities and plans and how he is helping communists gain power in Latin America.

"Guatemalan ex-president Arbenz is in Havana directing the overthrow of the present government.......

"Uruguay is the headquarters for Castroites and Soviet agents. Here money, literature and arms enter Latin America.....

"A haven for Communists is the University of Caracas in Venezuela.....

"Venezuelan students have Czech made, Castro supplied machine guns, pistols, and ammunition. Cartons of Castro propaganda are stacked in student buildings..."

So, by the USA putting Castro in a powerful position in Cuba, the US helped create chaos throughout Latin America in the 1960s and 1970s. It still seems that wherever the US intervenes in the political affairs of other countries (e.g. Iraq, Egypt, Libya, Afghanistan, the Philippines, Liberia),

more chaos and hatred are created. And the man on the street is poorer than ever before.

* * * *

In the beginning of my story about my India visit and my Masters' thesis subject, I talked about the race between India and China to feed their millions of people. So I continued to watch events in India, especially in relation to the food situation.

In the summer of 1964, there was a real food crisis in India. My July 31, 1964 article in *The Call* was headlined "India's Severe Food Crisis: Part Man-Made, Part Natural."

"India's present food shortage is partly man-made and partly nature's greatest problem. It is man-made because the population has been increasing at a phenomenal rate. Nine million Indians are born each year. ..

"The ban of killing cows has had a major effect on India's food situation. In India beef is largely eaten by the poor and a few Hindu castes. The ban has forced the people to eat more cereal grains, thus increasing pressure on available supplies. At the same time, the cattle, which are totally useless for draft animals or food, are wild, destroying crops and cover foliage.

"The present crisis is also a result of a failure of the monsoons for several consecutive years...

"To make matters worse, hoarding of food has led to sharp price increases and riots in which people have been killed and shops looted. Several cities have reported deaths from starvation."

The article also talks about the political governmental structure in India, which does not place responsibility and authority to act on any one segment. This meant that little was achieved, even though the central government made some decrees.

I also pointed out that "The US government has offered to give rice and some vegetable oils to India to ease the present shortage. However, neither port nor inland transportation facilities are modern, giving rise to the problem of getting the rice unloaded quickly and then transporting it to areas where it is needed."

* * * *

Given my close relation to the Nur family in Indonesia, I also kept a close eye on events there and the mood -- which led to my correct prediction of a political explosion.

In my May 11, 1964 article in *The Call*, headlined "Sukarno Keeps The Pot Boiling" I referred to the Malaysia-Indonesia disagreement and my September 1963 stay in Indonesia. Aside from describing how Sukarno was sending Indonesia soldiers into Malaysia, I reiterated my 1963 experience and private one-on-one interview with President Sukarno.

"Indonesia President Sukarno has been sending in battalions of armed soldiers into Sarawak, (part of Malaysia) since last summer in an attempt to crush the newly-formed state.

"However, officially he denied these were Indonesian soldiers....

"In fact, many (of these soldiers) --wet, hungry and weary of hiding in the jungle -- gave themselves up to the Dyaks (tribal headhunters). ....

The rest of this article talks about the events of Sept. 16, 1963, the day Malaysia came into existence and my watching a horde of Indonesian students (bussed in from the provinces) break into and burn the British Embassy. And my meeting with Sukarno, where he insisted "My people are now living well." And my pointing out how quickly the price of rice had gone up in the few days I had been in Djakarta.

The 1964 article continued "Some speculate that Sukarno creates crises in order to keep the mind of his people off their tragic plight. There is more to the problem. Whatever principles are for which he says he is fighting, he has placed his own power-seeking ego above the needs of his people. His ultimate desire is to recreate the ancient Indonesian empire, which included Malaysia and the Philippines. ..

"His word is law. He can create riots -- such as the burning of the British property last September -- or stop them -- as he did two days later -- simply by decreeing it...."

During the rest of 1964, Sukarno "kept the pot boiling" and pushed the country towards a more anti-American and anti-British policy and mood.

My October 24, 1964 article in *The Call*, headlined "Sukarno's Halloween Fun," describes all the things Sukarno did to promote a hatred of Americans. Sukarno deliberately fostered and orchestrated anti-Americanism. His fiery speeches denounced American imperialism.

"Indonesian President Sukarno has announced that American books and magazines will be burned on October 31 to mark the 36th anniversary of the Indonesia Youth Pledge Day.

"The announcement marks the culmination of an intensive hate America campaign that has been carefully created during the past six months.

"Sukarno in fiery speeches denounces Americans as imperialists. Students have taken to the streets of Djakarta,

Surabaya and Median in mass demonstrations carrying "Yankees go home" banners and singing national songs....

"This hate campaign was heightened by the withdrawal of US aid this spring and continued support of the British in Malaysia."

In addition to his hate American campaign, Sukarno wanted to push the British --who had strong power -- out of the area so that he (Sukarno) could reclaim the ancient Indonesian empire.

My article ended "Next week when Indonesians again mass in the streets, the possibility of their burning American property as well as books should not be discounted. For, as President Sukarno told me during a personal interview in 1963 "Material things can be replaced. We are fighting for a principle."

ANOTHER CORRECT REVOLUTION PREDICTED

Indonesia , September 1965

I've talked about my experiences in Indonesia in 1963 and the family with whom I stayed, the Nurs (Mohamed Nur el Ibrahimy). We kept in touch afterwards, although the mail system there was dicey. The Nurs had a hard time economically. I would put cash, a $10 or $20 bill in my letters. In the beginning they got the money. Then, I guess, the postal people saw the money and took it for themselves. So, I resorted to sending those one sheet air letters, which did get through. Once or twice I was able to get $$ through. From various news sources and talking with Indonesians here, I could see that the political situation -- the struggle between communists, the military, and national and Christian parties -

- was boiling. Sitting in New Jersey, in my gut, I could see an explosion in the near future. And I wanted to be there. Remember my prediction about the 1962 Chinese invading India?

In September 1965, I took off for Indonesia. However, I had not heard from the Nurs for a while. So I was glad an officer from Gen. Sabur's office met me at the airport and got me through customs. I decided to stay at the Hotel Indonesia because it had air conditioning and was clean.

After checking into the hotel, I sought out Kumar, my Indian driver from 1963. I hired him for however long I was to be there. As usual he was more than a driver because he knew what was going on and where key people lived. By that time he had several young children and faced hard economic times. Basics were so expensive that I would use the hotel's small cake of soap once or twice and then give it to Kumar for his family. And I would swipe cakes of soap and rolls of toilet paper from the cleaning cart.

By 1965, the Indonesian economy had deteriorated and basic consumer and household things were virtually absent. Or some were available on the black market for an exorbitant amount.

In those days you were allowed to check in two bags free. One suitcase was filled with the things the Nurs said they had trouble getting: towels, sheets, shampoo, soap, toothpaste and some cosmetics. I still have those suitcases.

The Nurs had four children. Susanna, the eldest, was in Paris studying French and had been there in 1963 so I had not met her. She was still in Paris in 1965. Nyazi was the next one and had been attending college in 1963. In Sept. 1965, he graduated from college while I was there. (Both Susanna and Nyazi played key roles in my future.)

Not having heard from the Nurs, I went to their house after settling in at the hotel. But they had moved. Their house had been confiscated by Sukarno for his Japanese mistress, and the Nurs had been forced to move. Gen. Sabur was able to locate the Nur's new house way out in the suburbs.

In the meantime on Sept. 13, 1965 Sukarno was at the hotel and gave a speech. I cornered him (yes, the correct word) afterwards and he did remember me from 1963. He said he would check his appointment book to see when he could see me.

A day or so later, the Nurs got me a front row seat at Ny's Graduation exercises at which Sukarno was the key speaker. He went on a tirade against America, shaking his fists, his face contorted. I wanted to get close up pictures of his face and so got up from my seat and moved closer to the podium. While I have some marvelous pictures, Sukarno was not happy to see me taking them and got mad at me. Even though my friend Gen. Sabur tried, Sukarno refused to see me. The only one who freely met with me was Aidit, the head of the communist party.

Because of the anti-American feelings, many leaders with whom I met in 1963 were afraid to talk with me... even though I checked with them on a regular basis. Sabur, however, was able to get me an appointment with Gen. Abdul Haris Nasution, Defense Minister, for the morning of October 1.

As I mentioned before, the Nurs had kept me up to date on happenings there, the unrest and anti-American sentiment. Letters from the Nurs indicated that the communists were gaining power. Unrest increased because of increases in food prices, and anti-American feelings prevailed. In 1965 these pressures seem to have jumped dramatically. I started writing about the problems early in 1965, and I've quoted from several of them previously.

Because Sukarno didn't like Americans, American journalists were taboo. But I got a visa. I think I may have gotten a press or tourist visa -- with the help of Gen. Sabur, head of Sukarno's security guard -- the one who got me the one-on-one interview with Sukarno in 1963. At any rate, I was the only American newspaper reporter in Indonesia at the time of the aborted communist coup on October 1.

Anti-Americanism was rife. A number of times I was asked if I was American, and I said "No, I'm from Canada." Even the Nurs, who were pro-American, felt the pressure and didn't come to the hotel to see me because they were afraid. I ventured to the suburbs, an hour out of the city with bumper to bumper traffic, only a few times during my 6-week stay there.

So much happened that September and October 1965 that it's difficult to sort out happenings in any chronological order. Before the coup, I followed the anti-American demonstrations and took hundreds of pictures, many of which appeared not only in *The Call and The Record*, but also *the NY Herald Tribune, the Far Eastern Economic Review, Plain Truth* magazine and *Life* magazine. However, I did not walk alongside of them. I stayed safely behind the fence at the American Embassy.

Once I settled down, I started what became my daily routine of visiting key officials. I revisited the Christian leader and learned that a New York University classmate of mine was there researching his Ph.D. dissertation. Stephen Sloan and I had been part of a close knit group of students majoring in international relations. The group partied together, spent a lot of time discussing what we would do differently when we would be 'adults', drank coffee in one of the 'hot' coffee houses, and rode the Staten Island Ferry back and forth during the hot summer months because it only cost $.05 (both ways if you stayed on the boat.)

At any rate, in Indonesia we spent time together and one night he took me to the China town there and introduced me to the delights of frog's legs. The nights after the coup he stayed at the hotel with me because we were afraid he would not be safe at the Christian leader's home.

Besides the Christian leaders, I revived my contacts with other leaders, including Subandrio, who was then Secretary of State. The head of the communist party, Dipsia N. Aidit told me there would be a coup soon, but wouldn't give me a date. In fact, I was the only reporter he would talk with. Every day or every other day I would make the rounds, gathering information and impressions.

Returning to NJ weeks later I wrote a series of articles on the coup, the aftermath and political ramifications. My articles appeared in *The Call, the Record, The Herald Tribune and Far Eastern Economic Review.*

I don't remember whether it was during my 1963 or 1965 visit when I met the most influential leader in the Muslim nationalist party, M. Soebchan. He was a major reliable source of information after the coup and took me to a secret political strategy meeting. In *The Call*'s third article Nov. 10, 1965 the political tensions and balancing problems that Sukarno faced after the coup were discussed.

"An integral part of this new power structure is the N.U., the largest political party in Indonesia. Suppressed by communist domination in the political arena for the past few years, the N.U. is making a comeback and can, with the leadership, maintain an anti-communist trend in the country's development.

"Its political philosophy is based on five principles: nationalism, internationalism, justice, belief in one god and humanity.

"While Suharto stands out in the military arena, the N.U. acting chairman, 36-year-old M. Soebchan, has come to the foreground in the political arena. An expert in economic development, he condemns both capitalism and communism and supports Sukarno's policy of establishing an Indonesian socialist state.

"I believe the government must play an important role in the proper distribution of national income and must provide certain guarantees of a reasonable standard of living," he said.

"We must give priority to mental construction over economic development. Many countries, for example those in Latin America, have bigger problems than we do but the state philosophy and mental development has not progressed.

"The development of political attitudes is more important than early material gains. A country must have political maturity before economic development can be successful."

I kept in touch with Soebchan after returning to the States, and learned several years later (1974) that he died of some sort of cancer, at a very young age.

THE COUP ITSELF

An Australian reporter, who was later killed in Vietnam, and I had become friends. He kept me up to date as much as he could and warned me that all of our telephone conversations were tapped. So, we wrapped the electrical wire from the table lamp around the telephone wire and put the light on. The electricity blocked the taping. Whoever was taping quickly caught on because every time I went out of my room, the electric wire was unwrapped. Frank had the same experience. We had some good laughs about this.

Tension had been building dramatically all week before that fateful night of Sept. 30 and early morning Oct. 1, 1965.

After the coup, The Indonesian society changed dramatically -- from a society where various different political groups coexisted to eventually a hard-nosed cruel, dictatorship under Suharto who allowed no discussion of politics.

The unrest before the coup was strongly anti-American, and many of my pictures of the demonstrators were published in a number of magazines, including *Life*. The unrest after the coup was strongly anti-communist and several months later thousands of communists were slaughtered.

I had an interview scheduled with Gen. Abdul Naris Nasution, Indonesia's Defense Minister, for the morning of Oct. 1. I went down to breakfast, and my driver, Kumar, came rushing over when he spotted me. "There's been a coup! There's been a coup!," he yelled. "No one knows where Sukarno is." No one seemed to know what was really happening. I ate breakfast, and we headed to army headquarters. Kumar was shaking but agreed to park next to the compound which was closed off by the army who had submachine guns guarding the area.

I had no fear in those days! I went up to the guards, who then pointed their guns right at me, and waved the appointment letter saying I wanted to see Nasution. They didn't speak English, but waved me inside. Chaos reigned. Everyone scurrying around. I finally found someone who spoke a little English. He said Nasution was not there -- even took me to his office. I think it was here that I learned that six other generals had been killed by the communist rebels.

No one knew where Sukarno was or what really was happening. Word was that the Air Force supported the communists and had taken over the airport (closed it down) and the national radio station. International communications were also shut down.

I stayed in Indonesia for six weeks, even though after the coup my editor through UPI wanted me out of harm's way. I refused to leave at that time. I wrote a long series of articles when I returned to New Jersey in October 1965.

According to the first article in my series, Nov. 8, 1965 from Nasution's office I went to the home of a Moslem leader who told me I shouldn't have come. '"They're watching, whoever they are. You may be in danger."

After visiting the Muslim leader, I went to the home of the Christian leader. Steve and I went back to the hotel. We stocked up on snack foods, juice, soda as we didn't know what to expect. Tanks with their guns pointed at the hotel surrounded the highway circle. The British Embassy was across the circle. I took pictures of the tanks using a strong telephoto lens and made sure the light didn't reflect off the lens. Frank had warned me to be careful, as the soldiers might think the lens was a gun.

We knew the Air Force sided with the communists and controlled the airport. We were afraid the communists would bomb the hotel. So, Steve and I slept in our clothes, kept our passport and money under the pillows, and had flashlights in case the power went off. It did in the middle of the night. The next morning confusion reigned and I don't think we left the hotel.

RIOTS & REVOLUTIONS

Djakarta, a city of 3 million was an armed camp with rumors flying. As I wrote in the Nov. 8, 1965 article "No one knew who was on what side. No one knew what the sides were."

Because the situation was very complex and confusing and after 45 years my memory somewhat fuzzy as to the details, I am going to include here parts of that first article.

"If there was confusion in high government and military circles that Friday, there was no confusion among the communists. As the hours ticked off and became days, the story of how they had engineered this attempt to take over the country began to fall in place.

"About 2 a.m. October 1 small bands of communists forced their way with guns blazing into the homes of the country's top generals. Six including Army Chief of Staff Lt. General Achmad Yani were dragged away. All were staunch nationalists and anti-communist.

"Either dead or badly wounded, they were taken to Halim, the Air Force base about 4 miles from Djakarta. According to some reports, communist women beheaded them and hacked up their remains. The bodies, which were thrown in a nearby well, were found 4 days later by the anti-communist military. Nasution's home had been one of those attacked. He escaped by leaping over the back fence and hiding in the Iraqi Embassy. But his 5 year old daughter was fatally wounded. One young aide, who reportedly had thrown on the general's jacket and dashed from the house to divert the communists' attention was mistaken for the general and mutilated beyond recognition."

The communist rebels were blood hungry and chopped up the six top generals. A blood bath never seen before in Indonesia. After the aborted coup the military massacred thousands of communists. There weren't any bloody pictures of the generals at that time. But the dismembered bodies received a state funeral, which I attended and photographed.

"The communist coup was directed by an unknown officer of the elite presidential bodyguard (the group headed by my friend Sabur) of 3,000 men. At 7 a.m., Lt. Col. Untung announced on Radio Indonesia that he had crushed what he called a general's coup against Sukarno. He said a purge had been made of members of the Council of Generals and that several had been arrested. He said communications facilities and other vital points in the capital had been seized and were controlled by his men, who comprised the 30 September Movement.

"Although Untung announced that Sukarno was alive and safe and still in control, the President's whereabouts remained a mystery. Afterwards, a high military official described Sukarno's movements to me."

According to my article, Sukarno, after spending the night with his 26-year-old Japanese wife Madame Devi (who lived at the house formerly owned by the Nurs) went to another palace."

I don't know if all the details bear repeating here but I feel the details have historic value.

With all the top generals gone, a lower level military official, Suharto, after being unable to get in touch with top leaders, rallied his men, among them the famed Siliwangi. Because of their extreme loyalty to Nasution, they had been targets of the Communists for many months.

"By 7 p.m. Suharto's men had surrounded the radio station and telecommunications office. Given an ultimatum, Untung's men fled after a few shots were fired.

"In Bogor (where Sukarno finally went) the Siliwangi moved in and Untung, his men and reportedly Aidit (head of the communist party) fled. At 9:45 Suharto over Radio Indonesia announced he had recaptured the government and that Sukarno and Nasution were both safe. He said the army was in his hands."

Suharto's troops moved into the city from outlying districts about 11 p.m. Steve, Frank and I watched all night as anti-aircraft guns, heavy tanks, and truckloads of soldiers proceeded to the palace and other strategic points.

The headline on my November 9, 1965 *Call* article, was "Reds Convinced Sukarno Generals Planned a Coup." I described the mindset of the communists leading up to the aborted coup as well as Sukarno's growing disenchantment with the military, which kept him in power. The military was strongly anti-communist. In the days after the coup, details of how carefully the communists planned and executed the attempt came to light. The Air Force was heavily involved and provided arms and information needed to storm all the generals' homes.

"The Indonesian Communists move to seize control of the government October 1 was made with President Sukarno's prior permission. Evidence indicates that the move was long planned, culminating months of tensions.

"Edi Martalogawa, communist party (PKI) member of Parliament and vice chairman of the Department of Foreign Affairs **told me after the coup,** "Communist leaders convinced Sukarno that the so-called Council of Generals was planning a coup October 5 (Armed Forces Day). ....

"The Council of Generals can be described as a military brain trust. It is an informal group of high ranking military officers, most of whom are staunch anti-communists. The six generals massacred October 1 belonged to this group. Although they continually opposed Sukarno's efforts to give the communists more jobs in the armed forces, there is no evidence the Army was plotting a coup October 5, as charged by the PKI.

"Martalogawa said he did not think the President knew exactly what the communists planned to do or when they planned to do it. He said he thinks Sukarno just wanted the generals neutralized so they couldn't oust him. Commenting about the massacre, he said, "I don't think Sukarno wanted them killed. He's too much of a humanist.'"

The aborted coup received strong support from China's leaders Premier Chou Enlai and Mao Tse-Tung. Before the coup a group of 20 top Indonesian military leaders was in Peking for talks with the Chinese. So they were unable to stop the communists from trying to take over.

According to my article, "One army general, after his return from Peking, told me that Chinese Premier Chou Enlai on Friday morning told them about the coup. The general also said that Mao Tse-tung during a talk on September 30, referred to the Indonesian revolution as being comparable to the Chinese period during Sun Yat-sen and Chaing Kai-skek. Mao said Indonesia is now going through the same transition period before becoming communist."

My series on the coup was written a few weeks after I returned from Indonesia. I had been in Djakarta long enough after the coup to see firsthand the domestic political repercussions. I walked alongside students who were delighted to see me. One of my pictures had the caption "Shoot to Kill." Angry Muslim students demand banning of communist party. They shouted "Kill Aidit." "Hang the communists." "Communists are traitors."

My November 10, 1965 article in *The Call* had the headline "Sukarno Image Blurs But He Still May Win Out."

"A week before the aborted Communist coup of October 1, an Indonesian leader told me 'There is only one man who rules this country -- Sukarno."

"Today, Sukarno is a master at surviving Indonesian political upheavals, has weathered the storm for the fifth time in the history of this young republic. But he is no longer the man who runs the country. His image is tarnished in the eyes of his people and his power has been deeply scarred. ....

"Christian groups joined the ensuing anti-communist melee that has sent chills of apprehension through anti-communists, officials and the diplomatic corps as well as the communists. Sukarno's pleas to stop the wanton destruction and senseless demonstrations have fallen on deaf ears. And the Muslim youth, with the apparent approval of the military, continue their wild escapades.

"The power struggle now going on in Indonesia cannot simply be described as a military takeover which ousted the communists. Whoever is in control or whoever wants power in that vast archipelago must consider Sukarno -- tarnished image and all.

"The communist massacre of six of the country's top generals unleashed the wildest anti-communist movement ever seen in this part of the world. It also tipped the scales of political power from communist party domination before the coup to military control after the coup.

"At the same time, Sukarno himself today is in a quandary. He has been the ladle that has stirred Indonesian politics into the consistency he felt desirable for the country. The ingredients consisted of national, religious, and communist groups and the military. For years he has maintained a balance between these groups and the military. In recent years, the PKI (the communists) was the stronger ingredient. Now the communists have been pulled out of the pot, which leaves Sukarno's consistency imperfect.

"A high military official said that Sukarno had trusted the communists and pro-Communists above everyone else."

The official said "In light of the evidence we've uncovered, which indicates the coup was carefully staged, Sukarno is bewildered. He still doesn't know how far he can trust the military.

"Before the PKI's activities were suspended, Martalogawa a communist leader, commented, "Sukarno lives between antagonisms. Politically Sukarno is more for the PKI than against it. If Sukarno banned the PKI it would upset the present political balance and Sukarno would be swamped by the Army.

"Sukarno cannot afford to ban the PKI. If so, he will ban himself..... Sukarno is still the head of state. For the time being at least, he will have to bargain to maintain his policies and may lose some ground. However, in the long run Sukarno will probably come out on top as he has so many times in the past.

"Wielding the military's power is tough Major General Suharto, commander of Army Strategic Reserve.....Suharto is a staunch nationalist, an anti-communist and a well-qualified and respected military man. He rallied the troops against the Communists and quickly recaptured Djakarta."

After Suharto was officially appointed Chief of Staff, the army "moved to crush the communists and arrested about 5,000. ... The military openly defied Sukarno." The military then banned all communist groups and activities. This was the beginning of the end of Sukarno's absolute power. My article continues, "He must go along with these military decisions if he wants to stay in power. In all instances in the past month, he has supported the military decisions after Suharto has made them public."

This was also the time when the Muslim party (the NU headed by Soebchan) gained more power. "Its political philosophy is based on five principles of Indonesia: nationalism, internationalism, justice, belief in one god, and humanity. ..."

According to my article, "Soebchan condemns both capitalism and communism and supports Sukarno's policy of establishing an Indonesian socialist state."

My article then described in-depth the domestic scene with the tug of war between the Muslim groups and the communists, who had gone underground, but who still had power among the poor and some student groups.

In my last article, November 11, 1965, in the series in *The Call* I dealt with the international ramifications and described the changed attitude toward Americans and the communists, and the Chinese who were thought to be communist. The headline read "Feelings Toward Americans Friendlier. US, Peking Switch Status in Indonesia."

During the first anti-communist rally in Djakarta after the aborted coup, Muslim students waved and called "Hello, Miss Carol" as I walked alongside them taking pictures.

"In September as an American, I would not have dared to walk alongside any demonstrators. At that time, demonstrations were communist led and those taking part jeered and shouted nasty slogans as they passed the United States Embassy or spotted an American. One day, when I wanted to take pictures of communist women who were protesting spiraling rice prices, hands were put in front of my camera lens. And I was promptly escorted from the headquarters of the communist women's group."

My November 11 article continued "Before the coup, China was the Rising Sun; now it is a fallen star. China once friend and ally of Indonesia is now damned as enemy and conspirator. At the same time, a friendly feeling toward Americans is stirring. ...."

"The shift towards Peking had been noticeable in the past year. According to communist leader Dipa N. Aidit, it was based on mutual interests between the two countries.

"We are Asian, China is fighting imperialism. China is an agrarian country; so are we. We are both near Vietnam. We are both threatened by the US 7th Fleet. We are both building a new society without capitalism," Aidit told me

The shift of feelings toward the Americans in a positive fashion did not happen overnight. As usual the American government expected a complete about face and the Indonesians to join the western bloc against Russia and China. This did not happen -- nor, quite frankly, should it have been expected to happen.

My article continued "The Americans are staging a comeback. This does not mean, however, that the Indonesians are going to change their whole foreign policy. Rather they will move to a more middle of the road and neutral position and will not have strong alliances with either China or the US.

"Before the coup, communist leader Aidit told me that the US has always supported Indonesia's enemies.

"You supported the Dutch. You support Malaysia. You support India's aggression against Pakistan."

At the same time, according to my article, "On the profit side for Americans and British interests is the fact that their investments, particularly in the oil companies, will be protected from nationalization. It is fairly certain that if the communist led trend continued the oil companies would have been nationalized by the end of the year. The military, now in control, as well as the Muslim parties, are opposed to nationalization."

The caveat here "Politically the US also has *much to gain if it acts wisely.* The military and the Muslim and Christian parties need much moral support rather than overt gestures at this time. Many believe the decision announced 10 days after the coup to remove American families came at the wrong time. There was no evidence that street fighting would break out in Djakarta and that Americans would be harmed.

"Indonesian military officials, including generals, called me into their offices while I was covering rallies. They wanted to know why the American government was sending their families out of the country.

"Don't they have confidence in us?" one general asked.

"My answer I am sure did not satisfy them. Nor did that of Ambassador Marshall Green, who said it was merely a continuation of the policy started earlier this year to reduce the number of Americans in Indonesia." This is the end of series of articles

* * * *

Communist leader Aidit actually fled to the Hotel Indonesia after the aborted coup and was in a room just down the hall from mine. Even after the coup he was willing -- even seemed glad -- to talk with me. We spent 2 1/2 hours as he filled me in on his dreams and future plans.

He said the communists were not weaker as a result of the failed coup. "Some communists have been arrested but our strength is not here in Djakarta. It is in Central and East Java." He said the communist organization (PKI) membership jumped from 10,000 to 3 million in 15 years.

"We had many new members who have had no bitter experiences in the struggle. They had to get more experience." He said the attempted coup was their training ground.

Aidit, shortly before the coup, told me that the Communists were first using an Indoctrination method to convert young people to communism. "As far as methods of gaining control are concerned, people can be changed." In the week before the coup he said he was still trying the indoctrination method. But he told me it didn't seem to be working so well because he could not swing the military and religious groups to his side. He said he would not hesitate to use force when he felt it was necessary.

As mentioned above, Aidit in the first interview told me there would be a coup -- and evidently he ran out of patience to try to make changes peacefully.

AFTER THE COUP

After Suharto and the military gained control, the airport was opened, but international communications was still shut down because of damage to the equipment. One international flight a day was allowed in. Frank and I would write our stories, and he managed to get out to the airport after dark and gave the copy to the pilots. Then they took the stories to the Western Union office in the first city they stopped at.

After several days, Suharto allowed several foreign reporters into the country. Two included Tom (I think) Friedman of the *NY Times* and John Hughes, *The Christian Science Monitor*. I don't remember if either had previously been in Indonesia. I do know they did not have the contacts among all the key players that I had!! While I made the rounds of key leaders every day, Friedman and Hughes commuted between the hotel and the American and British Embassies and relied on information from these sources for their stories. And the information was so far off base, it wasn't funny!!

I did not hang around with those "new" reporters. One morning, several days later, my driver Kumar was very upset when he came to pick me up. While he said there was no problem, by that time I knew him well enough to see that he was upset about something. He finally told me that the other reporters invited him into the hotel bar, started plying him with liquor so he would tell them where I went every day. His loyalty was to me and he didn't tell them anything. The reporters were frustrated -- and very cool to me.

When I returned to the States two weeks after the coup, I saw what they had written. Both Friedman and Hughes wrote drivel!! I was able to get an appointment with one of the top *NY Times* editors and told him that Friedman's articles were not accurate. I was told that Friedman was "a well-respected reporter and I was nothing." Hughes's articles were a little more accurate than Friedman's and Hughes won a Pulitzer Prize for journalism. To this day, I am upset about this!

* * * *

Near the US Embassy, a group of high military leaders established a coordinating center. Of course, I visited them, and they filled me in on what was happening. I think a lot of information came from these officers as well as from my old contacts.

For some reason, the American government did not pull out American families before the coup, even though anti-American sentiment was high for many months. But after the coup, when there was pro-American sentiment, American families were evacuated. I was called into the general's office and asked why Americans were told to leave. "Doesn't your government think we (the military) can protect them? Please tell the Ambassador that Americans are safe. We will be going after the communists," the general told me. I relayed the message to the US Ambassador (Marshall Green) - to no avail. I think I was told something about it taking months for the government to make the decision to evacuate and it would take more time to reverse that decision.

Actually I think the US government evacuated Americans because it didn't want a repeat of the trashing of dozens of British homes in 1963 during the Malaysian confrontation. And my NYU classmate Steve Sloan traveled to east Java a few weeks later where Indonesians compared the PKI (Communists) to the CIA. Signs read PKI=CIA.

* * * *

Indonesia was my first overseas trip (vacation) during my Call years. And I did have to return to W. Paterson, Little Falls and Totowa. Three reporters were assigned to my beat while I was on vacation -- a beat that I covered extremely well by myself.

I watched events in Indonesia after my 1965 visit and continued to monitor the political tug of war between Sukarno and Suharto. In February 1967, after a 17 month struggle to retain power, Sukarno was, in essence, overthrown by Suharto.

In my February 22, 1967 article in *The Call* and my February 23 article in *The Record*, I described the events since my September-October 1965 visit and recapped what happened when I was there. *The Call* headline read "Sukarno Surrenders Control of Indonesia. National Hero to National Goat." *The Record* headline was "People No Longer Leave It Up to Sukarno."

My *Call* article read "Today, after 40 years of fighting for what he believed was right for his people, an aging, a somewhat bitter and disillusioned Sukarno gave up. No longer would his people leave it up to him. ...."

Just before the October 1, 1965 aborted communist coup, "communist boss Dipa N. Aidit, sitting relaxed and confident in one of his several homes, told me " 'Communism is now the main stream of the Indonesian revolution'."

"Sukarno opened the flood gates, but was unable to stem the tide.

"The hero who did was Suharto, commander of the Army Strategic Reserve....

"Although Sukarno's image was tarnished in the eyes of his people and his power deeply scarred, military leaders after the coup could not afford to oust him. Whoever was in control of the world's fifth most populous nation had to consider Sukarno's popularity.

"Little by little his power and popularity was undermined by Suharto who did not see eye to eye with the President from the beginning...

"Two weeks after the coup, Suharto won his first political victory. In an after-curfew press conference Sukarno told us that Suharto had been appointed Army Chief of Staff.

"Shortly afterwards the anti-communist bloodbath began. And although Sukarno alternately pleaded and ranted that the killing should stop, no one listened."

In the *1967 Record* article, I talked about events in 1965 and also Sukarno's philosophy.

"The man, raised on Abraham Lincoln and Thomas Jefferson with Karl Marx thrown in, had fought the imperialist Dutch and British. He won. He played footsies with the Japanese and won. In 1963 he began the dangerous flirtation with the communists which triggered the 1965 coup. He got burned..."

One of the problems with American foreign policy has always been our tendency to push too hard on our values and not consider -- and respect -- values in other countries. In late November 1965 I gave a speech to the Totowa, Little Falls and W. Paterson Kiwanis Club. Another reporter covered my talk and according to that article, I pointed out

"Because a country does not agree with every American policy or criticizes us doesn't mean it is communist. Yet, we tend to look at them in this way. America must deal with these countries as equals and adults rather than as children. Yet, if a country doesn't agree with us on everything, we take away foreign aid. Adults just don't do this."

"Americans viewing other countries by American standards and values tend to create antagonism which pushes newly independent countries to the communist bloc.

"President Sukarno is not a communist as many Americans charge but is trying to build a socialist society, which in many ways is similar to the American society. .. Much of what Sukarno wants for his people and what he terms socialist is already in existence in the US. For example we have social security, Medicare, federal aid to education. These are things Sukarno wants for his people."

To establish an overall timeline of events, the following dates are important:

- October 6, 1965 -- Sukarno denounced the coup and said Major General Suharto was in control
- October 14 -- Suharto was appointed Army Chief of Staff
- October 15 -- the Chinese were accused of plotting and financing the coup and Chinese were attacked and killed
- October 24 -- Muslim vigilante groups massacred anyone believed to be a communist. Sukarno's supposed order to stop the massacres was ignored.
- November 22 -- Aidit was captured and executed. An estimated 400,000 were slaughtered
- Mar. 11, 1966 -- Sukarno officially turned over presidential powers to Suharto.
- Mar. 12, 1967 -- Indonesia State Assembly removed all powers from Sukarno and named Suharto Acting President.

CHAPTER 6

THE JEWEL OF AFRICA

My experience with Liberians started at the University of Wisconsin in 1955 and continues today. This experience very clearly shows that the **US government and American officials have absolutely no respect for other cultures, others' values and have no clear understanding of others' thought processes. My feelings from high school that the American people need accurate and fair information was re-enforced. It is very clear that a smart leader of a developing country can be both strong and democratic.**

Liberia is a prime example of "US arrogance and self-righteousness."

These are terms in the very beginning of my typed (on an old royal typewriter) article on my interviews with Liberia's President William Vacanarat Shadrach Tubman. I further stated that he said that "Americans think of and look at the world in terms of their own standards."

When I first met Oliver Bright he was in Wisconsin's prestigious Law School. He came from a prominent family. His father was a wealthy businessman and his mother was a fairly high official in the Liberian Dept. of Education. But when in college, Oliver became disillusioned with the system and started an anti-government movement. Because of his family's prominence, Liberia's President Tubman could not arrest him. The President gave Oliver a choice: leave the country and go to either the US or UK for graduate studies.

Oliver came to the US, the University if Wisconsin. He was active in UW's International Club, where I met him. After a couple of years, Oliver's brother also went to Wisconsin. The two rented a sizable house and often entertained.

In my senior year (1959), I was trying to figure out how to get all the things I had collected over the four years back to New Jersey. Oliver offered to let me drive his car to NJ. It was a stick shift. A blue and white Chevy. Although I learned to drive on an English Austin with a floor shift, my skills were so bad that Oliver finally said "forget it."

Because I lived in a small dorm, I hadn't been able to reciprocate all my party invitations. My father surprised me when he said he wanted to come out for my graduation. When Oliver heard my father was coming to my graduation, he offered his house for a party. We had such fun!! . It was a WOW one! I invited everyone I knew from the International Club.

Oliver and my father bonded immediately. When Oliver finished Law School, he stayed with my family in NJ for several weeks before returning to Liberia. He extended an open invitation to us all. My father said he'd visit when Oliver was sworn in as President of Liberia. This conversation -- the invitation and my father's answer - was repeated over the years. Unfortunately Oliver died in 1981.

When Oliver returned to Liberia, he was given a position in the State Department. Eventually, Oliver rose to Deputy Secretary of State. Later he became Secretary of Health, Education and Welfare and still later Attorney General.

Oliver left the US with $90, which he used to leverage a bank loan to buy a house in the outskirts of Monrovia (the capitol). He then rented it to a foreign diplomat. He parlayed

RIOTS & REVOLUTIONS

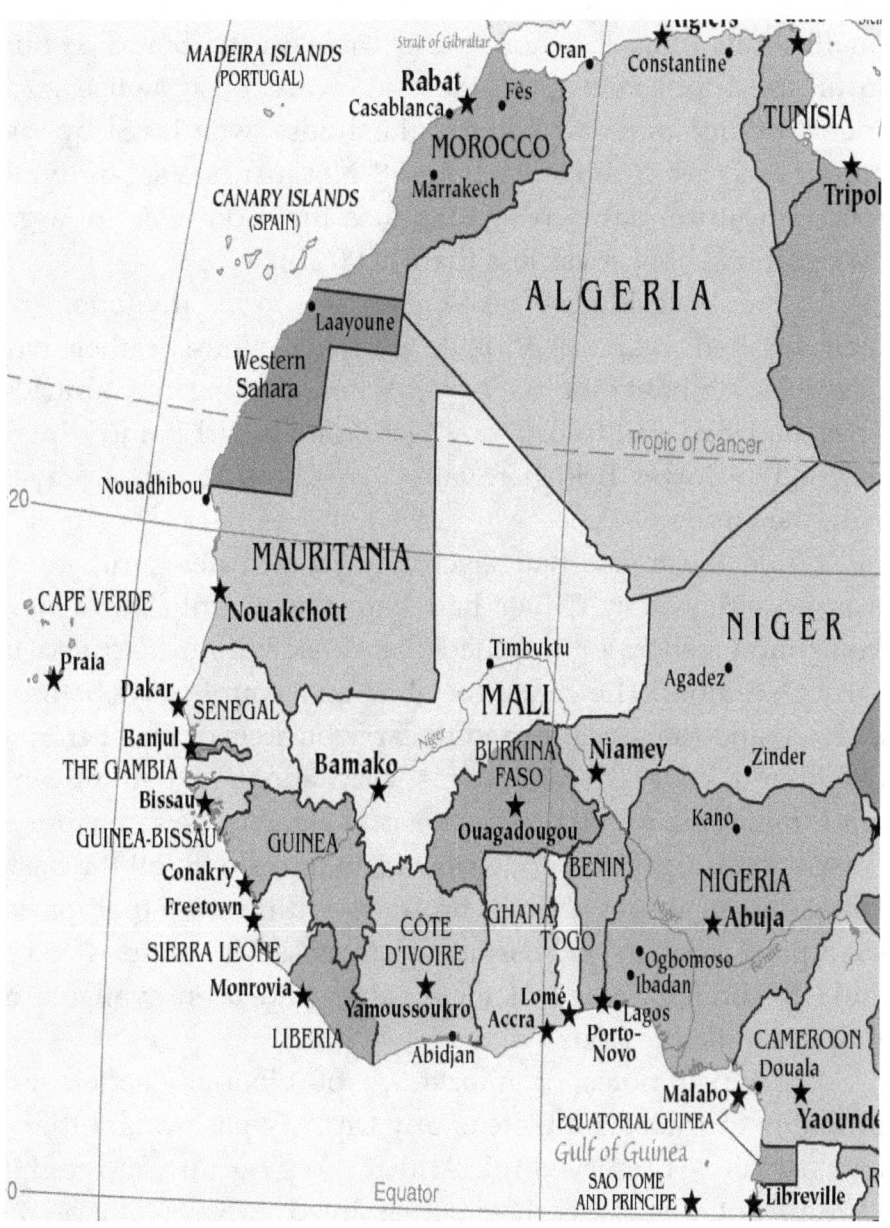

that one house to nine by the 1970s. In 1965 or early 1966 he finally built himself a house and came to the States to buy furniture. I took him to a wholesale warehouse owned by a friend of my parents. I knew the house was large by the amount of furniture Oliver bought! Not just one set of living room furniture, but two sets because the room was so large. (My parents' house was less than 1,000 sf.)

In 1966 I decided to take Oliver up on his invitation. By then he had married Violette Brewer, whose father was Liberia's Ambassador to several key European countries. They had two children, a boy Siafa, and a girl Baindu (now married to lower British royalty). Needless to say, I stayed with the family.

While the house had electricity from a new grid, there was no city water. Oliver had had a well dug and a new pump and generator installed the week before I arrived in early December. The generator blew up a couple days before I arrived, and the servants had to carry buckets of water from a neighbor's house. Again I was very adept at bathing and washing my hair with one bucket of water. At the same time, I was surprised to find modern supermarkets with all the basic amenities -- things I had brought with me - toothpaste, shampoo, toilet paper, tissues, cosmetics. Also canned foods and TV dinners. None of these items had been available in Indonesia the previous year.

My typed notes of interviews of Liberian leaders are probably the most complete of any trip. My pack-rat mother -- and myself -- preserved all. And my typing up my roughly written notes was because Oliver lived a ways out of the center part of the city. I was isolated and had plenty of otherwise empty time. Both Oliver and Violette (a pharmacist) worked full time.

RIOTS & REVOLUTIONS

All of Liberia's top officials were well-educated and most, like Oliver, overseas. Tubman was shrewd, and when any young Liberian returned home from overseas, Tubman gave the person a sound government job. Such a procedure eliminated unrest because those, like Oliver, who might have caused trouble, now had a stake in making the government work.

Most of the highest officials in Liberia at that time were educated in the US and knowledgeable about US democracy, rule of law, and citizen responsibilities. Liberia had come a long way by 1966 and had a long way to go. However, everyone with whom I spoke was aware of the basic problems and there was consensus on approach. I still shiver and get upset about the 1980 coup that brought economic and political chaos to this resource rich country and death to a number of Oliver's friends and people I had met.

FROM my Dec 3, 1966 handwritten notes:

Monrovia: greeted with blast of humidity and friends of Oliver's. Road from airport to town black-topped and first class and goes through Firestone Rubber plantations. Trees, older ones, are all bent in one direction as a result of years of winds coming, I think from the north. First impression is lush country -- everything green and growing. Welcome sign to Liberia is on poster-board advertising, Pall Mall and Camel cigarettes. Gas stations are American - Mobile, Shell, Esso.

City itself mixture of old and new. New buildings are of modern design, and white or pastel colored stucco. President's mansion is magnificent piece of modern architecture and most impressive with gardens and lawns in front. Most of the city is flat with few hills, which offer breathtaking view of the ocean. Luxury hotel is atop one of these hills, with kidney shaped pool, etc. Supermarket has everything imaginable - including tv dinners. Prices of goods are high - eg. toilet paper $.20 (20 cents) a roll; tissues $.52 (52 cents). Though cigarettes $.40 (40 cents) same as NY. People extremely friendly.

* * * *

While political stability provided a strong foundation for economic development, the actual building has been more difficult, Americans charge.

The basic infrastructure of any country -- transportation and communications, educational systems and a functioning civil service -- are still being built in Liberia.

And to build these things, money and educated people are needed.

According to my notes the basic problems of the country therefore were:

1. Being a producer of raw materials, international price fluctuations have a widespread repercussion on the nation's income.

2. Transportation and communication systems are totally inadequate; there are no public railroads anywhere in the country.

3. A 8 to 9% literacy rate is combined with inadequate school buildings and materials and generally unqualified teaching staff.

4. Civil service is practically nonexistent. Present laws provide only for clerical personnel.

5. Until recently, the country could not get long-term development loans.

6. Country is under populated. Thus there is a shortage of people at all work levels.
7. Corruption and 'materialistic' attitude among people.

Oliver Bright, my Wisconsin classmate, helped me get private interviews with President Vacanarat Shadrach Tubman (then 71 years old and in power 24 years) , the Finance Minister James Weeks (37), and Romeo Horton (43) , who was head of the equivalent of our Federal Bank. I also met and interviewed one-on-one Rudolph L. Grimes, (43), Secretary of State, and Anthony Weeks (37), Budget Planner.

I had trouble getting an appointment with the Secretary of Education, Augustus Caine (38), who did not like Americans. Oliver had a reputation for being anti-American because he had had several bad experiences in the States because he was black. However, when Caine heard I was staying with Oliver, he agreed to a one-on-one interview, which lasted more than two hours.

I always checked in with the American Embassy when I traveled. First to let them know I was in the country in case of an emergency or uprising. And second to glean as much information as possible about the country and what was going on. The press secretary and the political officers took me out to lunch. The Ambassador, Ben Hill Brown, when he heard I was going to see Tubman, called me into his office. The message I should take to Tubman: the American government was upset that Tubman had not put down on paper a Five-Year Development Plan, as had many other developing countries. Also, according to the Ambassador and political officer, Tubman was moving ahead "too slowly" with economic projects and "not the way we (Americans) do things." Liberia had rich natural resources, especially iron and rubber. They contended that corruption hampers projects as does the resistance to change from those in the establishment (American-Liberians).

* * * *

Again, as was my habit of traveling into the countryside of a foreign country, I went into the interior to visit several large iron ore mines -- a couple hundred miles into the jungle. The natives had never seen a white woman. There were several white male engineers, but never a woman. Again as was the custom of local people, the women and children surrounded me. The children wanted to touch my skin and hair, which were so different from theirs. I also visited a large rubber plantation owned by Firestone. At that time Firestone got most of its raw rubber from Liberia.

For several years, until I married in 1969 and moved to the Philippines, Oliver often came to the States and of course visited NJ. Romeo Horton, who was connected with banks in Liberia, came to NYC at least once a year. He always stayed at The Ritz. I would meet him, and we'd have dinner at a fancy restaurant. Then we'd go back to the Ritz, which had a very large dance floor and live band. Tables surrounded the floor and were on a raised part of the room. Most times there was an elderly couple who danced so gracefully that we simply enjoyed watching them. We talked with them and found out they were from either France or Australia and loved to dance, especially the waltz and the Latin American dances.

One time, Oliver, Horton and James Weeks (Finance) came to NYC for some conference. My parents and I invited them all out to Englewood for a family barbecue -- good ole US hot dogs and hamburgers, and beer. Of course, Oliver knew the family and had experienced this typical barbecue. Horton and Weeks had never before been "entertained" by an average American family, much less invited into an American home. They reveled in the warm environment.

MY NOTES: MY INTERVIEWS PRESIDENT VACANARAT SHADRACH TUBMAN:

One of the American official's biggest complaints was that Liberians had no sense of time. Americans like to set a time for a meeting and expect the meeting to take place accordingly. My copious notes clearly show the lack of importance of time by the repeated delays in my appointments with Tubman and at the same time my determination to spend time with him.

Hours were spent just waiting, and both the first and second interviews were seriously delayed. Before the second interview, as I waited hopefully, patiently, I talked with several men who had been waiting for 3 days to see The Old Man, as Tubman was called -- words of respect as THE head person.

I mentioned this to Tubman.

Re my observation that the government is very personalized in light of his seeing so many people, he said "it is a burden. It is most difficult. I have two administrative assistants, but the majority of people will not talk to them and even when they will talk to my assistants they still want to see me. I can't say I won't see them because what seems unimportant to me may mean a person's very existence."

Asked whether the culture had anything to do with this, he said "It was a tendency to go to the chief in the tribal areas."

Before my first meeting with Tubman, US Ambassador Brown had complained that Liberia wasn't developing as rapidly as some Americans would like.

As to the charge that things are going at a snail's pace, in my first one-on-one interview President Tubman snapped "I reject the opinion that we haven't developed fast enough. Considering the opportunities, the disadvantages, 100 years of threats from colonial powers and of internal dissension, all the country could do was to maintain its sovereignty and survive. And they talk about no development. I don't believe that those who criticize could have done so well in such a short time."

Tubman was a very calm person and understood his people. He told me that he had an overall plan in his head -- and he tapped his head with a finger. "I do a little here, a little there. And things get done. If I put my thoughts on paper, there would be so much discussion, things wouldn't get done. Tubman also acknowledged that he put extremely well educated and competent people (like Oliver) in key positions and that he trusted them to do a competent job.

As to corruption, the President said "You find corruption in every country. In every case the government has known about, the people have been prosecuted and in some cases imprisoned."

In relation to corruption and complaints from CARE volunteers, Tubman said "I have heard comments about supplies missing. They (CARE) control the distribution themselves. Our government has nothing to do with it. We don't approve of their methods, but have given them a free hand."

He said that it is evident the government at the higher echelons doesn't hear about all the cases. It is also true that many officials, even at the top, remain silent on some illegal and corrupt practices because they are part of the "establishment."

And while tribals are now breaking through the walls of the establishment, resistance to change is still widespread.

I asked what things or methods by Americans are not liked by the government, the President said "Some of these are making the US unpopular throughout Africa as a whole. The US is a big nation; some things, the way they do them, I would do differently." The president started to elaborate, but stopped. He said he would not say anything more.

In my interviews with President Tubman, we spent a lot of time talking about some of his achievements and his vision for the future.

"I took it piecemeal, step by step because I knew what I wanted to do would cause a fuss among the people.

1. I extended suffrage. This was carried out in spite of strong opposition from the elder group.

2. Three or 4 years later, I suggested that the tribal people have one representative in the legislature. This was submitted to referendum and passed.

3. Four or 5 years later, I suggested that another representative be added to the tribal districts. This was carried."

He described his vision for Liberia in such a way that no one could have disagreed.

"I would like to see Liberia a strongly united, industrialized nation with all of its population educated to the highest extent. I would like to see schools, colleges, universities, technical institutions throughout the country.

"I would like to see investigations and scientific explorations. I would like to see Liberia make inventions of sufficient import to become used universally.

"I would like to see the people and government strong in honor, morality and freedom without discrimination of any kind. If possible I would like Liberia to achieve the dawn of the day of Plato in his ideal republic.

"I hope someday this will come about even though I don't think it will occur in my life time. I'd like to be able to look down from the spirit world and see it."

Tubman was also realistic. "Politics is not necessarily righteousness. Sometimes you have to do things which may be wrong. If I have to do something wrong for the general good, for the sake of expediency, I pray for forgiveness. I want to keep my conscience alive."

Tubman's answers clearly underscored Americans lack of understanding of Liberia's cultural values! This was clearly shown by other interviews of Liberia's Cabinet officials.

* * * *

Although still primitive with underdeveloped infrastructure and electric power grids, Liberia had great potential. I was most impressed by Tubman's Vice-president William Talbot (who succeeded Tubman as President) and all the officials I met. I told the US Ambassador that he was wrong to pressure Tubman to "to do things like we do!" I don't think he appreciated the message.

My one-on-one interviews with various Cabinet ministers re-enforced my long held belief that Tubman's pragmatic approach to government and economic development should have been lauded by Americans and used as a model elsewhere. My friend Oliver was not the only government top official who was educated abroad and indoctrinated with democratic principles.

My own long held conclusions that Americans are closed to other peoples' values is borne out in the many interviews I had with Liberian leaders. In later years, the US interference in other countries because of this lack of understanding has created chaos that is negatively impacting society as a whole, lifestyles and basic human needs.

Misunderstanding probably was because there had been little socialization between Liberians and American officials. At most Liberian social affairs, I was the only white person and was made to feel welcome. Perhaps if there had been more personal interaction and exchange of ideas on an informal basis Liberian history might have been different.

* * * *

Rudolph Grimes, Secretary of State. I had two one-hour one-on-one interviews (Dec. 27 and 28, 1966) with Rudolph Grimes, Secretary of State and Oliver's boss. Discussions ranged from Liberia itself to world politics.

Grimes graduated from Harvard Law School and had a M.A. from Columbia University, School of International Affairs. Upon his return to Liberia in 1951, he set up the legal division of the State Department, organized the Law School at the University of Liberia, and then became Secretary of State in 1960, at the age of 37, the youngest in that position.

Liberia was THE first and only African country founded by and ruled by Africans, with no colonial (British or French) influence. Emphasis was on the rule of law, as exemplified by the numerous officials and business people educated in law in the U.S. and U.K.

As Grimes explained "The very fact that over a long period of time, in spite of difficulties, there existed an independent country run by Africans, this in itself was inspiration and helped fire inspiration of other Africans who wanted to become independent."

Grimes also noted a key difference in the Liberian constitution, which was modeled in large part by the US one. "In Liberia the Secretary of State takes over as Head of State when the President is out of town or the country. Liberians felt that any over ambitious vice-president could use the time the president was out of the city as a means of seizing office or fermenting trouble. When the President is out of town, the government is run by the Secretary of State and the Cabinet as a whole. The Cabinet, because it is appointed by the President, therefore can be relied upon to carry out the wishes of the President, while the VP is elected."

Asked how he sees the future role of Liberia, Grimes said "It is difficult to tell or assess what changes will come in Africa in light of the present instability. Some of the instability is directly related to underdeveloped countries. As you increase education, you increase the chance of ferment. Somewhere you have to strike a balance with economic development so people can play a more important role. The only way for this to happen is to increase education and training."

Grimes noted the special relationship Liberia has with the US. "Considering its peculiar historic position (Liberia was founded in 1847 by freed American slaves) people look to the US. This in light of experiences with France and Britain, both of whom sliced off territory. There is consequently an inclination to be suspicious of British and French motives. Many feel it was not mere coincidence that Britain and France stopped troubling Liberian officials after Firestone got concessions here. There is resentment because of the actions of some Americans. Even though we don't agree with everything the US does, we still look with favor upon the US. I myself don't judge the whole people by what some do."

Talking about political stability since Tubman became president, Grimes said "The personal popularity of Tubman is important. He is a very 'human' man. He will talk to anyone who has a problem, anywhere in the country. People like and respect him. In our culture, people are accustomed to taking their problems to the chief for solution.

"The President takes personal interest in other people's problems and tries to help. In some cases, he encourages people to come; he likes people and you couldn't keep him away from his people."

Grimes, like other Cabinet ministers, was realistic about the country's problems. "One thing those who help us must realize is that we are still developing our infrastructure, civil service, roads, water systems, sewage, communications, hospitals and clinics, controls for epidemics, education, pension and retirement benefits, adequate public buildings. All these have to be developed properly," he said.

"Most Americans don't understand our problems because they do not seek to understand other situations. You are brought up in the American way and naturally think in a certain way. You grow up in the US where basic facilities exist and are taken for granted. These facilities don't exist in other countries. As a result, there is the patronizing attitude of foreigners. This doesn't win friends. This attitude is found in Europeans as well as Americans," Grimes ended.

* * * *

James Milton Weeks, Secretary of Planning and Economic Affairs, had a B.S.C. and M.S.C. from the London School of Economics and a banking diploma from the Associate of Institute of Bankers in England.

While not educated in the US, Weeks was sensitive to the feelings many Liberians had about the US. He reiterated the reasons for the intellectual split.

"There is growing disillusionment among intellectuals because of their experiences in the US. Liberians have found that many Americans have no appreciation of our problems and values. They think of everything in terms of US standards. Therefore they get a distorted picture and unwittingly become offensive to Liberians.

"There used to be a tendency for US officials to continually tell us what they've done for us. We feel friendship cannot be measured in dollars and cents. Many intangibles are leading to growing resentment.

"We feel we should get special consideration because of our long time support of the US. During the world wars we opened up the country to American military.

"I am not talking about gifts. We don't want gifts. I am talking about a real effort to understand our problems and background, to help us overcome these problems. We are interested in loans being made available on better terms and quicker," Weeks emphasized.

* * * *

A. Romeo Horton, Secretary of Commerce, had a B.A. from Morehouse College, Atlanta, and a MEA from Wharton School of Finance. He was also the President of the Bank of Liberia. As head of the bank he frequently came to the US.

Horton repeated Weeks' comments about not being able to get long term loans. Liberia was able to get short term loans at high interest rates because the country had a high debt. He also said the US was no help. The high debt was due in large part to the fluctuation of prices of rubber and iron, the mainstay of Liberia's income.

Horton said that Tubman was "anxious to have the country industrialized as rapidly and soundly as possible... he believes in private initiative. The government's responsibility is to protect the rights of entrepreneurs, labor and consumers."

He also said "most Liberians had no identification with American or western values because their values are unknown in rural societies."

Horton pointed out that while most other African countries had support from Britain or France, Liberia had no help from other countries. In other African countries the colonial powers built basic infrastructure, roads and electricity.

* * * *

Augustus Caine, Secretary of Education, had a M.A. from Northwestern and a Ph.D. from Michigan State University.

Initially he refused to meet with me because of his bad experiences in the US and his distrust of Americans. He agreed to an interview only after he learned I was staying with Oliver Bright's family. Oliver had a reputation of being anti-American, even though he was like a son to my parents, the Goldsteins.

Caine was very honest in answering my tough and sometimes pointed questions about problems and corruption. We spent more than two hours, covering a wide range of subjects.

Education was a prime concern of Tubman, so Caine had much support in establishing schools throughout the country. In rural areas where there weren't enough children to support a teacher, classes were conducted by special radio programs.

He pointed to the progress made since Tubman took office in 1944.

In 1966, 13.8% of the national budget was spent on education. This percentage was high and probably no other country had the same ratio.

In 1944 there were 251 schools throughout the country; in 1966, over 900. In 1944 there were 19,000 students in the country; in 1966, more than 93,000. In 1944 there were 500 teachers; in 1965, 3,100. And in 1944 the Department of Education budget was $84,500. In 1966, $6.4 million.

Caine said "In the last 10 to 12 years the interest in education has increased. The investment benefits have been dramatized by the government. I feel education is paramount to bettering the lives of the people."

He said he "sees a hunger for education among the masses." He said that he tries to keep in touch with the masses. He walks through the streets and talks to people. He meets with young people whenever he can to hear their views and problems.

Caine identified the main problems as:
- trying to get more people to school;
- few schools had enough books;

- more people need to go to college and stay; and
- more Liberians need to go into teaching."

He said there were difficulties in fixing these problems.

"There is the problem of unqualified teachers. You can't compare teachers who have only an 8th grade education with those who have college education. They are functioning at entirely different levels."

Caine also pointed out a major problem which exists even today in other emerging countries.

"The textbooks are geared to <u>white middle class society</u>. The youngsters cannot identify themselves with what is in the books. <u>The content of instruction should be related to the native customs and culture as much as possible. The work in this area is just beginning.</u>"

Caine, like the other officials with whom I spoke, talked about the non-understanding of Liberian culture by Americans. "It is a source of frustration among Africans that Americans cannot transpose themselves from a technical society to our society. **I find them psychologically removed from our people and problems. They don't seem to truly understand and are incapable of realizing our problems.**"

Asked whether this attitude might lead to friction in the future, Caine said "Yes. This attitude would be a future factor as education spreads and as Africans become more nationalistic. National fervor is a recent thing as contact between other African states increases."

He also said "friction might arise because of Americans' refusal to understand that we don't want to be molded in their image. As education advances, this resentment will grow and the stereotype image of white arrogance will grow."

Caine, as did other officials as well as the American Ambassador, mentioned the fact that there was little socialization between Liberians and Americans. Why I do not know. Most often at the parties I attended, I was the only white person. Yet, I was always warmly received, especially when they learned I was staying with Oliver.

* * * *

James A. Pierre, Attorney General in 1966, was one of the few top officials not educated abroad. However he was very succinct in explaining the success of Tubman's policies.

Practically everyone with whom I spoke referred to Tubman's Unification Program, which brought tribal areas/people into the government. This eliminated tribal wars which plagued other newly independent African countries. Tribal wars across Africa continue unabated, and have left millions homeless, hungry and disease ridden.

My question to Pierre: "Why has Liberia been able to maintain stability and law and order, when other countries around her are going through traumatic times?

His answer, "When Tubman was first elected there were inter-tribal wars. With the Unification Program, there are no tribal wars and tribal troubles have ceased." (Refer back to Tubman's comments on this subject.)

The Unification Program, Pierre said "has so unified people that today we don't fear that anything major would happen which would tear the country apart. If the policy hadn't come about when it did, the country, like other African ones, might also have experienced chaos. The Unification Policy has given people a sense of belonging to the government and having direct participation in it."

He also said, "Our governmental experience of over 100 years may be a factor in stability in the post war period. New countries haven't had the opportunity to rule and hadn't been exposed to the type of experience Liberia has gained over the years. Perhaps we have avoided many of the pitfalls, because of our experience."

Toward the end of the meeting, Pierre said "American journalists have not understood the depth of the Unification Policy and its meaning."

* * * *

Ernest Eastman, Under Secretary of State, was a graduate of Columbia Law School and a close friend of my Wisconsin classmate Oliver Bright.

As several of the others had said, Eastman was clear about why Liberia was more stable than other newly independent African countries.

Eastman, Oliver, and an economist David Neal, drafted the basic document for the Organization of African Unity.

Because Liberia became an independent country in 1847, Eastman said "When Liberia became independent, the leaders said they were going to help liberate Africa. Edward James Brighton, former Ambassador to England in the 1800s, first used the term Africanization. From 1878 on other African countries drew inspiration from his writings.

Eastman pointed out that "During this time we lost one-half of our territory to Britain and France. Other countries looked to us as an independent oasis. We were a kind of stimulant. We have served to represent the embryo of the force towards independence.

"Other countries may consider us conservative. For the newly independent nations have nothing to preserve.

Therefore they have strong fervor. We have something to preserve because we have been a country for 100 years."

So his thoughts on the goals of Liberian leaders were different from other African countries that were trying to get a basic political system established. This is noteworthy -- especially as the US violated all of this in 1980.

"We differ as to goals in terms of priorities which gives way to struggle and definition of unity. We think the goal should not be political, but economic, social and health. These are the serious conditions. Especially health and education are things we feel we should struggle for," Eastman said.

In historic perspective, Eastman said, "The Liberia image of self reflects growth. We were founded by the American Colonization Society and not by any government. 95% of immigrants did not know how to read or write. The British came and we taxed them. The traders protested to the British government, who complained to the US government. The US asked us to declare independence to justify the taxes, and we did."

He also said -- as noted by the number of Liberian officials with law degrees --"Our survival depends on legal order. Therefore we stress law by giving it first priority."

Eastman and Tubman also stressed the religious beliefs. Eastman said, "Our forefathers were very religious. It is necessary to believe in something to set out to cross the Atlantic in small boats. Our Constitution appeals to God for faith and strength. This is a canister in our beliefs here."

As to the future, Eastman said, "I myself am very frightened by what has taken place in Africa. More than 30 countries have gained independence. There are questions of the consequences of this independence. In the last 10 years, Africa has assembled all the complexities that have happened in the world over a longer period of time. Capitalism vs communism; man vs man; religion vs religion. At the same time there is the struggle to become modern.

"None of the African countries have the strength like the US. Our strength is limited. We have to rely on the Organization of African Unity or other future organizations.

"Africa in less than 10 years has achieved more rapprochement among themselves than for instance in Europe. Therefore I don't know what role Liberia can play."

One hindrance was "Communications on the continent are limited. The US and USSR are vying for power. We (Liberia) have serious limitations."

Eastman ended the one-hour interview by saying, "Liberia represents the emancipation of cruel human evils. Yet in Liberia you do not find hatred against whites as found in other African countries which were colonized. We represent a synthesis of the kind of Africa that can be."

* * * *

Rudolph Grimes, Liberian Secretary of State (and Oliver's boss) was in New York City in October 1967, attending the UN General Assembly meetings.

After meeting with him one-on-one, I wrote in the October 23, 1967, articles in *The Call* and *Record* that "Secretary Grimes said "It is impossible for the UN to be effective politically when the US and Russia disagree. Peace can be kept only if they agree."

"The Secretary, who has been attending this session of the UN General Assembly, went on to say that peace is such an important thing that people lose sight of the other things the UN is doing."

Grimes -- and my article -- went on to list all the positive economic activities of the UN, in Africa in general and specifically in Liberia.

Grimes' visit was a few months after the 6 Day War in Israel in June 1967. His comments perhaps influenced me to go to Israel in December 1967 to see for myself the aftermath of the War.

My article said "While he would not comment on whether Secretary General U. Thant should have withdrawn the UN Force from Ghaza in June, Grimes said he didn't think the UN could have prevented the war. 'When Egypt was ready to move her troops to the front areas, it wouldn't have made any difference if the UN forces were there or not,' he said.

"Although the fighting has stopped, Russia doesn't have as much influence on the Arabs nor does the US on Israel as both might wish. The Arabs aren't going to listen to Russia and the Israelis aren't listening to the Western powers.

"Grimes said that while the Arabs publicly are unyielding, behind the scene they are not taking as hard a line.

"The big question is freedom of navigation and official recognition of Israel by the Arabs. The Arabs sit in the UN with Israel and that is recognition that the state exists."

Perhaps this last thought should be emphasized today as the Arabs become even more militant.

TURNABOUT: US SEEKS HELP FROM LIBERIA

In 1968, officials in the US government realized they could not change the negative image of the US in Africa without the help of Liberia's President William Tubman. The headline on my March 28, 1968 was: "US Seeks Tubman's Help to Change Our Africa Image." The caption on my picture of Tubman in full African regalia reads "...Tubman...often stands as lone symbol of pro-Americanism in changing Africa."

My article discussed Tubman's positive influence in African politics as well as his seeking American help for major economic projects in Liberia.

"Liberian President William Tubman, now on an official state visit in Washington, will be asked to help improve America's image in Africa.

"Tubman, in his 25th year as chief executive of one of Africa's smallest and richest nations, was invited here by Vice President Hubert Humphrey. The invitation was extended when Humphrey attended Tubman's inauguration in Monrovia in January.

"Just the other day, the Old Man as Liberians affectionately call their leader, ended a two year dispute between Joseph Ankrah, head of Ghana, and Sekou Toure, President of Guinea. The two countries have been at odds since the beginning of 1966 when Ghanians deposed Kwane Nkrumah. At that time, Toure gave Nkrumah asylum in Guinea.

"As a result of Tubman's tact, Ankrah and Toure will now sit at the same table later this month at a Heads of State Conference in Monrovia. The conference may lead to the first concrete steps in regional economic cooperation and development in emerging Africa.

"Thus President Johnson and Secretary of State Dean Rusk will ask Liberia's elder statesman to quietly round up support for the US policies in the Middle East and Vietnam.

"In exchange for drumming up American support, Tubman will undoubtedly get more government financial aid.

"Uppermost in Tubman's mind is construction of a multimillion dollar port at Cape Palmas, the southern tip of Liberia. Such a port would open up the entire southeastern region which abounds in hard timber and minerals. ...."

I have previously stated that I thought Tubman was "a shrewd leader and his own man." My article here clearly showed that Tubman went far beyond just getting foreign money to invest in Liberia. When all is said and done, and in spite of the luxury in which he lived, Tubman really was a man of the people.

My article continued "Tubman has also consistently demanded that private investors do something for Liberia. Foreign companies are required to build housing, hospitals, clinics and schools for their workers.

"Foreign companies must also train the natives who will eventually replace all imported foreign workers.

"Liberia finds itself in the position of having many industrialists interested in investing there. The leaders are therefore in a more flexible position than a resource-poor country.

"This is something that American officials must understand. If Americans press Tubman too far in demanding more vocal African support for their policies in exchange for more foreign aid, they might find it backfires.....

"Officials here cannot overlook the fact that Tubman does not particularly like some of the way Americans do things. Some of these ways are making the United States unpopular throughout Africa as a whole" Tubman told me during my 1966 visit and one-on-one meeting.

"All anti-Americans call us American stooges, But I know I am not,' he told me.

"And American officials may find this out too late."

I have repeated here several times that Americans do not understand the values of other cultures. And the American press usually supports the US governmental policies and views regardless of whether or not these views are even factually accurate.

* * * *

After Tubman died, *Newsweek* (Aug. 2, 1971) ran an extensive negative article headlined "The Passing of Uncle Shad." I had had no input into the content but my picture of Tubman in full African clothes was used. I was appalled about the tone of the article and re-reading it now rankles me. I wondered whether the writer had ever been in Liberia.

Newsweek's description included the following

"Like the leaders of most of Liberia's aristocratic families, ranging from Ambassador Charles T.O. King in Paris to Army Chief of Staff Maj. Gen. George T. Washington, Tubman amassed a large personal fortune. But while the President and the rest of the black Yankee upper crust lived in style, the huge majority of Liberian people -- despite Tubman's development programs -- subsisted in squalor.

"For all the opulence of its stately mansions, moreover, Tubman's Monrovia remained a ramshackle city where cabdrivers pointed out to visitors the numerous sons and daughters of their virile President."

My Note here: In those days poverty in every developing country was visible. But in Liberia there was no starvation like that found in India and China.

And the *Newsweek* writer even admitted that "Despite his freewheeling style, Tubman was in many ways more enlightened than most of his fellow African leaders. By throwing open Liberia to foreign investment, he helped give the country one of the fastest growth rates in the underdeveloped world and an annual per capita income of $220 -- double the average for the continent. He introduced schools into the bush, and above all sought to reduce class differences between the American-Liberians and the indigenous people. Over all, Tubman ran a stable government and indulged in much less brutality than some of his left-wing African critics."

The article described Tubman and his uniqueness, which had come out in my interviews with him.

"Among the leaders of contemporary Africa, William Tubman, President of West African Republic of Liberia, was a bizarre anachronism. A bespeckled, cocoa-colored man, Tubman often appeared in the blazing sun of his capital of Monrovia turned out in a gleaming top hat and cutaway. With a glass of scotch in one hand and a big Havana cigar in the other, he ran Liberia for 27 years as if the country were his private plantation. His passing leaves a vacuum that will not be easy to fill. Said one Liberian sadly, 'We've never known any other President than Uncle Shad. He took care of us'."

There were more negatives in that *Newsweek* article, which I will forego here. But the lengthy article ends with "And for all his shortcomings, Tubman was a beguiling man who was genuinely liked by most of his people. Courteous and open, he had the reputation of being available to the humblest of his countrymen. And when it came right down to it, Liberians also liked the show he put on -- his party giving, his drum playing, the quadrilles he sometimes danced with his daughter Coocoo. 'In a sense, he was legitimately a man of the people,' said a Western diplomat. 'The trouble was that President Tubman, like Liberia, was so touchingly out of date.'

This diplomat's comment clearly shows that Americans did not understand the culture of Liberia.

UNITED STATES CREATES CHAOS

Forward to the 1980 coup that is still another example of the American government not properly connecting "the dots," interfering in the political affairs of another country (which was not a threat to our national security), and creating both political and economic chaos that has lasted for decades.

I've already talked about the American dissatisfaction in 1966 with President Tubman. Tubman died July 23, 1971 and his duly elected Vice-President William R. Talbot took over and was later elected President.

However, the Americans did not like Talbot, who like Tubman, was his own man. The American government then supported a coup which occurred on April 12, 1980 and in which Talbot was killed when rebels stormed the palace.

An illiterate army sergeant Samuel K. Doe took over the country. I won't go into the political ramifications here, but will talk about the coup from a personal venue.

Oliver was in the US when the coup erupted. His two oldest children, Baindu and Siafa, were at a boarding school in New Hampshire. His wife, Violette, and four year old Wyanie were in Liberia. Because Oliver, as Attorney General, had had to call in the army to quell food riots in 1978, he was on a "Kill" list with a number (I think total of 10) of other top officials. Those caught were publicly executed on a beach outside of Monrovia.

Violette and Wyanie first hid at the Nigerian Embassy, but had to move around so they were not arrested.

Oliver was in Atlanta on business. He had left the Liberian government after the 1978 food riots and started a private law practice. Violette's brother, Herbert Brewer, was Liberian Ambassador to the US and in Washington, DC. We had Oliver's telephone number and called to tell him to come to our house in New Jersey. He said he was ok and went to the Embassy in DC. We were still worried. Then the Embassy was invaded by Liberian students who supported the coup. Oliver got on the first plane he could and landed at JFK and called us. He rented a car and came to stay with us for four months.

Oliver was beside himself because Violette and Wyanie couldn't get out of Liberia and he couldn't get them out from here. He was ready to hire a private plane and go back to Liberia, but my husband, Angel, took Oliver's passport and hid it.

Finally on July 4, 1980 Volette and Wyanie were able to sneak out of Liberia and arrived here. For several months Oliver's whole family stayed with us.

Over the years before the coup Oliver had put money into a bank in NYC. He had accumulated several hundred thousand dollars. But a year or so before the coup, he bought some sort of plantation.

So, at the time of the coup, Oliver had only $40,000 in a bank in NYC. I went into NYC with him and he took out the cash and closed the account. We had to wait until Monday to go to the bank here and we were worried about having so much cash in the house. All of his Liberian properties (including the nine houses and investments in a rubber plantation) were confiscated. He had nothing left in Liberia.

The rest of this story is long, and I won't go into details here. Briefly, Oliver died in early 1981 from a very aggressive form of leukemia. His uncle Richard was here and had money. Richard supported Violette and the children and paid for Baindu and Siafia's college.

In late 1982, Violette was able to get back several houses and returned to Liberia with Wyanie. In the summer of 1990, there was another coup. Violette and Wyanie fled to the Ivory Coast. After three months Wyanie got a US visa. Violette already had a multiple entry one. Wyanie came to stay with me in NJ and attended Marlboro High School.

Needless to say, given my relation with Oliver and his family, I kept up to date on happenings there and wrote about them. Because top Liberian officials were well educated (either here or in England) they were respected on the international scene. Their evaluation of international political affairs was insightful. Liberians also were staunch supporters of the UN and the US.

Sitting here reading these articles about Grimes and Tubman's visits to the US, I can clearly see that my earlier comments that the US does not understand and respect values of other cultures were re-enforced. And the events in 1980 and 1990 further support my conclusions and feelings.

CHAPTER 7

THE MIDDLE EAST IN TURMOIL

Even though in 1967 my primary focus as a *Call* reporter was on Paterson, I watched events unfold in the Middle East. And of course my conversation with Liberia's Secretary of State Rudolph Grimes further peaked my interest.

Six months had passed after the Six Day War, in which Israel captured Gaza and much of Sinai, the West Bank of Jordan, and the Golan Heights of Syria. I wanted to see for myself. In early December I headed to Israel.

Because of the political situation it was impossible to get interviews with top Israeli officials. Even journalists who had been in Israel for years did not have access to top officials.

However, I traveled freely throughout the three areas captured by the Israelis -- Gaza (Egypt), the West Bank and East Jerusalem (Jordan), and the Golan Heights, (Syria.) No one questioned either my driver or me.

Egyptian President Nasser started playing games in May (16) 1967 by moving tanks and troops into Sinai. By May 24, Egypt had blockaded the Strait of Tiran, thus prohibiting Israel's access to the Red Sea. According to news reports here, Egypt also moved 9,000 men and 200 tanks to the edge of the Gaza Strip near the town of Rafah. While Nasser threatened to attack Israel, his strategy (Announced June 2) was to push Israel to strike first. On June 5, 1967 Israel did strike and sent troops and tanks 100 miles into Sinai. There were 13 Egyptian air bases, 23 radar stations, anti-aircraft sites and 107 airplanes (according to US news sources.) All of these had been supplied by Russia. All of which were taken by Israel.

On June 9, Israel attacked and took over the Golan Heights. On June 10, the Israelis routed the Egyptians in the Sinai and Egyptian soldiers fled - mostly on foot.

The famous Six Day War ended with Israel "owning" all of Gaza plus a large part of the Sinai, the Golan Heights, and the West Bank (which had been an integral part of Jordan.) On August 1, 1967 Israel took over East Jerusalem, bringing together the Holy City for the first time in 20 years.

I stayed with my brother-in-law's parents in Netanya, a resort suburb of Tel Aviv. One of my brother-in-law's cousins was a travel agent, who arranged a car and driver, who spoke English, Hebrew and Arabic. We traveled through the occupied areas, and I interviewed leaders and refugees. I wrote a series of articles that appeared in *The Call* and *The Record* with information no other journalist had.

I think it very important to say upfront that the refugee camps that existed for 20 years after Israeli's independence were established by the Arabs to keep Palestinians isolated and were not set up by Israel or the US! This is critical as the Arabs always seem to blame the US for their situation!

The Egyptians established the refugee camps in Gaza, built very high concrete walls around each camp, and kept the occupants virtual prisoners. No one was allowed out -- and few allowed in. So two new generations of Arabs were born in those camps.

What did I find? The land was poor, mostly sand, and there was no attempt to cultivate for food. Refugees were dependent on the good will of international organizations for everything.

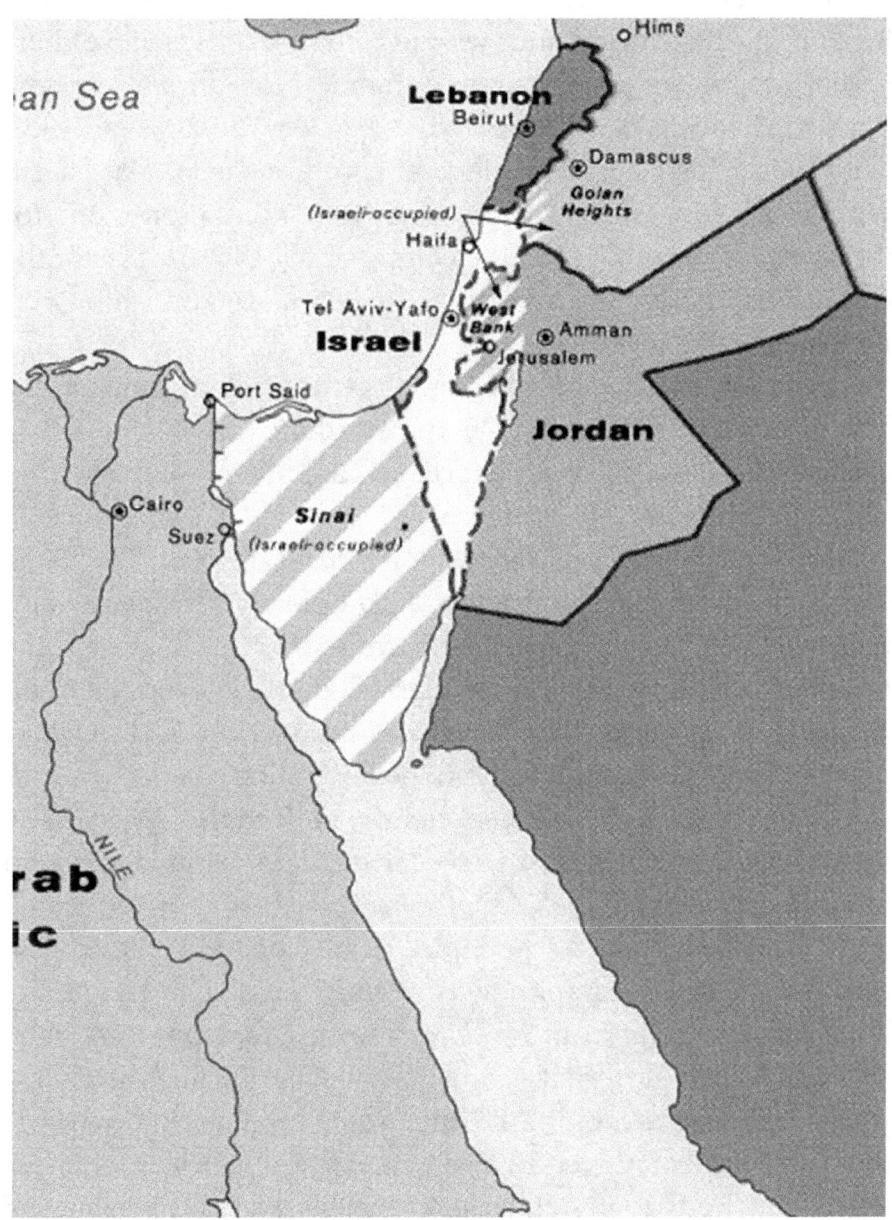

What else did I find? A restless, hopeless feeling people, fearful of the future and worried that the Israeli soldiers would come in and massacre them. Not an atmosphere conducive for peace.

I was allowed into the largest camp and spoke at length with the 'leader' who was an Arab doctor -- the only one for thousands of people. I left the camp feeling that in spite of the conditions there that a positive working relationship with Israel could be developed.

Outside the camps, the Israeli army ruled. One of the officers took me around. On the northern coast of Gaza, a couple from the Bronx had started a cafe business. Interesting place for Americans to settle.

What was fascinating was a trip out into the Sinai (Egyptian territory) desert -- completely desolate and undeveloped! We followed the trail of the escape of the Egyptian soldiers. As the soldiers fled, they dropped their guns, some shoes, belt, canteens and more. They had to travel several hundred miles to Egyptian civilization.

There were also refugee camps in Jordan's West Bank area. But the society itself was -- and still is -- much different than the Egyptian Gaza. Here the people were more educated and shrewd business people. One of my Wisconsin classmates, Essam Ibrahim, was from E. Jerusalem. His family owned a hotel right on the border with Israel. My first stop. The hotel was deserted, with a few workers in the area. I wandered around hoping I'd find someone who knew where the family was. A well-dressed man came up to me, and I found out he was my classmate's uncle. He said Essam and his family were in the U.S. The uncle owned another hotel in E. Jerusalem and took me there. The hotel had been taken over by the Israeli army. The uncle had positive words for the

Israelis, who paid their bills on time and didn't cause any problems with the Jordanians. Over coffee at his hotel, he filled me in on happenings both before and after the Six Day War.

* * * *

Again the atmosphere seemed very conducive to an acceptable political settlement with Israel.

We (driver and I) then visited Nazareth and Bethlehem, where we stayed overnight. It was Christmas Eve, and the first time since independence that a Christmas mass was said with Arab families from Israel joining their relatives there. The atmosphere was joyful -- and hopeful.

Looking back, I can better understand why the extremists today have found more support in Gaza than the West Bank. The people in Gaza were -- and still are -- basically uneducated and unsophisticated compared to the Jordanians. The desert had not been developed, still hasn't been and the lack of jobs has frustrated the people. If the Arabs in Gaza had developed the land the same way Israel did after 1947, the economic and political situation would have been very different.

The Arab leaders in the area's other countries fell down on their responsibilities, yet still blame the Israelis and the Americans for today's problems. If the Arabs had accepted the Palestinians into their countries, the hatred against Israel would not exist.

The third segment of the occupied lands was the Golan Heights, Syria, a strip of land bordering the northern part of Israel. Some agriculture had been developed here, but the main thrust was the missile bunkers along the border.

Missiles were constantly sent down onto the Israeli settlements below. When I visited the area it was virtually deserted. Only a few Israeli soldiers were stationed there to protect the settlements below.

At the end of that trip peace seemed possible.

* * * *

The possibility of accommodation between the Arabs and Israelis, however, was burst, I believe, by the Brooklyn Rabbi Kahana, who moved to Israel, got elected to Parliament and actively developed strong anti-Arab emotions among the Jews. Kahana's activities were the nails in the peace coffin! **It seems Americans have a great propensity for creating chaos in other countries. The examples of this include Cuba, Iran, Liberia, the Philippines, Iraq, Afghanistan and more!**

My articles from the 1967 trip, published early 1968 in *The Call* and *Record*, show the mood and the reaction of the Arabs to me as an American (very friendly) and to the Israelis (distrustful).

My articles clearly showed hope in Gaza, but distrust in Jordan.

My first article appeared January 1, 1968 with a front page promo picture and "Ban Lifted. Palestinian refugees get new hope as Israeli authorities lift the 20-year dusk-to-dawn curfew in the narrow Gaza Strip."

The headline read "Israel Lifts Curfew On Refugees."

"The curfew, instituted by the Egyptians in 1948, was lifted on a temporary basis at the beginning of the Muslim Ramadan celebration earlier this month. If the present calm and Arab cooperation continues, Israeli officials said it will be permanently abolished.

"The move to abolish the law, which kept 300,000 refugees virtual prisoners, comes just months after the Israelis captured the city in a 25-minute battle.

"Since the blitz, the Israelis:
- have begun wiping out gangs and criminals who use the refugee camps as bases.
- have created a local Red Crescent (a self-help type organization).
- are setting up a joint program between their government and the UNRA, the International Red Cross, and CARE.
- are establishing close daily relations with the Arabs and the refugees.
- have instituted a "food for work" program.

"The refugees have existed for 20 years on rations from UNRA. They have been confined to a small strip of land 40 miles by 3 miles along the Mediterranean. They were allowed to enter Gaza and other cities in the strip during the day only. They could not enter Sinai or Egyptian territory west of the Suez Canal. Few have worked."

As a journalist I never took 'sides' in any situation and never 'blamed' anyone or particular group for problems and high emotions. But before adding here some more about Gaza, I have to say that I believed after my 1967 visit, that the blame for today's situation between Palestinians and Israelis sits in the hands of Egyptians as well as other Arab countries. The refugees could have been taken in and absorbed by the surrounding Arab countries. Only the rich were able to get out during the Independence War, fleeing to Lebanon, Cairo, and Europe.

My article read:

"A generation of young people has grown up in this atmosphere. Fear and distrust for both the Israelis and the Egyptians were fostered in the schools in the UN controlled refugee camps."

"The Israelis found paintings done by refugee youngsters vividly depicting brutal acts of murder and rape by Israeli soldiers on Arabs. The paintings also show a bloody victory by the Arabs over the Israelis."

A number of these pictures appeared with my article. The caption read "Refugee children painted these pictures of the atrocities of war. They are frightening testimonials to the plight of the refugees and the terror of children trapped in a tinderbox."

And while no one group should be labeled negatively, I do have to say here that Arabs seem to have more brutal tendencies against their own people than many other groups. Brutality then and still today. I doubt that will ever change.

My article also read:

"These feelings were apparent when Israeli authorities first began to investigate crimes by gangs (one led by a woman), who commit murder, rape, robberies and various tortuous acts to extort money."

"One Israeli official told the following story:

"Members of a gang kidnapped a young girl, tied her to a table, and plunged knives into her hands so that her mother would give them money. When the Israelis went in to investigate, none of the refugees would talk.

"Finally the Israelis found a relative who cooperated. The men involved have been arrested and sentenced to life imprisonment.

RIOTS & REVOLUTIONS

"The Egyptians, the official said, never did anything about these gangs. "They were afraid to go into the camps. And they never dealt with the people. ....."

"In building up better relations with the people in Gaza, the Israeli civil authorities make themselves readily available to the people. The government building has a continual stream of people seeking help and answers."

While there seemed to be some hope in Gaza, in other areas daily life had deteriorated - specifically on the West Bank, where previously residents (those outside the camps) had free access to all of Jordan, which meant jobs and a thriving economy. There was a booming tourist industry in East Jerusalem and Bethlehem. Tourists stopped coming after Israel took over the area.

As in Gaza, faced with criminal and terrorist elements, the Israelis were faced by increasing activity of El Fatah, one of the earliest 20th century terrorist groups. Consequently they tried to eradicate El Fatah, who hid in the hills and in some villages.

My next article describes the dilemma.

Headline: "Arabs Rap Refugee Treatment."

"Arab officials are charging Israel with undue harassment and destruction of property in the Jordanian sector. They say that economic conditions in the cities and refugee camps are worse today than they were before the June war.

"An official in one of the refugee camps south of Jerusalem said he felt that the Israelis wanted peace, but pointed out the razing of villages was after the fighting stopped. ...

"This the most horrible thing,' the Arab said. The El Fatah come from the East Bank and hide in the hills. The people in general shouldn't be blamed. Why should I be blamed for the actions of those people? We want to live in peace.

"We are against the El Fatah, but we ourselves can't prevent them. They'd kill us.

"Israeli military officials in the area admit that sometimes a house is messed up during an investigation.

"We know they are there, but sometimes don't know exactly which house. It's like when you lose something and look for it. Sometimes you disturb things.

"The officials said the Israelis do not search homes unless it's necessary. 'We don't do it for sport. We must do it.' ...

"The Israeli official said the El Fatah are dangerous to the Arabs as well as the Jews. He said they don't care if they shoot civilians or soldiers. Last week a mine was found near an Arab house where 6 young children were sleeping.

"The Israeli said that the El Fatah demand money from the Arabs. 'They are paid to come here to sabotage. They do damage and go back to the East Bank.'

"The El Fatah, which use Jordan as a base, are the most active saboteurs. Night incidents along the Israeli-Jordanian border are expected.... Certain areas, including the famous Allenby Bridge, have been closed to everyone, unless a military permit has been issued.

"While Israelis have tried to get daily life back to normal for the Arabs, most Arabs claim economic conditions have drastically deteriorated. ....

"Before June, the refugees could work in the East Bank or other parts of Jordan. Or they could get money from relatives. Now this is all cut off,' he said

"Unemployment is estimated between 75 and 90%. ....

RIOTS & REVOLUTIONS

"Hardest hit is the tourist business, particularly in Jerusalem. Hotel owners are faced with empty rooms. Shop keepers with no customers. ...."

Because the economy on the West Bank and East Jerusalem had been to some extent thriving, the mood in the West Bank was more negative than in Gaza. Comments made by Arabs with whom I spoke highlighted the problems and viewpoint. The anti-Israeli feelings on the West Bank have been heightened over the years by the vast settlements built by the Israelis right in the middle of the area.

My January 3, 1968 article in *The Call* was headlined "Bridge of Sighs Unites War-Split Arab Families."

It talks about the role the Allenby Bridge, Jericho, played at that time in the lives of Arab families -- some split apart by the June war and others 20 years before.

"They come to the bridge only on Monday and Fridays.

"They embrace, they cry. They say hello and then good bye. They are Arab families. Some were separated by the war six months ago. Others were split 20 years ago during Israel's fight for independence. ......

"As wrinkled-faced old women hug rose-checked youngsters, the regular flow of traffic across the bridge -- the only link between Israel and Jordan, north of Jerusalem -- stops. It is the bridge used by thousands of refugees who fled during both wars. Today it is used to reunite families and ease the flow of products (particularly fruits) between the two countries

"After a 15 to 20 minute visit, families are separated by police and soldiers. Reluctantly they depart.

"During the reunion trucks line up on both sides of the bridge. Among them are those laden with citrus fruits from Gaza. Small farmers, who do not have the facilities to export, have been allowed to transport their produce to Jordan and then return to Gaza.

"This is the first time in 20 years that many of these farmers have left the narrow strip of Gaza. ....

"All said the fate of the Middle East rests in the hands of the United States. They said unless Russia and the US agree, there will be no peace.

"A doctor in the Gaza refugee camp said that the Israelis must withdraw before the Arabs would sit down at the conference table. 'We will not even discuss the situation if we are forced to under the present circumstances.'

"He and others said the key to any settlement is the refugee problem. 'They must be allowed to return to their homes.'

"The doctor also said the creation of a Palestinian state on the West Bank would not solve the problem. 'Since 1948 it is not a local problem. It involves the whole Middle East,' he said.

"Everyone I spoke with agreed that Israel must withdraw from the territory it took in June. They also said Arabs would not agree to any solution unless Jerusalem was returned to them. They said they would not go along with internationalizing the city.....

"While the Arabs are looking to the US for an answer, the Israelis say they can rely on no one but themselves."

According to my article the third territorial area captured by the Israelis was the Golan Heights, Syria, a narrow strip of land overlooking rich agricultural fields in Israel.

My January 5, 1968 article head was "Israel Bolsters Claim to Syrian Mountains."

"A new kibbutz on top of the Syrian captured mountain has been established to give the Israelis a permanent claim in the area.

"It's center is at Kuneitra, the largest Syrian town on the mountains. There are 20 homes formerly occupied by Russian advisers to the Syrian army and newly planted fields.

"The mountain strip, where some of the fiercest fighting took place, was the most heavily fortified area and most troublesome of all of Israel's former borders. The gray Syrian mountains tower above several kibbutzim nestled at the foothills and the Sea of Galilee.

"From here the Syrians lobbed mortars at the farmers and fishermen below for 20 years......

"One of the volunteers on the kibbutz at Kuneitra said the Syrian civilians must have started leaving the villages three days before the fighting began. He said it would take that long for the 5,000 inhabitants to leave taking with them all their possessions. All that remains now are dozens of hungry mewing cats at the entrances of camps of the Syrian army officers. ....

"The strategic importance of the Heights to Israel can best be understood when one ascends steep winding roads, drives along the top of the mountains and looks below.

"The fertile plateau atop the mountain, several miles wide, has been cultivated a little. The outstanding features are deserted army camps and fortifications. Fields are sprinkled with underground dugouts used to store arms. Stone fortifications line the ridge of the Heights. Mosques in the village were used as lookouts and had caches of arms.

"As one volunteer said, 'We walk along the fields and step on Russian machine guns. We pick them up every day.' The volunteer estimated that there are still 5 tons of ammunition and small arms (all Russian made) in the fortifications scattered throughout the area.....

"With the Syrians on top of them, those in the Israeli kibbutzim had no peace for 20 years. For some, the past six months have meant undisturbed sleep for the first time since independence."

* * * *

During the time in early 1968 when I was writing the articles about my December trip, Israel's Prime Minister Levi Eshkol came to Washington to seek stronger backing from the US in relation to the whole situation there and to get arms. My article in *The Call,* Jan 4, 1968 combines what I learned while in Israel with Eshkol's objective.

The headline read "Arms for Israel Is Eshkol's Main Aim in US."

"Prime Minister Eshkol is seeking an American guarantee that Israel will not be isolated in the Mideast arms race and continued escalation. ...

"The problem of replacing the military equipment lost in the fighting has been compounded for the Israelis by a French as well as American embargo.

"As a result of French President de Gaul's backing of the Arabs, the Israelis would like the US to become the major supplier of military equipment. ...

"Since June there has been what Israeli officials describe as a 'dribble' of arms coming into the country.

"On the other hand, Israeli officials contend that Russia has replaced most of the Egyptian equipment lost in Sinai. Officials here say that the equipment now in the hands of the Arabs is far superior to what they had before the war. ....

"Undoubtedly the two leaders will also look for ways to unlock the Arab refusal to negotiate with Israel.

"Officials here, while optimistic that such negotiations can take place, admit that neither the Arabs nor the Russians have made any signs of changing their adamant policy.

"A foreign ministry spokesman said the crux of **the problem is Russia's desire to get a foothold in the Mideast.' If it weren't for her intervention, Egypt would not have been egged on to fight.'** "

NOTE: Russia and now China continue to arm and egg on the Arabs against Israel. The Arab market is so much bigger than that of Israel that China has become active in wooing the Arabs. -- and in arming them.

MORE REMEMBRANCES

While my trip in Israel was serious business -- I was THE only foreign journalist to visit all three occupied territories and write about the human aspects of the area -- there was also some fun experiences.

There is an artists' colony in northern Israel and I have always loved to roam through art galleries and craft shops. I met a French couple who were living in Western Australia and teaching French -- Professor and Mrs. Leon Tauman. They were going to stop for one day in NYC on their way back to Australia. I gave them *The Call* card and told them to call me. In early July, they did! They were only going to be in NYC that one night. I invited them to dinner and drove into the city from work. I took them to the Rainbow Room in Rockefeller Center. I had heard of the Room, but had never been there and had no idea how expensive it was.

I had $36 in cash and my checkbook. In those days, no credit card. Well, the Room was very fancy, stark white linen table clothes, waiters in tuxes and a price-fixed dinner of $9. That meant dinner was a basic $27 before drinks and tip. I also had to pay for parking and the toll on the George Washington Bridge to get home. I did not know if they would take a check -- and didn't ask, figuring that they probably would accept a check at the end of the meal.

I called *The Call* office in New Jersey and spoke with one of the reporters who lived in NYC (Murray Zuckoff). I asked if he had any cash. Yes, a little. Again no charge card. (What would we do today without them?) He managed to get to the restaurant when we were having dessert and coffee and bailed me out.

I've always wanted to go to Australia, but...

NOTE: I have repeatedly said that (1) I do not understand why supposedly human beings cannot learn from events and the past to solve human problems and (2) Americans do not understand the thinking and values of other peoples. The Middle East today is a cauldron boiling over. One would think that problems existing 45 years ago could have somehow been solved.

CHAPTER 8

ASIA: A LITTLE HERE, A LITTLE THERE

In 1968 events and tensions both in the US (racial) and Vietnam escalated. On Jan. 31, 1968 the Americans started what was called the Tet Offensive. A Wisconsin colleague, Hasso Rudt Von Collenberg, was an official in the German Embassy in Saigon. Originally I planned to go to Vietnam. But then Hasso was killed, and the war was too hot even for me. Hasso and I had spent time together in London in 1959 and kept in touch.

In the fall of 1968, my "vacation" took me through southeast Asia -- Burma, Thailand, Sabah, Hong Kong and Taiwan. A month in all these places didn't allow me to stay long in any one country. The longest stay was in Burma. This differed from my usual practice of going to one country for a month, which gave me time to get to understand the politics, economics, and family values.

* * * *

Burma's leader Gen. Ne Win was America's "friend" because he was anti-Communist. Burma interested me because of what I had been hearing from Fred Swarte, a VP of Singer Sewing Machine Company. Swarte was in charge of all Asian rim countries.

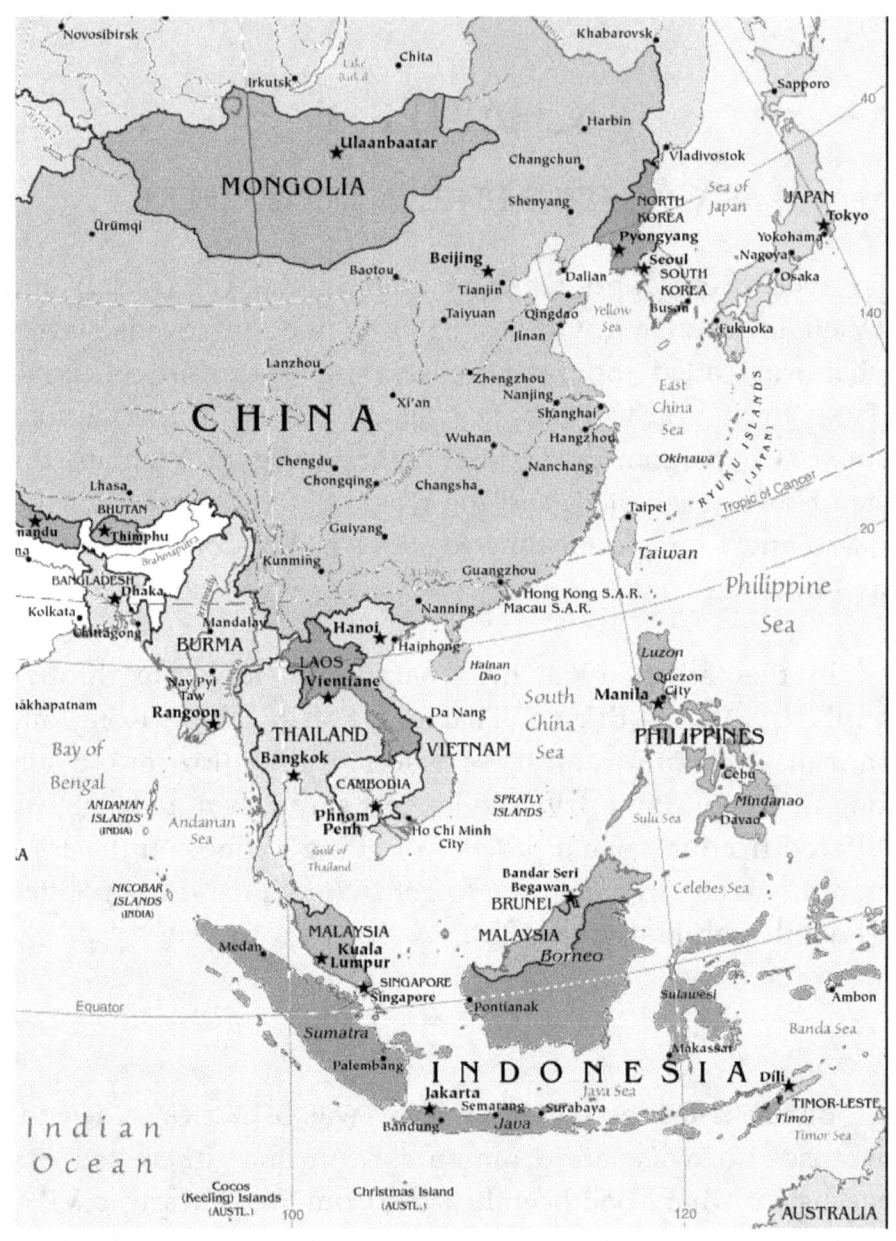

RIOTS & REVOLUTIONS

When Ne Win took over in a coup in 1962, he threw out all the Indians (who were the backbone of the economy) and banned all foreigners from entering the country. Swarte was only allowed to meet his employees at the airport. He told me about the economic chaos in Rangoon and beyond -- even though American officials said Ne Win was a "good guy."

For three years, I tried to get a visa. Turned down, repeatedly! I was THE first foreign journalist finally allowed into Burma since the coup and allowed to travel freely. What a coup for me!! A good kind of coup!! Swarte's employees arranged for my stay, and one of the managers, a woman named Bernie Raphael, acted as my guide. We traveled north almost to the area where the communists were very active.

I got the visa to Burma, even though Ne Win had banned all foreigners, using the name of Singer's head of the Rangoon office, Auong Thein. At that time Fred felt the Burmese government would be more amiable to an American journalist because Ne Win was planning a trip to the US.

In Swarte's letter Dec. 6, 1968 written from Indonesia he said, "I was pleased to read that you had safely returned from your trip to Burma, because you never can tell in these funny countries what can happen to you. You must have found it as I told you, very depressing, practically no more private enterprises, with the exception of some peanut vendors perhaps.

"We have no plans whatsoever to start any kind of business in that country (Burma). I just use my small staff to keep a foot in the door and to get some business from the government. They have their government clothing factories, shoe factories, parachute factory and all these need new sewing machines from time to time, and as we are the only sewing machine company represented in Burma we get all the orders.

"I am playing a waiting game, which does not cost me a penny because we still have quite an amount of un-remittable Chats in the bank. The money I use in Burma is invisible remittance ...." He also said he wanted his staff to have a job given the tough economy.

* * * *

I can still see the poverty -- the decay of the buildings in Rangoon, the falling pieces of cement from the buildings, the open-air food markets with little food available, the empty shelves in stores, all kinds of stores.

As was my custom, I checked in at the American Embassy. The press and political affairs officers briefed me. I also met with the American Ambassador privately, who told me that Ne Win was our ally and I should respect this. The political officer warned me (very strongly) not to write anything negative about the country. How could I write only positive things given the abject poverty? I couldn't and didn't.

As I said earlier, the Indians, many of whom had lived in Burma for generations, were thrown out of the country after Ne Win took over. They really had no place to go and weren't allowed to take anything with them. Some went to India, others to Ceylon. Without the Indians, the Burmese economy tanked quickly. Businesses -- especially food stores -- closed. So people were hungry. The transportation and distribution systems had been run by the Indians. So food and gasoline and kerosene weren't distributed throughout the country in a timely fashion. More problems! As a result, a black market developed and basic goods were sometimes (note I say sometimes) available at a high cost. US dollars were a premium, and I took advantage of this black market.

None of this mattered to American officials! Ne Win was anti-communist, therefore he was "good." Good for whom? I could never figure this out!

Ne Win had established a closed society. No one dared to voice anything negative for fear of arrest. The government nationalized everything and put people in charge who had no idea how to manage the transportation and distribution businesses. The government also took over much of the commercial real estate without compensating the owners.

My Singer friends made sure we were totally alone or far away from another table at a restaurant before they talked with me. They knew I was a journalist, and to this day, I admire them for being so honest with me. They said people were afraid to voice anything against the government for fear of being arrested. They would not even voice negatives to other family members or friends. Spies were everywhere, they told me. Even the students were quiet. Too many had been arrested and just "disappeared."

TRAVELING IN BURMA

Singer's Bernie Raphael and I flew up to Mandalay and were picked up by a driver. We went to the town of Pagan, which had -- and still has -- hundreds of pagodas (temples) from different cultures and times.

On the way to Pagan, we periodically stopped along the desolate road to "use" the bushes. Luckily I had plenty of tissues! We came to a small village and spotted a sign that indicated a medical clinic. "Oh boy," we said, "Maybe a clean bathroom!" Bernie knocked on the door, explained she had an American guest, and asked if we could use the bathroom. As everywhere else, the Burmese were hospitable even to complete strangers. But the bathroom (a hole in the floor) was filthy dirty!! Flies and odors unbearable! Before we got back into the car, we looked at each other and both said "From now on, the bushes!"

Pagan still intrigues me because I have been unable to trace the history of all those temples, each with different architecture and decorations. The reason I am still intrigued is that I saw the same style in North and South American Indian villages. I could identify Inca, Aztec, Pueblo, and more. I still haven't found out how all these different styles and peoples found their way to the Americas or how or why all these different styles are in Pagan.

We traveled further north to a hydroelectric plant and dam project under development. One of the lead engineers was a European who worked for the UN. We stayed at a government guest house that was very clean.

Again, as happened in the interior in Liberia, villagers here had never seen a white woman. Women and children came to meet me, to touch my skin and hair. They were also fascinated by my clothes. A group actually camped outside my room watching everything I did.

My room had mosquito netting around the bed. I was told to be very careful as the bugs at night were terrible. Besides tissues, I always traveled to these countries with a can of Off. Unfortunately Bernie's room did not have the netting. In the middle of the night, Bernie woke me saying she was getting bitten alive. I went to her room and sprayed. The next night I made sure she had netting around her bed.

Because this area was jungle and had lots of vegetation, basic fruits and vegetables, were plentiful. So there was no starvation as was the case in Rangoon. But clothing was sparse and amenities - as we know them - virtually nonexistent.

My articles appeared in *The Call, The Record,* and *The Washington Post*. They provide further insight about the Burmese people and economy.

The Burmese were a gentle and peaceful people, stemming from their Buddhist heritage. The women were shy, yet friendly. Actually everywhere I went, people smiled at me.

From my article Oct. 24, 1968 in *The Call*.

"An old woman looks up from prayer and smiles.

"A young girl turns from whispering with friends and smiles.

"A boy swimming nude in the hot sun stops splashing long enough to smile.

"The national characteristic of the Burmese is the ever-present smile. They are an easy going, open hearted people and they wear hospitality on their sleeves.

"As one scholar here put it, Buddhism emphasizes giving to others. So everyone gives everything to everyone else. It doesn't matter."

* * * *

Because Ne Win, Burma's president, was preparing to visit the US for the first time, I couldn't get an appointment with him. But the country's second-in-command U Ba Nyein and I had a long opened-ended conversation. I was very surprised to see how open he was as he described the deteriorating economy and the emergence of a strong black market.

The Far Eastern Economic Review, Jan 2, 1969, headlined my story "Human Errors." This head was based on my lengthy two-hour exclusive interview with U Ba Nyein, Economic Advisor to Ne Win and second in command in the government, as well as events after I left Burma.

"Burma has moved a step nearer its goal of creating a socialist economy. The Government has just nationalized a further 168 concerns, industries ranging from textiles to foodstuffs, and from chemicals to engineering. These new state takeovers followed the nationalization last month of sawmills and cinemas.......

"These developments highlight the problems which Burma is grappling with and remedies it has espoused for its economic headaches.

"The two major obstacles to the development programs so far, the country's economic advisor, U Ba Nyein admitted are inefficiency on the part of government workers and black-marketeering "

"Inefficiency stems from two factors, U Ba Nyein said: lack of administrative experience and some lack of interest by government employees."

The following comes from my article in *The Washington Post* dated Nov. 17, 1968:

"Resentment of changes, inefficiency of government workers and black-marketing has slowed Burmese development to a crawl, according to the chief economic advisor to the six year Revolutionary Government.

U Ba Nyein said "Former landowners and businessmen resent nationalization because they lose all their profits.

Monks resent nationalization because they can't get as much money from those who formerly had been wealthy. Workers don't like the changes because now they have to punch time clocks and can't loaf. Opium poppy growers oppose eradication of cultivation of their crop because they'd have to grow something else."

"U Nyein, one of the creators of the new Burmese Socialism and known among the foreign diplomatic community as an extreme leftist, admits agricultural and industrial production, per capita income, and exports and imports have declined drastically in the past three years. He said the country is going through a transition from a capitalistic economy controlled by foreigners to a social state run by the Burmese.

"Socialism, according to U Nyein, is 'ownership by the people as a whole and not by individuals of all of the means of production. The profits must be appropriated for the benefit of the entire people, not for any individual."

This philosophy seems to me to be Marxist. So why Burma was considered an ally, is beyond me. At that time, I did not editorialize, I just wrote the interview and the conditions from a factual point of view.

He admitted that black-marketing was flourishing because of the shortage of basic consumer goods and some foods. Prices at government shops are low, as low as the supplies. For example, one can buy a loaf of bread for one cent and can sell it to someone else outside for 30 cents."

U Nyein went on to tell me more stories of the economic problems, examples of which appeared in this article.

U Nyein said the problems were part of the transition to a socialist state.

* * * *

However, according to my article in the January 1969 *Far Eastern Economic Review* "Several former Burmese leaders disagreed. A former Finance Minister, not unnaturally, was anxious to interpret the economic failures as a novel form of political opposition to the present administration. He argued that the economy has slowed down not so much because of unintended inefficiency, but because of a very conscious noncooperation and passive resistance campaign on the part of the people."

U Nyein had known I was an American journalist, yet spoke freely. I wrote accordingly. The US State Department was furious that I dared to write the truth, which of course was "negative" in their eyes. Remember the US Ambassador and the political and press officers urged me to write only positives because Ne Win was "our friend." *The Washington Post* article was sent to the US Ambassador in Rangoon, who was also furious. My Singer friends were approached in an angry manner. "How could your friend do this?" Bernie was asked. She wrote to me, upset, and somehow I managed to get that article and the others to her.

ON THE RIM

I can't remember now my exact itinerary for the rest of that trip -- Thailand first and then Sabah? or Sabah first and then Thailand? Then Hong Kong and Taiwan.

In Thailand I was strictly a tourist, for only a few days. Bangkok was a pretty city, uncomplicated as a city could be where water transportation dominated. The flower boats, the

RIOTS & REVOLUTIONS

fruits and vegetables boats, even household goods boats. Boats were the distribution system of the region.

I can still remember:
- the magnificent temples with all the gold, the incense, and orange robed monks.
- the baby elephant that roamed the hallways of my hotel - The Erawan Hotel, the only 4-star one at that time.
- the beautiful raw silk -- purple, rose, navy -- that I bought and had made into outfits, which I wore for years.

As I said somewhere in the beginning of this saga, I am a pack rat. So when I thought of my trip to northern Thailand, I "visited" my very old address book to see if I could find the name of the woman who took me to visit her family. Lo, behold, her card is in the beginning of the book -- Khunying Kanitha Wichiencharoen, Executive Secretary of the Thai-American Technical Cooperation Association.

We took the train -- modern for those days -- through the countryside dominated by lush vegetation. Everywhere I traveled, no matter where, people were always friendly and willing to share their life and goods with me.

I remember my train trip - alone - back to Bangkok. A sleazy Chinese (sorry about this) man started harassing me. I moved, and he followed. I moved again, and he followed. I spotted two American soldiers and moved to the seat behind them. I told them what was happening, and they stared down the Chinese man. One of the soldiers then took me to dinner and a casino. I lucked out at a slot machine and ended up filling my purse with US nickels. We used the nickels to pay the taxi driver when we returned to the hotel. The driver couldn't believe all those nickels. We laughed....

* * * *

My old clips are a mecca of information and my impressions. As I wrote the above -- about the train ride back to Bangkok and meeting the American soldiers -- I wondered why American soldiers were in Thailand. There was no war there! My article of Dec. 4, 1968 in *The Call* answered that question and provided an interesting perspective of life there and the economy.

First I described Bangkok. "The country's only real city is modern and has dozens of multi storied, air conditioned hotels and apartment houses. The city's streets are in top condition and are clean of the garbage and dirt so often found in other Asian cities. The people are well-dressed and look healthy. There are few, if any, beggars." The end of the article noted that Thailand was a flourishing tourist mecca and a shopper's paradise.

Second, my question about the presence of American soldiers was answered. Thousands of US troops flew in and out of Bangkok each week for R&R from the battle fields of Vietnam.

According to my article, "The Thais are good business men. They see lots of money in the pockets of lonely soldiers 10,000 miles away from home. Both the travel business here and prostitution are scientifically organized and tied together. The tourist agency not only makes arrangements for soldiers to take a boat ride through Bangkok's canals and floating markets or see a Thai boxing match, but also provides a young female "companion."

The girls are generally in their late teens or early 20s and have been lured to this wealthy, modern city from the poorer countryside."

I'm a people person, so spoke with a number of these young girls. Because of the British influence, most Thais spoke a least some English. Enough English to talk to the just as young US sailors and soldiers, who were lonely.

In the *Far Eastern Economic Review* article, I wrote "One extremely pretty girl with long, jet black hair and flawless Asian complexion said she had been in Bangkok a year, but really didn't like it.

"In the country the people are happier," she said, "Here it's too busy."

The girls told me that the government gave them periodic medical exams to make sure they were "clean." We probably discussed birth control. I would, however, guess there are hundreds of Thais today who don't know their American fathers or grandfathers.

THE LAST SULTAN

Just a few days before I started this trip, I received a call from my photo agent, Walter Schrenck of Keystone Press Agency. "I want you to go to Sabah," he said. "Why? What's there?" I asked. "I don't know," he said, "but I'm hearing rumblings and I want you to find out what's going on."

What was "going on" was a dispute between Malaysia and the Philippines, both of which claimed to own Sabah. Sabah occupies about half of the island of North Borneo and is today a state in Malaysia. The dispute stemmed from a lease in 1963 given to the Philippines, signed by a nephew of the last undisputed Sultan of Sulu, who died in 1936.

According to my January 10, 1969 articles in *The Call* and *The Record*, "I flew into remote Sabah recently expecting a primitive Malaysian state with thatched huts and few modern conveniences.

"Instead I found a rapidly developing young state of 600,000 persons with a standard of living in Asia second only to Japan. I found a serenity and sense of peace I've felt in few countries in today's whizzing 20th century.....

"As I walked through the two main cities and numerous villages I got a stiff neck looking up at high rise apartments, peaking through windows into just built low-income one-family stilted houses with all modern conveniences, and snapping pictures of giggling female workers and shy children. New clinics and schools are scattered over the countryside and construction is continuing at a rapid pace.

"Surrounded by such abundance, the people seldom think about the dispute with the Philippines. But as soon as you mention the subject you are fiercely told that no one wants anything to do with the Philippines."

In order to better understand the dispute, I went to Sabah's press information office and was introduced to four officials. One of them was always there as my guide. They were very protective of the fact that I was a woman traveling alone. I think my main guide was Chen Dudley, an assistant information officer. One of them, I don't remember if it was Dudley, introduced me to the supposed last Sultan of Sulu -- Datu Mohammad Julaspi Sultan Kiram, then 69. My cover story in *The Far Eastern Economic Review*, of Jan. 23, 1969, discussed in depth and at length the controversy between Malaysia and the Philippines, the history of the conflict, and my exclusive interview with the Sultan.

The situation was complicated as there were three branches of the family, and few had ever heard of Datu Julaspi. The entire story is complicated. Julaspi claimed to be the only legitimate son of the last legal Sultan of Sulu, Jamalul Kiram, who died in 1936.

According to my lengthy *Far Eastern Economic Review* cover story "Evidence of his identity, as offered to me by Datu Julaspi, in an exclusive interview at his modern, wooden, stilted home, is sketchy and inconclusive. But his story makes fascinating reading. Although Kota Kinabalu government officials will not publicly grant credence to his claim, privately they confirm Datu Julaspi's heredity.

"Datu Julaspi, with a wispy build, told me that at the time of his father's death, he was leading a gang of bandits in the hills of North Borneo, and therefore was unable to claim the throne. Julaspi moved to Sabah in 1963 just after his cousin Esmal Kiram had proclaimed himself the new Sultan of Sulu and ruler of Sabah and had "leased" the territory to the Philippines. "I came here to avoid killing him," Julaspi told me. "I would have if I had stayed there." ....

When Malaysia and Singapore (then part of Malaysia) refused to acknowledge the Philippines claim, the International Court of Justice, in 1963, decreed that Sabah become a state in Malaysia.

The details of Datu Julaspi's life growing up are in this article, as is the controversy among family members. Given the economic prosperity of Sabah, it is no wonder that the Philippines wanted control. And also given the political situation in the Philippines (where murder of non-friends was common) many Filipinos who lived in Sabah did not want anything to do with the Philippines.

I left Sabah reluctantly. I would have liked to stay longer. My momento of Sabah is a nickel-sized Mabie grayish/blue pearl. My thought when I bought it was to have a ring made with diamonds circling the pearl. The pearl remains in its original form, in its original little box.

CAROL ABAYA

BUSTLING AND UNPLEASANT

Hong Kong was and still is -- the financial and business center of Asia. I hated it! And stayed only a few days, and extended my Taiwan stay.

Hong Kong was crowded, noisy, dirty, polluted and smelly. The only thing in favor was my father's tailor. I had bought Thai raw silk -- purple, rose, navy -- and had my father's tailor make me three business outfits -- dresses with jackets -- which I wore for years. This tailor visited New Jersey/New York every year and my parents had matching suits made. My father also had his long sleeve white shirts made to order.

CAPITALISM AT WORK: TAIWAN

Taiwan was then called the Republic of China. In 1967 or early 1968, my mother was president of the local (Englewood/Tenafly, NJ) chapter of Zonta International, a professional women's organization. As part of an exchange program, a Taiwanese Senator, Mo Tan-yun, visited NJ and stayed with my parents. Senator Mo was also a fairly high official in the Taiwan Dept. of Education. She acted as my hostess there -- arranged for me to stay at a government guest house, had lunches for me with various government officials (though none major) and helped make arrangements for me to travel around the island. I learned to be competent with chopsticks there, and the people I met were pleased that I even tried to use chopsticks.

At that time, a former *Call* reporter, Bob Green, was working for NBC, covering the area (mainland and Taiwan politics). He joined me at these various functions. After several days of lavish Chinese lunches and dinners we headed to the American Embassy cafe for American hamburgers with sautéed onions. Bob wanted to take a vacation, but needed someone to cover for him. He asked me if I would stay there for 4 to 6 weeks so he could vacation in the US.

Chinese drivers used the kamikaze method of driving -- everyone was his own boss on the road. There was only one traffic light in Taipei. Aside from the fact I couldn't stay away from *The Call* for another month, I was afraid to cross any street. So, I said, "thanks, but no thanks." While the traffic here was just as crazy as in Hong Kong, here the city streets and sidewalks were clean and the air did not smell bad.

* * * *

Most developing countries in those days had a primitive infrastructure and even more outdated ideas on the role of government, business and the world. As Senator Mo told me, the Taiwanese government, controlled by China mainland expatriots, was ahead of its time. Many of the Chinese were able to get gold and jewels out of the mainland. So there was money to fund new projects.

Senator Mo told me her family hid their jewels in their backyard well so the communist rebel enemies couldn't take them. She said the family was never able to go back and get the jewels out.

* * * *

Taiwan was a democratic country and very strongly capitalist. The government fostered economic development and foreign capital investment. It created a tax-free zone at the port of Kaohsiung.

Kaohsiung, Taiwan's largest port, was the site of the Kaohsiung Export Processing Zone (KEPZ).

The factories were modern and had a clean working environment. Workers were well paid and had decent housing, education, and medical care. I can still remember being very impressed. Senator Mo had arranged for me to meet and be taken around by top port officials.

My article in *Far Eastern Economic Review* on Kaohsiung is lengthy. The numbers attributed to the port -- number of acres, 69, square footage of warehouses and dollar exports -- are very small in today's economy. Even a local super market here can be 100,000 s/f, and houses can be as large as their largest warehouse. But in 1968, the numbers were significant.

I can still remember that I was very impressed by Kaohsiung.

The article reads "Near the southern tip of Taiwan, the city of Kaohsiung straddles a sluggish stream called the Love River. Nothing else is sluggish about Kaohsiung. It's the second largest (733,000) and fastest growing city in Taiwan. It's the island's number one port, handling 1,000,000 metric tons of goods a year, and one of the most booming industrial cities in Asia....

"KEPZ is a waterfront free trade zone that combines the best of industrial and port facilities needed for export production. Built on 69 acres of reclaimed land, it opened its doors in 1966. Last year (1969) it exported US$60 million worth of goods to 28 countries -- everything from wigs and cosmetics to sophisticated electronic products and refined petroleum.....

RIOTS & REVOLUTIONS

"One of the most awesome things is the equipment along the shore that loads and unloads cargo 24 hours a day. .. You get a stiff neck looking up at the giant cranes that make workers look like midgets.....

"If you visit the zone in the early morning before workers arrive at the plants, you will suddenly hear the silence of dawn broken by a low hum -- bicycle spokes in the wind -- that suddenly gets louder and is soon an unbelievable din. Then you see 10,000 bicycles pedaled by pretty Chinese girls. One of the most striking features of the labor force is its youth and high percentage of females. Some 12,000 of the workers are between 16 and 19. About 86% are female.

"The invasion of bicycles is followed by scores of buses, their engines roaring. In a few minutes all have passed and the streets are quiet again. Now the noise is within -- the 117 factories -- where 32,700 workers begin a day's work."

In my article I also describe a number of parks that were built by the government to provide a nature retreat for the workers. A unique concept in those days -- to give workers a calm and beautiful environment in which to spend time.

I ended my article, "While the bustle of the factories and the serenity of the parks seem vastly different things, they really aren't. The leaders of Kaohsiung realized they are both aspects of the development of a model community. And what is a model community? Confucius had an answer, and maybe that is what the planners of Kaohsiung had in mind. Said the Chinese sage, "A community is good when those in it are happy and those far off are attracted to it."

"Kaohsiung could pass that test."

* * * *

From the port, I traveled by train to the mountain area, where native Taiwanese lived.

In Taiwan, I bought a wood carving and several small jade figurines, which still grace my curio cabinet. I have always loved the facial expressions of the figures.

I returned to Taipai and said my goodbyes. My mother and I kept in touch with Senator Mo until she passed away.

CHAPTER 9

LEADING TO THE FUTURE

Remember the Nur family from my 1963 and 1965 visits to Indonesia? Susanna (the daughter who was studying in Paris) and Nyazi (the older son) would play important roles in my future.

In 1967 Susanna finished her studies in Paris and on her way home stopped in the States -- New Jersey to be exact. My mother and Susanna bonded right away. When Susanna expressed an interest in staying in the US, my mother got her a job teaching French at the prestigious Dwight School for Girls in Englewood Cliffs, New Jersey. Besides earning American dollars, Susanna was given room and board at the school. She was able to send money home. The Nurs were having a tough time economically and often didn't even have enough food.

Nyazi was able to get a minor position in the government. Officials realized Ny was bright and in 1968 sent Ny to school in the States -- a special economic development program at Williams College in Massachusetts. The program was geared to government officials who would have, in the future, important decision making positions. The various governments paid all the expenses plus a stipend. The students had to promise to return to their native country and work for the government for two years.

In January or February 1969, Susanna and I went up to Williams because the college was having a special Indian celebration. There I met my future husband -- Angel Francisco Ortanez y Abaya, who was on Philippines President Marcos' Presidential Economic Staff.

I had just returned from that very memorable swing through Asia -- Burma, Thailand, Sabah, Hong Kong and Taiwan. The Philippines was claiming that Sabah really belonged to it, rather than Malaysia. Having met the last Sultan of Sulu, I didn't think the Philippines had any rights to Sabah. So Angel and I spent the night talking about Asian politics. I don't think either of us was aware of all the activity around us.

In May, Susanna, my mother and I went up to Williams for Nyazi's graduation. The "students" received a Master's degree in economic policy and development. I saw Angel only briefly because he had a bad cold. (This was Angel's second Masters. He had a M.A. in Theology from Ateneo University in the Philippines.)

After graduation, the program participants spent time visiting various US nonprofit and governmental agencies. Ny and Angel were assigned to an agency in the Bronx. Both stayed at my parents' house after the Bronx assignment and before going to the next place they were to visit.

The four of us (Susanna, Nyazi, Angel and myself) spent the weekend together -- Bear Mountain, New York City, the shopping malls. Then dinner and dancing at a nightclub in Englewood Cliffs. Angel and I "clicked" and the chemistry was strong. (My knees were weak -- from dancing?? or something else.) (To relate this is difficult for me even though Angel has been "gone" since 2003.)

Before Angel left for his next assignment in Washington, DC, he asked if he could come back to see me the following weekend. I said "Yes." We spent the weekend together -- can't remember doing what. Then he had another place to visit and returned to NJ again. When he had telephoned to confirm our 'date' he said, "We have a lot to talk about." I sort of shrugged to myself. To make this a short story, Angel proposed that weekend and the end of July we were married. Ten days later we left for the Philippines. We had pushed up the date because his mother was dying of cancer.

* * * *

At home, besides my assignments at *The Call* and overseas trips, the Civil Rights Movement gained momentum. President Johnson, who knew how to move Congress, was able to get the Anti-Poverty Bill passed in 1968. By that time I was tired of having to deal with a bigoted editor and of sitting on the outside of events. Reporters in those days reported happenings and did not, like today, create stories.

My covering boards of education and the Paterson High School sit-in sharpened my feelings that education was the key to the American dream. I wanted to play an active part in making those changes happen.

Because Paterson was one of the first cities to have race riots and had a large low-income population component, Mayor Lawrence (Pat) Kramer applied for a multi-million dollar Model Cities grant. I had expressed interest in working in the Program. I knew the black community and there was mutual respect all around. So, when the final proposal was sent in, I was plugged in to handle Community Outreach and Education programs.

But Washington kept going back and forth, always asking for more details. In early 1969, word from Washington was that Paterson had received preliminary approval. But the wait for final approval continued.

In the meantime, events were progressing in relation to my romance. In mid-June, the two events merged. Angel's proposal and the final approval of Paterson's grant came together. I became engaged to Angel and subsequently quit *The Call*. I also had to tell the mayor the news. He was stunned.

Because Angel's mother was dying of cancer and he had to return to Manila to fulfill his government obligations, we did not plan a large wedding. Just immediate family for dinner after being married by Paterson's bachelor judge, Ervan Kushner. When I asked him to perform the ceremony, his initial reaction was (being the bachelor he was) "Why are you doing something stupid like that?" By that time he had forgotten my confrontation with him during that child abuse case. He had been the defendant's lawyer.

Kushner married us in his small office - crowded with my parents, my sister, and witnesses Judy Megaro and Mark Stuart, both now "gone." I wore a white linen sleeveless dress, and the only picture we had was one of my back and jiggling rear end. That picture got lost in the shipment back to the US in 1972.

The night of the ceremony we had a dinner just for the immediate family -- my father's sister, Mary Albert and her second husband Sam, my mother's cousins Leah and Julie Katz and Rose and Irving Siegal, my mother's uncle Izzy Katz (Julie's father). I can't remember who else, and Leah can't remember either.

Originally we had planned to spend our first night at a resort in NY state just across the NJ border. We ended up at a sleazy motel in Hackensack. At 3 a.m. we were hungry and I can still remember going to Holly's, a favorite ice cream and breakfast restaurant. I had my favorite - waffles, chocolate chip mint ice cream, hot fudge sauce, lots of green, yellow and pink whipped cream, and of course cherries.

So, the next phrase began.

TO THE PHILIPPINES! SUMMER 1969

I didn't have much time to pack what I wanted to ship, buy various appliances (refrigerator, washing machine, air conditioner) and close up my apartment. I had just signed another 3-year lease, but the landlord, a friend of my parents, didn't care. The apartment was sought after because of its location right next to a bus stop where my great-uncle's buses stopped virtually at the door. Many people worked in NYC.

Our "honeymoon" consisted of a quick trip to New Hampshire. Angel wanted to start an export business -- selling Filipino wood crafts to the US. We met with a couple who was interested in importing and developing the US market. Over time, the venture did not succeed because (1) the Filipino manufacturers were not reliable, (2) the quality was not up to high standards, and (3) the 1972 'revolution' cut off any opportunities. I still have a number of pieces we had made up to our designs.

We arrived in the Philippines in August as Angel's mother was dying of cancer. She 'waited' until she could see her older son again. She opened her eyes as the family stood around her bed, squeezed Angel's hand and closed her eyes. She passed that night. The wake lasted a week, with someone from the immediate family always sitting near the casket. Food was brought into the church, and young children played in the aisles.

We stayed in the same hotel I had been in during my 1963 visit. We learned it was owned by the father of one of Angel's "arty" friends. We stayed almost two months because we had difficulty finding an apartment that met some of my basic standards -- clean environment. The apartment complexes in the Manila suburbs were all surrounded by 8 or 10 foot concrete walls. Outside the walls, usually on either side of the entrance road, were piles and piles of garbage, covered with thousands of flies and very bad smells. Not acceptable to me!

We finally found a clean complex (Palm Village -- still there) in Makati, an upscale suburb of Manila. The owner had the garbage picked up at each apartment on a regular basis and hauled away. We would call the apartment a town house -- two stories, postage sized back yard (actually concrete) and a front patch of grass. No garage, but a carport.

Downstairs was one large room which served as a living and dining room, a small kitchen, a small maid's room and bathroom. Cinder block walls. Upstairs were three bedrooms and a bathroom. We knocked down the wall between two rooms and so had a strange L-shaped master bedroom with two doors and two sets of closets.

In those days most furniture was made to order. Aside from my favorite orange triangle chair, we did not ship any furniture. We did ship, besides the appliances, my car -- an 8 cylinder Chevy II -- pots, dishes, glasses, flatware, a toaster oven, linens and books. I had told the packers and shippers in NJ to remove the new appliances from their original cartons and repack them in crates. So we had made-to-order living room, dining room, bedroom and den furniture. Solid wood! Much better quality than was available reasonably here.

The Philippines had been ruled by the US from 1898 until its independence in 1946.

So, it was not unusual that American companies had major investments there. Makati, where we settled, had a sizable modern supermarket with all the basic consumer goods - from toilet paper, tissues, cleaning materials, laundry detergent, soap, toothpaste, shampoo, canned goods and soda. All were manufactured in the Philippines by American companies -- Dole, Procter & Gamble, Scott, J&J, Colgate.

The Philippines was at that time THE only developing country that manufactured its own basic consumer products. All of the other developing countries imported all these items. And like in Indonesia, these products were hard to find in other developing countries.

Periodically Luz (our live in maid) and I would go to the open air market for fresh fruits and vegetables. Fish there was really fresh. I would have the fish de-boned. And Luz insisted on keeping the head -- considered a delicacy.

So that Luz would know what to cook and food was not wasted, I developed the habit of making out dinner menus for a week. This also gave us a balanced variety. I still try to plan menus ahead of time because it drives me crazy to be hungry and not know what I want to eat. I do have to admit, these 'menus' are often ignored.

GRAFT WAS PREVALENT

The items shipped from NYC took two months to get to Manila. So we timed moving into the apartment to the arrival of the shipment.

A cousin of Angel's brother-in-law was a shipping agent, and we used him (Sal) to get everything through customs. After two days of Sal's employee being unable to do anything,

I stepped in. The graft -- as is the case in all these countries -- was unbelievable. But I was not going to pay even one peso! After all, it was transfer of household, which meant no duties were due. Except for the car.

One of Sal's employees and I went to the dock warehouse to get things through customs. We had shipped "transfer of household" because Angel had been out of the Philippines for more than a year. As we were waiting for the customs official to review the shipment and fill in the papers, a man came over and started talking with me. He said his name was Abaya. No relation. We chatted awhile, and then Sal's man took me aside. "He's a spy and wants to be paid off," he said, "Don't talk to him."

The customs official finally came over. Unfortunately the shipper had not taken the new appliances out of their original cartons. So the official gave me a rough time, wanting thousands of pesos in duty. No way! I was not going to pay anything! Besides which, we didn't have any money to pay, even if it was o.k. with me.

Angel had gone back to work after his mother's funeral. Early on, I had checked in at the US Embassy, right near the hotel, and with Marcos' press secretary and private secretary, who had also been the previous president's secretary. I reconnected!

From the pier I headed to Malacagang (the Palace) and the private secretary. I explained that (1) we shipped as transfer of household, therefore no duties should be due, and (2) Angel worked on the President's Economic Staff (PES). The Secretary gave me a letter on Marcos' stationery with a royal embossed seal saying that no duties were to be paid. Back to the pier. By that time, Sal's truck had arrived. After I showed the letter to the customs officials, our things were quickly loaded up. As we left the dock area, the man who was supposed to be a spy, came over to me and asked how much I paid. He wanted his cut! I said, "I paid nothing!" He had a hard time believing me.

That was Wednesday.

The car was at a different location and still had to be gotten from that pier and through customs. We had been prepared to pay duty on the car because Angel did not have diplomatic privileges. I think it was 2,000 or 3,000 pesos.

Thursday we were back at the pier. In order to get the car out, a number of other customs officials had to sign various papers. Sal's rep had been unable to do anything as the officials ignored him because they wanted to be paid off. So, again I stepped in. When I think back, I did have a lot of "balls" in those days. Sal's rep took me from office to office, where I waved the papers directly in front of the customs guys. Office by office, the same procedure. "Please sign," I said as I waved the papers virtually under the official's nose. Most of them were just sitting reading the newspaper and drinking coffee. By the end of the day, all the papers were signed. But it was too late to get the car moved to the exit gate.

On Friday, we were back at the pier, with me waving all the signed papers. Sal had told me that we needed to get the car out that day. If the car was left on the pier over the weekend, it would have been vandalized -- everything salable stripped off.

The car was finally brought to the exit area very late in the afternoon -- but it had no gas. The gas had been taken out before shipping to avoid a fire. So we couldn't start it and there wasn't a gas station near the pier. I can remember we had to push the car out the exit gate. For some reason, two times clamor in my head: 11:15 a.m. and 4:15 p.m. Maybe we arrived at the pier at 11:15 a.m. and finally pushed the car out at 4:15 p.m. just before everything was locked up for the weekend. Five hours to get the car out!

* * * *

While I had had four servants in India, none lived in the apartment. So I told Angel, we could get in some day help. I never liked house cleaning or cooking on a regular basis. Day help was not the custom in the Philippines -- so I was told. Live-in help, yes. Live-in because there was insufficient good living quarters for help elsewhere.

My eldest sister-in-law, Chong, a nun, was at that time a principal of a Catholic school located in the provinces -- miles from Manila. The family "cooked" things between them and sent Luz Fortes to us -- without asking us first.

Our apartment had a small maid's room and full bathroom downstairs, off of the minute kitchen. No room even for a stove! We had a 3-burner device that was placed on the sole kitchen counter. No oven. The toaster oven I brought with us had to suffice. No room inside for the washing machine. We had a wooden shed built in the back "yard." It was built on a raised platform because the yard flooded during heavy rains. Many times, Luz and I had to bail out the water and bring the buckets of water into the kitchen sink and toilet.

Because of the climate, cockroaches and ants abounded. And those little lizards (geckos) climbed the walls and ran across the ceiling. All food had to be either refrigerated or stored in glass jars or containers.

The cockroaches weren't as huge as those in Indonesia, but were just as plentiful. And the geckos unsettled me. Every time I saw one or the other, I screamed. After a couple of weeks, Luz asked me "Don't you have bugs in the States" "Yes," I said, "but not inside our houses." (At that time I guess I was unaware of the problems in our cities.)

Fortunately the apartment had both 110 watt (US standard) and 220 (Philippines standard) electricity. So, some plugs were 110 and others 220.

We settled in and established our daily routine. The days were not exciting or dangerous.

* * * *

After 18 months or so, Luz said she'd like to go to college to become a teacher. One reason my sister-in-law chose Luz was because Luz was bright and Chong thought she should have the opportunity to better herself. We paid Luz's tuition and books, enabling her to go to school every day. She would dust downstairs before we got up (dirt was a major problem), made us breakfast, cleaned upstairs while we ate breakfast, cleaned the dishes. Then she would spend the day at school. Even after we returned to the US in 1972, we continued to pay her college costs. Twenty years later, I brought her to the US.

Communications were still primitive in the Philippines and there were not enough land telephone lines to accommodate demand. For the general public, there was a long waiting line and several years passed before one could get a telephone.

Angel had a phone in his name at his family's house, so he couldn't get another one, even though he worked for the government. I was using my maiden name, Goldstein, because I did not want to get Angel in trouble if I wrote anything negative about the government and the unrest. I used my press credentials and got two phones (one upstairs and one downstairs) within a few days. The previous tenant, a Japanese businessman, had a phone in the apartment and wanted to sell it to us for hundreds of dollars. We refused. But for a couple of weeks we had two numbers/lines. I would use the upstairs phone to call the other number downstairs to let the maid know when we wanted breakfast. Like an intercom system, but not a "system."

Of course, the weather was much different from that of New Jersey. Manila's weather is hot and humid all year round. I can still clearly remember the headlines in the *Manila Times* one December day: "Manilans Shiver as Temperatures Plummet." The temperature was 70' that night. Even Angel, who spent the 1969 winter in Williams, MA., laughed. " Cold certainly is relative."

Angel's family welcomed me and made me feel at home. He was the second eldest of seven and had five sisters and one brother. Apparently he had a reputation for being arrogant -- though he was far from that. Early on, I was watching one of my sisters-in-law (Macri, I think) cook as I wanted to learn about Filipino dishes. "How do you put up with his bossiness?" The she said something else -- I don't remember what. I do remember saying "I just don't let him get away with it." (Whatever "it" was.) Macri laughed and called another sister into the kitchen and told her the conversation. They both laughed. "Good," they said.

Remembering is sad. Angel died in 2003. His eldest sister (Chong, the nun) died in 2009 and his brother Luke in 2010. Two other sisters (Pufi and Macri) died in 2015.

While Angel's family welcomed me, this contrasted with how Romi Abello's family (he was a second or third cousin) treated his American wife, Mary Ann. Romi, a doctor, had done his residency in the US and Mary Ann was a nurse. His family did not accept Mary Ann and did not even talk to her. They ended up returning to the States in 1970 or 1971 and settled in Pennsylvania.

NEW ROLE

When we were still living in the hotel, I contacted the US Press Attaché and other foreign journalists. The Press Club had regular meetings, and I went as often as I could. Early on, one of the former reporters (Anthony Polski) from *The Record* (which owned *The Call*) was in Asia, representing McGraw-Hill World News. McGraw-Hill, besides Business Week, had some 25+ special interest and industry magazines. Tony was also an editor at *The Far Eastern Economic Review*. Tony hired me on the spot to work in the Philippines for McGraw Hill World News.

As time went on, I began to develop a relationship with the directors at MGH and certain editors. When we visited the States in 1971, I made it a point to meet with as many editors as possible. This helped me better understand the needs and focus of various magazines. I returned to the Philippines with a number of specific assignments. So the last year in the Philippines was more productive. Payment was per word actually published and expenses on a specific assignment. I think it was 25 or maybe 50 cents per word.

Newspapers there provided basic event information and important business news. I regularly read every paper I could find. After identifying magazine interests I established relationships with people in that industry.

Aside from the telephone, the only communications with other countries was Western Union. The equipment was very old, probably 1940s (maybe 1950s) time frame. My articles were hand typed into the WU machine and sent to New York via Ticker tapes that were printed out. Usually I dropped off copy at night and let a WU employee do the typing. However, as the political situation became unstable, I typed in my own copy and took the ticker tape after the story was sent. This way the government had no way of knowing what I sent.

MGH had several magazines that covered the utility industries, among them *Electrical World and Engineering News Record*. I covered events and trends. There was a big international utility conference in Manila, which I attended. One of Angel's uncles owned a power plant on one of the other larger islands. The uncle attended the luncheon, and when he spotted me, put his arm around me, saying he wanted to introduce me to his friends. He said to them "I'd like you to meet my niece. She's a reporter." Mouths opened as his friends tried to understand how an American could be his niece. Note here that he didn't refer to me as "my nephew's wife." As I've said earlier, Angel's family made me feel I *was* a part of the family.

Besides McGraw-Hill, I also contacted *Far Eastern Economic Review*, headquartered in Hong Kong, and again started writing for them.

Even though the economy really was thriving, there was political unrest fostered by students of the wealthy, who demonstrated on a regular basis. The issues: corruption, high prices of food, especially rice, high taxes (not really) and lack of law and order.

(As an aside -- political opponents during Filipino elections often killed one another and then went to "confession." Catholic confession wiped out the crime, and no one was ever prosecuted.)

While I had walked alongside Indonesian demonstrators in 1963 and after the coup in 1965, I did not physically cover the Philippines marches. The Filipino students had no respect for the press, smashed cameras and roughed up reporters.

* * * *

Marcos had first been elected President in 1965. I still have the letter he sent me after I sent him a congratulations note. So when we arrived in August 1969 the reelection campaign was in full swing. The election tactics consisted of strong "black propaganda." Marcos' opponent Sergio Osmena had been convicted of being a traitor during WWII because he sold equipment to the Japanese (who had killed one of his relatives and threatened to kill more). He was sentenced. But he later received amnesty.

In an exclusive interview for *The Far Eastern Economic Review*, Osmena told me he was running "to help liberate the country from Marcos." Osmena's wife objected to his running, but he told me "if I get out of the election who will the people turn to? The people are suffering, they are hungry. Four years of Marcos has made them suffer."

He said, "The country is facing a crucial election in the sense the result will determine its course -- whether it will go communist or tow the democratic line." He described Marcos' leadership as "incompetent" and "impotent."

Marcos, according to one of my 1969 *Far Eastern Economic Review* articles, was accused of having "one of the most criminally-abusive careers in the exercise of the pursuit of power in the story of the Republic."

* * * *

Marcos was reelected by a wide margin. Students were still demonstrating. So, after my first stories, FEER wanted me to interview Marcos. The holidays in 1969 intervened, and I was given all kinds of excuses. Then the State of the State speech was coming up. (Angel was one of the speech writers.) More excuses. I finally told the Press Secretary that FEER was pressuring me for a story and said "If I don't get an interview soon, I will write the story and say Marcos refused to comment." "Blackmail," said the Press Secretary. "So, be it," I said. I got the one-on-one interview within a week. The Press Secretary wanted a list of questions beforehand. I have always refused to do this, regardless of who I interviewed!

Marcos had seen me at press conferences in the previous few months and also remembered me from my 1963 visit and dinner at his house. We chatted some and then started talking about the unrest.

Marcos said he had always had a "vision for my people." "I feel I am fulfilling a kind of task, a vision.... of implementing my dream. It is a soul satisfying, difficult and sometimes thankless job. It needs capabilities, endless patience and stamina. But I find it exhilarating."

In the middle of our talk, Imelda came prancing in (yes, the correct word). At that time (1970) the diamond tennis bracelets were the new vogue. Someone had given one to Imelda. She whirled around the room, showing off the awesome bracelet. Her very short skirt whirled around, showing her underpants.

After that, I had easier access to Marcos -- especially when he learned Angel was on his economics staff.

* * * *

Sitting here writing this book , I remember
- Yes, the corruption was rife, but not as bad as it was before Marcos took office. And corruption was -- and still is -- in every country, especially today in China and India, the two up-and-coming economic superpowers.
- Prices were rising, and there was some hunger in some areas, but not everywhere. But there was no abject poverty like in India and China or outright starvation.
- Law and order was another issue. While goons roamed in some provincial areas, one of the first things I had noticed when we arrived in August 1969 was that there were no armed goons or beggars in downtown Manila as was the case in 1963. I felt safer, never felt threatened or afraid to either drive or walk around the area.

The student demonstrations faded away as the 1970 school year ended. Without the school as a rallying point, the students became quieter.

However, the seeds were planted in Marcos' thinking and in the US officials minds that the communists (called Maoists or Huks) wanted a revolution.

Actually, the government had expanded education and health programs -- some initiated from Angel's recommendations. We felt the government was making inroads into solving problems.

* * * *

Angel and I, together with Angel's brother Lujud (Luke Jude), discounted the Maoist threat. First, Lujud, a Christian Brothers intern (I guess the word is) worked in the rural areas. (He hadn't taken his final vows.) Lujud said a few Maoists might be vocal in 1970 in the Manila student demonstrations, but the communists were unorganized, had very little financial backing, and no weapons.

In early 1970, Angel had reached out to the key student groups. We met secretly (yes, I was there) several times with the leaders to see if a "real threat" actually existed. And of course I wanted material for my FEER articles.

Marcos' (and later the US's) perception was different from mine and Angel's.

In my March 26, 1970 FEER article, written after my exclusive interview with Marcos, I wrote:

"As further student trouble hit Manila last week, President Marcos was sticking firmly to his own opinion on the cause of the recent strife. Plain and simple. The communists want to take over the government. They are utilizing the students to advance the communist ideology." This was his stand after the first violent clashes in January, and he reiterated it in my exclusive interview.

"After talking to many students from a variety of organizations, it seems there may be Maoists among them. However, the number spouting a rigidly communist line -- and those who actually favor a communist government -- are few.

"Convincing President Marcos of this, however, is another matter. Security around Malacagang Palace has been tightened considerably.......

"Marcos, drawn and pale, does not hide his concern as he discusses the situation. He distinguishes between moderate students and what he calls the communists and radicals. "Those who use violence have no legitimate gripes because they are not content with the redress of any grievance. They will be satisfied only with a communist takeover.'

"Students were quick to reject this claim.......

"The students deny they want to overthrow the government. The aim was to 'refine it into a democracy. Now it is a plutocracy -- the rule of a select few for a select few. We want to re-instate true democracy.'

"And they claim that while they may be using tactics employed by communist revolutionaries, they themselves are not communists."

There is more in that article. But the bottom line is that the communists posed no real threat to the government and were not in any position -- financially or with arms -- to overthrow the government. They were a nuisance, with a weak rallying point in the provinces where land reform was indeed needed.

* * * *

Beginning with our arrival in Manila in August 1969, I used my maiden name, Goldstein, when writing for overseas media. I did not want anyone to connect myself with Angel's position on Marcos' staff. Nor did I want anyone to think that Angel was giving me classified information. So the March 1970 FEER article -- quoted above -- used my Goldstein by-line. In the beginning only a few people knew about the connection.

However, Angel did bring home -- for me to read and use for articles -- a 300 page report done by the RAND Corporation, headquartered then in Santa Monica, California. The study, paid for by the US government, was titled "A

Crisis in Ambiguity: Political and Economic Development in the Philippines." While the statistics were gathered in early 1969, the basic factors and conclusion, I believed --and so did Angel -- were still valid in 1970 -- even though the students were more active.

For my April FEER article the by-line (purposely) was "By a Correspondent in Manila."

I did not want Angel to get into trouble.

The Report supported Angel, Lujud and my conclusions that the communists were not in a position to even try to overthrow the government. After all, there may have been only several hundred hard-core rebels in a country of 35 million. Unfortunately, neither Marcos nor the US government believed the Report's conclusions.

MISCONNECTION OF THOSE IMPORTANT POLITICAL DOTS

According to my FEER article, "The Report says crime is not mounting, that the economy is growing respectably, and the polity appears stable. It (the Report) chastises both foreigners and Philippine decision-makers for their misperception of the problems and the attitudes of the people."

The Report stated that "the crisis of crime has been overstated...... Dissidence and insurgency are not new to the Philippines, but at this time, 'the Huks do not appear to be an organization that could mobilize and exploit any dissatisfaction.'" The report concluded that the Huks "will continue to be a major nuisance, adding, however, the Huks 'feed on terror and coercion rather than on the popular discontent imputed to tenants."

The Report concluded that the communists "do not appear to pose a revolutionary threat to the government because it is very difficult to find large-scale popular support for them even in their home areas. They should not be characterized as having a single objective of overthrowing the government. In fact, the organization works with and through local politicians. It does not behave like a classical insurgent organization. Part of the organization appears motivated by personal gains, part by political ideology."

This report was lengthy and my article went into more detail.

The unrest settled down in the spring of 1970, and Marcos began his second and last allowable term.

INTERNATIONAL FRIENDS

Both my college degrees (B.A. & M.A.) are in international relations. And my social life at both University of Wisconsin and New York University was comprised of friends from all over the world. This international theme continued as life went on in the Philippines.

We had a varied social network with several completely different groups. There was the mixed marriage group, consisting of several couples where, like Angel and me, the men were Filipino and the women American. Key in this group were Kathy and Ernie Montemayor, who lived several doors down from us. There were two Filipino doctors who had done their residency in the US and married American nurses: Mario and Carol Garcia, and Romi and Mary Ann

Abello. Because of the men's doctoring schedules we did not go out together often. But Carol and I were (and still are) particularly close.

Ernie had an export business and met Kathy while traveling as she had been an airline hostess. Ernie's grandfather had been an American soldier in the Philippines during the 1898 war. Kathy decided she wanted to become a doctor and so went to medical school in the Philippines -- in-between having two of their three daughters. Kathy did her residency in NJ in the 1980s and then settled in Florida, opening a pediatrics practice.

At that time, (1970) there weren't many porn movies available to the general public. Ernie, somehow, got a few such movies and a projector. The kids and maids were sent over to our house. The four of us (Ernie, Kathy, Angel and I) closeted ourselves in the Montemayor's bedroom, locked the door, and watched. I think this was my one and only porn movie. Today's general public movies actually show much more skin, sex, kissing, groping, if not more, than did those old movies.

As Kathy was from Philadelphia, she loved Jewish bagels. Through one of the wives of an Embassy officer, I had access to the US Commissary -- a store that was exclusive to Americans and offered items not found in the Filipino supermarkets. I had lamented about missing bagels. One day I received a call that Lender bagels had arrived, and my friend had bought two bags for me! Needless to say, I rushed to get them. When I got home, I called Kathy, only to get a continuous busy signal. Finally I sent our maid down to Kathy, with a note "I have real live bagels. Come on over!" Even before the maid returned, Kathy was at the door. I didn't have any cream cheese, but we pigged out on toasted bagels with butter. Bagels never tasted so good!

Then one weekend we decided to go to the country. Rain had been intense the previous week and the country (dirt) roads were slick and muddy. The roads were also built up through the rice paddies. Ernie was driving, and the car slid off the road into a ditch filled with mud and water. At least 12 men tried to push or pull the car out of the ditch -- to no avail. Finally, a huge water buffalo was tied to the car, and eventually the car was pulled back onto the road. I was glad Ernie was driving his car.

* * * *

Kathy's parents and mine came over for the 1970-1971 Christmas and New Year's season. We all went out New Year's Eve to our favorite Mexican restaurant, and Mario's parents joined us. I still remember our bringing our parents 'home' and then going to some Filipino park celebration that Carol Garcia had read about. She was very adventuresome. Then we went to their apartment, getting home around 7 a.m., just as our maid went out to mass.

Because we were married in the States and none of Angel's family was at the ceremony, we had a reception for all of Angel's family -- sisters, aunts, uncles, cousins and more.

Everyone welcomed my parents. Then Angel's mother's family and father's family each invited my parents to dinner.

Ernie's mother also warmly welcomed Kathy's parents, and Mario's parents were very kind to Carol.

At the same time, both Carol and Mary Ann had trouble understanding the closeness of their husbands to their parents, aunts, uncles and extended family. Because I grew up in a close-knit Jewish extended family environment I better understood family ties and relationships. The Filipino and Jewish cultures were more alike than that of American Christian families, which tended to focus more on the immediate family - parents and children.

All four of the mixed marriage couples ended coming back to the US. Two ended in divorce.

* * * *

The second social group consisted of Angel's friends, with whom he had gone to elementary school through Ateneo University and the Seminary. All of the men had dropped out of the seminary, and several married after Angel and I moved to the Philippines. We were particularly friendly with two couples, Pete and Lucy Alejandrino and Percy and MaLou ___

None of us had any money to spend on nightclubs or even out for a nice dinner. We gathered at one of our apartments, just listened to music and talked. But two happenings still make me laugh.

Pete's father had retired from the railroad and started a pig farm. He really wasn't a businessman, and after a couple of years had more pigs than he could sell. So he had a luau. When we arrived at the farm, Mr. Alejandrino grabbed my arm, and said, "Come meet all my friends." He meant the pigs. He had a favorite -- a 300 pound sow, who squealed making all kinds of grunting sounds when she spotted Mr. A. The sow loved to be scratched behind her ears and made more approving sounds when scratched. What a feast we had! Even 40 years later I still picture that sow whenever I see live pigs, or even pigs in cartoons.

RIOTS & REVOLUTIONS

Shortly before we returned to the US for a visit in 1971, Percy and Malou had a baby girl. Malou had gone to school in Connecticut and was snobby pro-American. Everything American was better than a Filipino item. We had to bring something back and bought a frilly little pink organdy dress that really was beautifully made. After returning to my parents' house, I took out the dress to show my mother. The label read "Made in the Philippines." I cut the label out so Malou would think it was American! The dress -- minus the label -- was a big hit!

* * * *

Another group was what I call "the arty" group -- a wide range of creative people who Angel had known for many years. One was the daughter of the man who owned the hotel in which we had stayed when we first arrived in Manila. Others were artists -- all media --, writers, poets, musicians. Those in this group had money, so we didn't go out with them as much as we'd have liked.

I can still picture in my mind the winning "picture" that one of the men had entered in a multi-media art show. He won first prize with a white toilet seat mounted on a piece of plywood. Nothing else was on the board, just the toilet seat. Reminded me of that picture in the Guggenheim Museum in NYC which had a very large canvas with three squares on it, red, blue and yellow, and nothing else. I still have a hard time viewing either of these as 'art.'

Several of the group were into theater -- various elements, from acting to set design to the music. The then new round Cultural Center opened, and we were invited to the pre-performance dinner and then the program. The inside of the theater was round, and the lobby was encircled with lots of windows. All the theater lights were turned off. The darkness remained. You could not even see shadows -- just complete, pitch darkness. I can remember sitting there (at age 30+) thinking "I would never want to be blind. I would rather be deaf." Even then I loved to read and write.

One weekend, we all went to one of the beach resorts, where one of the couple's family had a summer complex. There were several buildings, with open camp like rooms with rows of beds. Women on one side, men on the other side. At that point I did not like nor eat pork. Because the facilities were primitive we ate a lot of canned foods or cooked over an open fire. Everyone knew I was Jewish and didn't eat pork. The women had brought canned corn beef, spam, and tuna fish. The Spam label said it had pork in it. The label 'magically' disappeared before they thought I saw it.

This trip was a great treat. Another way of seeing the beauty of the Philippines. The water was completely clear and pure. I sat in the shallow water feasting on the various fish that swam by. The colors, the shapes were fascinating. Believe it or not, I can still picture the beach and the fish.

It is amazing how fast one becomes spoiled with civilization's amenities. Before we left the States, I had air conditioning put into my car. Angel had pooh-poohed this. Yet whenever there were problems with the air conditioning, Angel took off from work to get the car fixed. At the beach resort, there were ceiling fans, but no air conditioning. After all, the buildings were all open. Angel was not happy after the first night and wanted to go home. I talked him into staying. But after the second night he insisted we return to Manila! He missed the air conditioning -- or maybe missed me in his bed. We always had a 'sleeping pill' at night.

When one of the couples in this group married, I again was 'hit' with the differences in culture, religious attitudes and beliefs. As the priest pronounced the couple husband and wife, he deliberately addressed the wife saying, "Now you must love your husband through fear of God!" Wow! I was shocked! "Fear of God!"

Jews are taught to love - not fear - God. When we first arrived in Manila, it was shortly before the Jewish High Holy Days. I took Angel to the Kol Nildre service (the night of Yom Kippur). The service message, of course, was to love God and ask for his forgiveness of any 'sins' we may have committed the previous year.

So, after Angel's friend was married and the priest talked about fear of God, I was turned off of Catholicism. Angel went to mass on an irregular basis, and I never went, even during the holidays.

* * * *

Early on -- and maybe because of my press credentials -- I was able to go to the Army-Navy Club, which was international in its membership. I would go during the day, when Angel was at the office. I became friendly with a woman, Annette, from the Bronx. Annette was married to a German (Otto Dumbach) and did not work. So she spent a lot of time at the Club.

In the spring of 1972 Angel and I were thinking of moving to a regular house, and I wanted to get a dog. One day at lunch, I told Annette I wanted a black lab. Coming from the Bronx, Annette had no idea what a lab looked like. She asked if it was big. I said, "Yes." "Oh, I know someone who has one," she said. "Let's go over there now." Unannounced we went to the house of an Israeli family. Annette rang the bell, and a maid answered and invited us in. We were standing at one end of a very large living room, when a huge black dog came bounding toward us -- a totally black Great Dane. I went white! And froze! Afterwards, Annette laughed at me.

* * * *

And of course, there was Angel's family. We often had Sunday lunch at either his parents' (then deceased) house where two of his younger sisters and aunt lived or at Pufi and Joey's (Almeda) house. Pufi and Joey had one son when we arrived, then later on another son and then a daughter.

Regardless of where we ate, they always made sure there were pork dishes, as they knew I did not have pork in the house. As did all upper class Filipino families, Pufi and Joey had a number of servants. I could never keep track of how many. But one time there was a Filipino holiday, and Pufi wanted to go with the servants to some sort of celebration. I offered to baby sit. After all, I had taken care of my niece Ruth in the US on many occasions. Jo-Jo was maybe 18 months old and spoke a few sentences but not many. We were upstairs in my office and after reading him some books he said something I could not understand. He finally became frustrated with me and took my hand, led me downstairs into the kitchen, opened the refrigerator door, and pointed to his bottle of milk. He was thirsty. I can still see him in his diaper and little sandals pulling me down the stairs.

I think sometime in that first year there was an earthquake and then several tremors in the days afterwards.

The first quake was on a Saturday, and Angel and I were taking a nap in the afternoon. I felt the bed vibrate and thought Angel was getting up. But he wasn't even in the room. We learned later that there had been a quake with some damage to both roads and buildings in Manila.

The next day we had Angel's family for lunch. We were sitting around talking about the quake. Angel's aunt was telling about quakes during WWII. She said that people should stay inside during a quake because concrete cinder block buildings were protection.

I can still remember sitting there feeling some vibrations. I said, "I think there is another tremor." Angel's aunt was the first one out the door.

Several days later I was in the pool at the Army-Navy Club. I looked up to see the light fixtures around the pool sway and the water rolled from one side to the other. Only a few seconds... So, no one even got out of the pool.

Sitting here now, it really is amazing what one remembers so clearly. I remember a lighthearted lifestyle. None of us had any excess money, but we enjoyed ourselves.

After we were in the Philippines a year or so, I got a call from a Jewish couple from California, Sophie and Leonard Haimowitz.

They said they liked to look up Jewish people in the countries in which they traveled. They found me (Carol Goldstein) in the Manila telephone directory. We met and took them out to dinner -- a typical Filipino one. We remained friends for years, even after the coup.

So, in 1972 they met me at the LA airport. I became hysterical when I saw them. I stayed with them overnight before my flight east. Angel was already in the US, staying with my parents in Englewood, NJ. I have to say here that for years afterwards whenever I heard the Star Spangled Banner or God Bless America I would cry.

A NEW DIRECTION

The summer of 1972 was critical in our lives and the Philippines. Angel headed a delegation to Washington DC to seek $13 million from the World Bank..

The monsoons that year were really bad, and the entire Manila area was flooded. PES (Presidential Economic Staff) sent three vehicles to get Angel to the airport -- hoping that at least one would get through the flooded streets. Two got to the apartment, but only one made it to the airport. As we neared the airport, water poured into the car and reached almost to the top of the seats. We sat with our feet up against the front seat. The airport itself was fairly dry, so the plane took off. The driver took me home. The only reason his car didn't stall out was that the driver had put plastic baggies over the carburetor and other key car components.

The World Bank was willing to match funds provided by the Philippines government. Somewhere Angel had found $13 million hidden in some department's account. Consequently the World Bank loan was approved. Angel returned from DC elated about getting the money from the World Bank.

Before we married, Angel said he wanted to remain in the Philippines and never return permanently to the states to live or work. When he returned from this trip, his attitude had changed. One of his seminary friends had a high position in Morelco -- the country's largest utility, owned by the Vice-President Fernando Lopez's family -- and wanted Angel to join him. Angel planned to leave the government and get at least two years' experience in the private sector. Then he said he would consider going back to the US. I liked living in the Philippines (with all those maids and services), so it was up to him.

* * * *

In the fall, political tensions -- especially in the provinces -- were increasing, according to Luke, Angel's brother. Luke said that Marcos would do something drastic -- probably in 1973 -- before his term ended. The Philippines Constitution had adopted our four-year term limit for Presidents. Marcos could not run for a third term.

A couple of weeks after Angel returned from DC he left for Malaysia to speak at an international economics conference. My brother-in-law Joey Almeda was traveling around Asia as head of Far East operations for Diebold, a large banking equipment company. He had returned to Manila for a few days to see his newest baby -- finally a girl, Michelle. And then left for Taiwan. Ernie Montemayor (our neighbor) was in Texas, trying to further develop his export business.

The three of us women were on our own when the coup erupted.

* * * *

7 a.m. Friday, Sept. 21, 1972. My sister-in-law Chong, a nun, (then an administrator at a Catholic College in Manila) called. The College was located just outside the gates of Malacagang Palace. "There's been a coup! Soldiers are in the streets. They closed off the street and the Palace," she said. "We don't know what is going on." I think she also said something about the possibility that grocery stores would run out of food.

I turned on the TV, a 19" black and white -- no color in those days. And as I did so, I yelled for Luz (our maid) and grabbed whatever cash I had. I had not picked up Angel's pay the day before. So I just took my check book, which was how I usually paid the supermarket.

We headed to the Makati Supermarket. We got there just as they were opening. More and more people came. We filled two shopping carts with everything from toilet paper to canned foods (especially tuna fish, meats and juices) and water to whatever fresh food we could get out hands on. And milk and baby food for Pufi's new baby, Michelle.

The lines were long. And people were pushing and shoving, grabbing what they could. Suddenly a sign was put up at the cash register. "Cash only." No one knew what would happen to the banks. I did not have enough cash to pay. I tracked down the manager and talked him into approving my check. By the time we left the supermarket, the store was mobbed and shelves quickly emptied.

I can remember that my emotions those first hours -- and then the next days -- were like a roller coaster. I was scared stiff, but determined.... If I didn't appear calm, my maids, Pufi and her servants would freak out. I guess in times of strife one's inner resources are dredged up. We all had to remain calm. Like when Steve and I faced those first days during the 1965 Indonesia communist coup. We didn't know what was happening. So saying we were all scared doesn't really describe our feelings.

Back home I turned on the TV. Cartoons on the only working channel. Periodically a voice announced that everything was ok, that everyone should stay home and be calm. This announcement played during the day as did the cartoons.

RIOTS & REVOLUTIONS

Somehow earlier in the day I was able to contact Angel on the phone and told him not to return to the Philippines. Pufi and Kathy were also able to get word to Joey and Ernie. Then ALL telephone communications was cut! And a curfew started.

I stayed at Pufi's during the day because of the baby and the kids. Because telephones had been closed off, I had gone over to make sure she was ok. Many of her servants had fled, leaving only one or two. I had left my house and two maids. (Luz's sister Paring had joined our household.)

Pufi had had 4 or 5 servants, only a couple of male stayed. So just before the curfew I returned home. Kathy and I got together to make sure everyone was ok. I think Ernie's mother had sent over a couple of male servants.

The cartoons went on all day and well into the night.

Using my experience from the Indonesia coup, I wrote a brief message to McGraw-Hill and took it to the Intercontinental Hotel which was located near us. Several American pilots were just leaving, and they successfully took my message to the Western Union office at their first stop. That was the last plane that left the Philippines and none returned for several days.

So at that point, not only were telephone and telegraph communications cut, but the airport was closed. Cartoons continued!

Sitting here 45 years later, it's difficult to remember the chain of events in the second and third days. I guess McGraw-Hill got word to Angel that he should go to Singapore and stay with MGH correspondent Colin Gibson. Colin had visited the Philippines, so Angel knew him. Angel hid out there for more than a week. He said afterwards that every time the doorbell rang, he hid in a closet.

Sometime during the weekend, Marcos appeared on TV, announced he had foiled a communist coup and declared martial law -- thus throwing out the constitution that prohibited him from running again. Communications were still cut off with the outside world. Also, there was a ban on Filipinos leaving the country. Because the Philippines consists of hundreds of islands, travel to other countries was impossible except by plane or boat.

On Monday, even local telephone communications were still cut off. I can still see myself getting into my car and cautiously driving through the soldier-lined streets to Angel's office. I hoped his boss (Alejandro Melchor) would be able to tell me what was going on. He confirmed that Marcos had declared martial law and said that everything was "O.K."

Angel's boss asked me when Angel was returning as he (Angel) would be getting a key position in the new government. I think I gave a vague answer.

We talked about the travel ban and how it would impact Angel and my export business. I was told that once Angel returned he would not be able to leave the country -- that only I could go back to the States for business. The ban was for an indefinite time. Planes were still grounded or prohibited from landing.

I returned home again passing through those soldier lined streets. The large automatic weapons looked frightening.

Given Angel's reaction to the charges of corruption in the government and his plans to leave the government, I knew he would not like working for a dictator. So, Kathy (then in medical school) and I conferenced. She finally came up with the story that Angel had infectious hepatitis and was in a hospital in Singapore.

Shortly afterwards, I guess, internal phone service was restored. So I called Angel's boss, giving him the hepatitis story. The next day Melchor called to ask the name of the hospital so that the Ambassador in Singapore could visit and make sure Angel was getting the proper treatment. I said I didn't know the name. After all, Angel was really hiding in Colin's apartment. Everything happened very quickly over several days. We all were very worried and glad we had enough food and water for a couple of weeks. We even rationed what we ate to make sure we did not run out.

Somehow we got word to Joey that he should not return to the Philippines. His job depended on his ability to travel freely in and out of Manila. And somehow Kathy got word to Ernie (in Texas) that he should not return.

Outside communications were finally returned. I remember going to the Western Union office and keying in information and sending the info to McGraw Hill as events unfolded.

As I've said earlier, telegraph equipment was primitive. I typed on a typewriter like keyboard and a ticker-tape like paper came out -- maybe 1" to 2" in width. Then the tape was put through another machine that sent the message. After supervising the sending of the message I took the tape so that no one in the government would know what I sent. Then I burned the tape.

Whatever the sequence of events, once Angel was in Singapore, he knew he did not want to work for a dictator. So we decided he should go on to the States. My mother wired him money for the air fare. This "process" took several days -- not like the instant sending of cash today. He had a diplomatic passport, so didn't need a special visa. We had to keep his defection secret because we were afraid Marcos would stop him. Ten days later, Angel arrived in the US safely.

My activity was frantic. What was I to do with all the stuff we had collected in the three years we lived there?

I sold the refrigerator, the air conditioners, the TV, the washing machine. I left the dishes, glasses and flatware for my sisters-in-law. I kept the linens, towels, and pots and still have some of them. I packed up the books and various collectibles.

My car was a bigger problem. I certainly did not want to ship it back. I left it with the General Motors dealership, with instructions to give the money to my in-laws. They then gave the money to Sal to pay for the shipping of our things. I can't remember how long the port was closed, but Marcos realized he had to keep the economy going. I remember a long conversation with the GM manager. He talked a lot about WW2 and the Japanese occupation, that the Japanese were very tough business people and "would sell the shirt off their mother's back if they could gain money." He also said something that startled me then -- and still makes me wonder -- that in any business transactions "the Japanese would Jew you down." I doubt he had ever met a Jew other than myself, and I certainly did not mention the fact. He handled the sale very well, and the amount covered the original cost of the car, the shipping and the duty. So after three years of having the car, I certainly did well.

After a few days, communications and airplane activity resumed. Reporters from several countries arrived. Marcos had a press conference, again saying he saved the country from the communists. (Nonsense of course!! He just didn't want to give up power.)

RIOTS & REVOLUTIONS

An Australian reporter kept asking about the corruption and crime. Marcos fenced and did not answer. Finally, Marcos finished the conference. But even as Marcos was leaving, this reporter continued to harass the President. Marcos spotted me, smiled and pointed at me and said to the reporter, "Ask this lady. She has all the answers."

I certainly did not have all the answers! Then or now!

(I learned from this reporter that my Australian reporter friend (Frank) from Indonesia days had been killed in Vietnam. I really felt -- and still feel -- bad about this. He was a superb reporter.)

The situation in the Philippines in 1972 **is another prime example of political dots not being connected correctly.**

In spite of the RAND report and our (Angel, Luke and myself) conclusion that the communists were not a real threat, Marcos was convinced that there was a threat. I could not convince him otherwise. Yes, I tried. Maybe the demonstration headlines in the newspapers and the pictures on TV made the situation seem worse that it was.

In one of my *Far East Economic Review* articles, noted above, Marcos was convinced there was a danger. And he convinced the American Ambassador Henry A. Byroade who convinced Washington. The Ambassador was at the Manila airport the night before the coup, supervising the unloading of heavy arms.

* * * *

Well before the coup, the US Embassy was looking for a communications specialist. I applied for the job and was initially told I had the job. Then Washington cut funds. After the coup, I received a call from the Embassy saying I had the job. Of course, I refused. I don't know why funds were suddenly available. I suspected then -- and still do -- that they felt I could give them inside-the-Palace information because of Angel's position.

I learned from other reporters that airport security looked through all the papers the reporters carried. I had three years of information in my 4-drawer file cabinet. A lot sensitive. I did not want the government to see the sensitive information I had collected. I spent days going through folders. We set up a burning process in the postage stamp back yard. While I sorted out sensitive information, Luz and Paring burned the papers in metal wastepaper baskets.

I really hated having to leave. I can still remember driving around, my hands tightly gripping the wheel, saying to myself "I don't want to leave. I like it here." Actually I felt more at home in the Philippines than I did when I visited Israel in 1959 and 1967. I did not feel a Jewish identity there. Maybe because Israeli street signs and newspapers were all in Hebrew. In the Philippines, English was the predominant and official language.

When I finally left, ten days after the coup, I closely held certain files and refused to give them to airport security people. Just after I got out, the government banned travel for permanent residents as well as their own citizens. If I had stayed one more day, I would have been trapped.

* * * *

Some of the above was recaptured in an article in *The Record* (New Jersey) written in 1986 after Marcos was ousted. Following is part of my story, as related in that article, written by Mark Stuart, my former city editor (the one who said my story "stank" when I was new at *The Call.*

The headline read "**I'm used to riots and revolution**". The text read:

"When I first met Carol Goldstein in 1964, she was a very effective reporter covering Totowa, Little Falls and West Paterson. That summer, one of the worst race riots in the city's history erupted in Paterson, and Carol insisted on covering it.

"Come on, Carol," I said. "You think I'm going to send you out into that raging mob?"

"But I'm used to riots and revolutions, "Carol persisted.

"I hadn't notice any commotion in Little Falls lately," he shot back."

"I was then given a lesson in the pitfalls of presumptive male chauvinism. Carol Goldstein, all 5 feet 1 inch of her, had been on the scene in the early sixties when serious trouble broken out in India and when revolution erupted in Indonesia."

Mark's article continued: "I didn't send her out to cover the Paterson riot. I still didn't believe she'd been quite so close to revolutions -- until I attended a reception at the Indonesian Mission to the United Nations a month or so later, at Carol's invitation.

"When I saw the Indonesian ambassador embrace her effusively, I knew I'd made a mistake. I didn't know how big a booboo until the ambassador spent 15 minutes telling me how much he admired Carol's talent and how pleased President Sukarno would be when he learned that Carol had been at the reception. (NOTE: I had had - as reported here earlier a one-on-one interview with Sukarno in 1963, interviews with Philippines President Marcos and other leaders).

I have talked about the 1972 coup earlier here. But Mark's article was even more specific:

"I remember the night Marcos took over. It was a Friday. Marcos closed down all TV and radio stations and forbid newspapers from printing. The one TV station allowed to operate ran cartoons from 7 a.m. to 7 p.m. Every once in a while a voice would interrupt the cartoon to tell everyone to remain calm, that everything would be all right.

"Almost immediately Marcos began gobbling up everything in sight. One example: The country's electric utility was owned by the family of his vice president Fernando Lopez. They had invested something like $15 million to build it. Marcos nationalized the company and paid the Lopez family $1,500 for taking it away. Then he put his cronies and relatives in jobs where they could steal from it for his benefit."

I have related earlier here the details of Angel's trip to Malaysia and then to Singapore, and my leaving the country before Marcos banned those with permanent residency visas.

Mark's article continued: "It didn't matter that Marcos was a fan of Carol's ever since she had interviewed him in 1963 when he was senate president.

I was quoted "I still remember a press conference Marcos held after taking power in 1972. An Australian correspondent kept badgering Marcos about corruption in the government. Marcos fenced with the guy without giving him a direct answer. The Australian persisted with his questions even as Marcos got up to leave. As he walked toward the door with the last question hanging in the air, Marcos spotted me in the group.

"Go talk to that lady," he said to the Australian. "She has all the answers."

"Carol Goldstein Abaya usually did. END of Mark's article.

* * * *

The plane went from Manila, to Hong Kong, to Dykarta, to Guam and then Honolulu where we went through customs.

Directly in front of me was an older couple who had been traveling in Asia and got on the plane in Hong Kong. In front of them was a young man who had been in Indonesia for a year teaching. And in front of him was a young couple who had been on their honeymoon.

By that time I had traveled a lot and been through customs many times. I had never seen custom officials literally take apart every bag and all the contents. Even opening up makeup and breaking apart lipstick. The young man had brought a very large painting, which was carefully wrapped in brown paper and tied up. The official tore apart the paper with no regard to preserving the painting.

I was petrified. I knew that if my suitcase was opened, I would not be able to close it again. And my other bags were also fully stuffed. Hoping for compassion, I put my press card in my passport. The official looked at it and said they had had a tip that drugs were being brought in. He said he had to at least open some bag or he would get into trouble. I pointed to the carry on, which he opened but did not go through the contents. He asked what else he could open. I said my camera case. My attaché case also had to be sat on to get it closed. So, he cooperated with me.

CAROL ABAYA

THE PHILIPPINES - POST-1972.

Joey (Pufi's husband and Angel's brother-in-law) who worked for Diebold (a bank safe company) was in Taiwan, where I met him on my way to the US. He went to Singapore and did not return to Manila. He established residency in Singapore and in the spring of 1973 was finally able to get Pufi and the three children out of the Philippines. There was still a travel ban.

Ernie Montemayor stayed in Texas only a short time and then went back to Manila.

The Philippines government finally realized that Angel was not returning and he was labeled a traitor. Because of my family's connection to Congressman Frank Osmers, Angel was able to get permission to work here almost immediately and a green card was issued within six months.

However, we were careful not to let too many people know where he was. For years we kept major assets --eg when we bought my current house in Marlboro in December 1973 -- in my name only.

Needless to say, McGraw-Hill was very interested in our story and impressions of what happened and why was in the *Far East Economic Review*.

Unfortunately, American businessmen in the Philippines hooked into the Maoist over throw theory and were upset by all the corruption. Corruption was rife, but no more so than in previous years. And the businessmen did not believe the RAND report's conclusions.

Angel, Luke (Angel's brother who worked in the provinces) and I felt the RAND report's conclusions did represent the situation. Angel at that time was the Director of Health, Education and Welfare on Marcos' Presidential

Economic Staff. So we knew that major strides had been made in these areas, thereby improving the quality of life for middle and lower income families. Much more did need to be done

And while there had been some bombings of private buildings these acts were not supported by the students who had started the demonstrations and with whom we had talked.

American businessmen, however, did not look at the progress that had been made, even in the three years in which we were there. Major US companies that had $2 billion investments in the Philippines included Ford, Mobil Oil, Squibb, J&J, Colgate-Palmolive and Jersey Standard Oil.

In a November 4, 1972 *Business Week* article, American businessmen described the demonstrators as from a "militant middle class" that had ties with "family oligarchs. They also were upset by the fact that the Philippines was $2 billion in debt -- mostly to US banks -- and that the Philippines Congress had not approved allocating money to pay for the July flood damages. So Americans supported martial law and hoped for better times in the future.

The *Business Week* article reads "In the six weeks since Marcos declared martial law, "American Businessmen have become increasingly sanguine about their future. Marcos, employing dictatorial power, has imposed a sort of order in a country wracked by civil unrest. In doing so, he has made it abundantly clear that he wants to help American business as much as domestic politics will allow......

Robert Wales, President Mobil Oil Philippines is quoted as saying "Something drastic had to be done. If martial law will instill some discipline and solve the law and order problems the temporary loss of freedom of speech is not important."

The BW article also reads:

"The question is whether only Marcos' adversaries are corrupt. The President and his close associates are hardly free from suspicion..... It is also well known that Marcos has demanded that he and his associates in the government be cut into the profits of local businesses..."

I think I said earlier that the US backing Marcos in the declaration of martial law was another prime example of the "dots" not being correctly connected. He gobbled up key businesses and fired thousands of civil servants. He did to the Philippines what Gen. Ne Win did in Burma in the early 1960s. The one difference here was that the Philippines had many more well educated people.

But the corruption got worse in the 14 years in which Marcos controlled under martial law and where there had been poverty before, now there was starvation and extreme poverty.

POST NOTE: The first trunk of my life's tree is now over..... as is this story.

www.ingramcontent.com/pod-product-compliance
Lightning Source LLC
Chambersburg PA
CBHW070048080526
44586CB00013B/964